8-

LADIES OF THE GOLDFIELD STOCK EXCHANGE

LADIES OF THE GOLDFIELD STOCK EXCHANGE

Sybil Downing

A TOM DOHERTY ASSOCIATES BOOK
New York

A Forge Book
Published by Tom Doherty Associates, Inc.
175 Fifth Avenue
New York, NY 10010

Forge® is a registered trademark of Tom Doherty Associates, Inc.

Design by Helene Wald Berinsky

Library of Congress Cataloging-in-Publication Data

Downing, Sybil.
Ladies of the Goldfield Stock Exchange / Sybil Downing.—1st ed.
p.   cm.
"A Tom Doherty Associates book."
ISBN 0-312-86331-4
1. Stock exchanges—West (U.S.)—Fiction.   2. Women stockbrokers—West
(U.S.)—Fiction.   3. Gold mines and mining—West (U.S.)—Fiction.
4. Frontier and pioneer life—West (U.S.)—Fiction.   I. Title.
PS3554.O9348L34   1997
813'.54—dc21   97-730   CIP

First Edition: July 1997

Printed in the United States of America

0 9 8 7 6 5 4 3 2

This book is dedicated to my husband.

ACKNOWLEDGMENTS

The list of people who offered me their encouragement and advice for this project is long. Particular thanks must go to Margaret Coel, Jane Valentine Barker, Jerrie Hurd, and Elizabeth Downing. I also wish to acknowledge with gratitude the following individuals and institutions for providing technical advice and historical background: Harold A. Backer; Jerry Beaber; Richard N. Hall; Carol Krisman; Claudia Reidhead of the Beatty, Nevada, Museum and Historical Society; Dr. Warren Gillette; Dean William Baughm; Lesley Kellas Payne, the Government Documents department of the Norlin library and the School of Business library, University of Colorado at Boulder; the Nevada State Library, Carson City, Nevada.

AUTHOR'S NOTE

Although this novel is based on historical events surrounding the famous gold rush that took place from 1904 to 1907 in Goldfield, Nevada, it is a work of imagination.

The idea was born while I was doing research for another project and I came across an article, in a 1907 issue of the *Los Angeles Times*, about a women's stock exchange, established in Goldfield, Nevada, at the height of that mining camp's gold rush. Immediately, I became intrigued.

Further research revealed that though it was compared with the fabled 1859 Comstock lode, the strike in the Goldfield area was also a creature of the twentieth century. Automobiles competed with mule teams to haul freight. Electric lights shone next door to kerosene lamps. Telephones relayed the news of the latest gold finds. Nevada had not yet granted women the right to vote, but Wyoming and Colorado and Idaho had. The Populist movement of the 1890s had given women leadership roles. Women were going to college in rising numbers. By 1900, one out of five women were employed outside the home. Thirteen percent of the women living in the American West at the time were professionals— doctors, lawyers, engineers. A stock exchange established by women did not seem far-fetched. Indeed, I discovered at least one other women's mining stock exchange, which was formed in 1896 in Colorado Springs, Colorado.

At the time, a woman could buy and sell stock through a broker for a fee. She could not, however, own a seat on a stock exchange and, thus, could not be a broker. She was cut off from "making a market" (selling shares of new mining ventures). In addition, the commission fee schedules were so arranged that the trade of a small number of low-priced shares—the type most women could afford—was very expensive. Women were as eager as men to make their fortunes by trading mining stock. Clearly, the logical way to do that was to form their own stock exchange.

Sally Zanjani, in her excellent book *Goldfield: The Last Goldrush on the Western Frontier* (Athens, Ohio: Swallow Press, Ohio University Press, 1992) wrote of the men and women who flocked to the otherwise impoverished and desolate stretch of desert: "They cast aside the moralities and the suffocating dos and don'ts of small town society along with the discarded rigs and empty bottles that littered the roads leading to Goldfield and adopted the free and tolerant ways of a gold rusher." That a group of women established a stock exchange, however briefly, should come as no surprise.

The women who establish the women's stock exchange in my novel are fictional, as are other characters. A few were suggested by actual players in the events: George Graham Rice, a stock promoter; George Winfield, an Oregon cowboy turned gambler; and Senator George Nixon. Careful research was done to present them accurately. Only those who knew them at the time, however, can be certain whether the characterization is as precise as it might have been.

PROLOGUE

On a warm May morning a few days after her twelfth birthday, Meg Kendall leaned against the old cottonwood on the edge of Boulder Creek, a length of rope in her hands. The taunts of the boys on the opposite side drifted over the roar of the icy spring runoff hurtling over rocks and nearly spilling over banks partially eaten away by the power of the water.

"Sissy," one shouted.

Slowly, she played out a loop of the rope as she'd seen trick ropers do in the wild west show. "You bet I can't jump it?" The broad jump was her specialty.

On the other side, the boys exchanged glances, laughed, then bent their heads together, conferred. A moment later, they looked up, grinning as if they'd outsmarted her. "A dollar," they called in unison, cupping their hands around their mouths.

"A dollar it is."

She stepped back from the bank's edge a half-dozen yards, unlaced her high-topped shoes, and took them off. She lifted her skirts and petticoats up around her waist, tied them out of her way with the rope. She was ready.

She crouched, took her stance. She leaned forward onto the

balls of her stocking feet, then straightened and ran in long, sure strides across the thick grass to the very edge of the shelf above the bank. Working her arms like a windmill, she lifted off, stretching, reaching, soaring over the jumble of rocks and spray, until she landed on the opposite bank.

*   *   *

The midday sun streaming through the window of the front parlor, Tess Wallace aimed the six-gun she'd stolen from her Pa at the dark-haired man holding her daughter on his lap. "I said put her down."

"We're just cuddlin'," the man said, stroking Jenny Lynn's little legs with a beefy hand.

"I'll count to three." Tess drew back the hammer. "One."

The man turned his head, spat toward Miss Nell's brass spittoon. "I dunno why you're so riled, Tess. We're in a whorehouse after all."

"Two."

Jenny Lynn's blue eyes were wide with terror. She began to cry.

"Shut up," the man snarled, then shoved the child to the floor.

"Jenny Lynn, come here to Mama," Tess said softly but firmly.

The little girl sniffed, crawled to Tess, clung to her skirts.

"Three." Tess fired.

The man grabbed his right arm, howled. But he didn't move.

Tess still held the revolver, now aimed directly at his heart.

*   *   *

Verna Bates stood in the shadows, gazing at the bear. He looked more like a huge, moth-eaten dog than a black bear as he lay on the hard dirt, chained to a post at the back of Pitkin's Silver Age Saloon. His owner, a mean-looking, scruffy man, had brought him to the camp earlier in the day. He'd jerked him from one saloon to the next, poking him with a stick to make him do tricks like sitting up and begging, rolling over, growling. Some of the people they passed and customers at saloons tossed silver dollars into the man's filthy derby.

Verna stepped out of the shadows and cautiously walked toward the bear. The animal lifted his head, eyed her. Her heart pounded. A bear was nothing to fool with, but she couldn't stop now.

She saw the chain had been looped over the post. She took the meat she'd brought with her from her pocket, held it out to him. He lifted his head, sniffed, lumbered to his feet. She stopped, her heart thudding in her chest, tossed the meat on the ground some distance from the post.

The bear moved toward it. She stepped back, never taking her eyes off him until she reached the post.

The door to the saloon opened. The bear looked up, eyeing the splash of light spilling out into the darkness.

Verna froze. Then as if the bear knew what she'd come to do, he glanced around at her, not moving. She slid the chain up over the post, let it drop to the ground, and fled.

1906

⎯⎯ᢒᡠᢒ⎯⎯

CHAPTER 1

*M*eg Kendall watched the bright yellow Rambler touring car and its driver disappear around the corner in a plume of dust, pulled open the screen door, and went inside. Weaving ever so slightly, she unpinned her new leghorn hat and tossed it on the newel post at the foot of the staircase in the narrow hall.

The August afternoon was warm, aggravating her lightheaded-ness from all the French champagne she'd downed at the garden reception of Boulder's fanciest wedding of the season. Tents had protected guests, gathered around pink linen-covered tables as they nibbled at salmon aspic, tomatoes vinaigrette, and croissants, a string quartet playing quietly in the background. On the tables, in every corner, no matter where one looked, had been flowers and more flowers—all of them pink and white.

Meg had sat with the usher who owned the yellow Rambler, sipping champagne, laughing lightly at his compliments, aware of the impression she was making. She knew she was pretty, even beautiful. Men had told her so often enough. Three had proposed marriage, but none were men with whom she wanted to spend a lifetime. So, as the saying went, always the bridesmaid, never the bride. Today she hadn't even been a bridesmaid.

Nuts. She hated weddings, and she didn't care a fig how important Adele Richards and her parents thought they were. Dear, sweet Adele. She'd be the perfect wife—obedient, agreeable, boring. Just like most of the girls Meg knew. Few of them had gone to college, and most had set their sights squarely on catching a man. It wasn't that she was against marriage, but from what she'd observed, the moment a woman married, her independence went out the window and her husband became the lord and master. The thought was distinctly unappealing.

When someone at the reception had asked her what she would be doing in the fall now that she'd graduated from college, she'd announced her acceptance to Johns Hopkins Medical School with casual indifference, as if to imply, given her brains and abilities, it was only to be expected. Oohs and aahs of congratulations had followed. She'd smiled, caught in others' eyes the mixture of astonishment and disapproval she'd seen so often before.

Her science professors had given her As yet had written half-hearted letters of recommendation for medical school. Even Dr. Mauer, her aunt's doctor and a family friend, continued to warn Meg about the impenetrable wall of prejudice against women practicing medicine. Meg, however, had imagined herself as a woman of accomplishment for a long time.

The house was quiet, empty. Her aunt had gone to the mountains for the weekend with friends. Meg's head began to clear. She supposed she should change, and there was the trunk in the spare bedroom, clothes waiting to be packed. Medical school would begin in three weeks. Her aunt looked forward to going with her as far as Washington, D.C., where they'd visit distant relatives before Meg went on to Baltimore.

She went into the parlor, conscious as she always was of how Aunt Hilary had arranged the sofa, the rocker, the two reception chairs, so their slightly shabby coverings weren't quite so apparent. Brussels lace curtains, bought from Sears Roebuck instead of Denver's Daniels and Fishers Department Store, hung at the windows. In the center of the room, beneath a brass electric chandelier, was a round table piled with back issues of the *Goldfield Tat-tler*. The latest one had arrived yesterday and still lay, unopened, in its brown wrapper.

Meg picked it up. The sight of her name and address in her father's familiar scrawl made her smile. She slid off the wrapper, unfolded the paper, looking forward to reading the note he always enclosed. The newspapers and notes, sent from wherever he happened to be working, were her father's substitute for lengthy letters he seldom wrote. When she'd been six, he'd given up on trying to raise his motherless child in the mining camps and brought her to live with his sister Hilary.

Though without formal training, her father prided himself on his skill as a mining engineer, on his experience and his instincts about ore. Once they had been enough, but Meg knew that in recent years he'd had to struggle to keep up with the young know-it-alls, as he called them, with college degrees.

Meg scanned the front page, noting the inch-high headlines. "World Lightweight Championship Fight Set for Goldfield." She smiled. Goldfield, Nevada, was said to be the site of the greatest gold rush since the Comstock lode. She could picture the frenzied types streaming across the Nevada desert to make their fortune. A championship prize fight was right up their alley.

She turned the page, and the expected piece of notepaper fell out, fluttered to the carpet. She picked it up, moved to the window for better light.

> *Dear Meg,*
> *If something should happen to me, watch out for Nolan and Winters, and for God's sake hold onto the stock until you talk to Pete Eckles.*
> *Your loving Dad.*

Meg's heart skipped a beat as she stared at the words, stark and abrupt, as if he had no time for further explanation. She read them again. Her father was frightened, enough to believe his life was in danger; two men named Nolan and Winters were somehow involved. It didn't make sense. As far as she knew he'd always been well liked wherever he worked.

After she'd written him in the spring about being admitted to medical school, he'd sent her a telegram of congratulations. Her aunt had huffed that for once in his life he could have taken the time to write his daughter a proper letter, but Meg knew her father was proud of her. She'd never take the place of her mother, who had died a week after Meg had been born, but she had never doubted his love. He'd always led a vagabond life. It certainly wasn't how most fathers lived, but she didn't care. In fact, she envied him a little.

Still, in a week or so she'd be on her way to medical school. Four years at Johns Hopkins School of Medicine, a year of internship in the East, five years total of rules and traditions as inflexible as cement. But when it was over, she'd be able to make her own way in the world, with style, and she'd be someone.

She walked back down the dimly lit hall to the bottom of the stairs, still unable to make sense of the letter in her hand. The urgency of it worried her, worried her a lot. She could write and ask him to tell her what it was all about, but it would take days for the letter to get to Goldfield. By the time she received a reply—if she received a reply—she'd already be in Baltimore.

There was nothing to do but go see him. The trip would take two days each way. She had time, barely.

She'd started up the stairs when the thought occurred to her she might not have enough money for a ticket. Then she remembered the twenty dollars she'd drawn out of her savings account on Friday to buy some new boots and a winter coat before she left for school. Their purchase was a necessity, not a fashionable luxury. She shrugged, decided she'd make do without them somehow. Added to the five dollars she had in her pocketbook, the amount would be enough for a round-trip ticket to Goldfield, with a little extra for meals.

Aunt Hilary wouldn't approve of her going. She'd always believed her younger brother had shirked his fatherly duties. Meg didn't agree. Her father had done his best by her. He had believed in her, shared his love for mining and its importance with her. She had to find out what had happened in Goldfield serious enough to make him send her a warning note.

* * *

Her heart pounding with a mixture of excitement and apprehension, Meg plied her way through the mob of humanity pushing and shoving its way alongside the train. She had to duck out of the way of a parasol being carried by a tall, redheaded woman who exuded the scent of expensive perfume. The hot air filled with shouts, and laughter reverberated with expectancy, as if something extraordinary were about to happen, everyone here a part of something special. A man elbowed past her, nearly causing her to drop her valise. A boot heel tromped on the toes of her right foot. She stumbled, gasped with pain, moved on.

A thermometer nailed to a telephone pole registered 110 degrees. Sweat streamed from under her arms down her sides. Her camisole was soaked. Her pale-blue traveling suit was wilted beyond saving. The wind had only a stultifying effect.

Meg hadn't been in a mining camp for fifteen years, but the smells and sounds were as familiar as if she'd left one yesterday—the stench of garbage rotting in the sun, of overflowing outhouses, the crack of a freighter's bullwhip, the steady crash of stamps against ore, beating like giant hearts. All of it felt charged with electricity, and she understood why her father couldn't live without it.

Not even the tedious, dusty, bone-jarring misery of the thousand-mile train trip with all its stops and changes had made her regret her decision to come. Now that she was finally here, she was anxious to find her father and get to the bottom of the mystery.

She felt a firm tap on her shoulder, started, glanced around. It was the older woman from the train with the reassuring blue eyes and ready smile who had introduced herself as Verna Bates, newspaperwoman.

"Good luck," she mouthed in the din, then disappeared into the crowd.

"Thank you. Same to you," shouted Meg, too late.

The pain in her foot was fading; the heat was not. She wondered how far it was to wherever her father lived, only to realize she had no idea where that was. The obvious place to inquire was the post office. Or maybe she should go to the office of the mining company where he had mentioned he worked. At the moment, all she wanted was to get out of the sun and collect herself.

Just ahead was a garage, its doors yawning wide. Blessed shade. As she began to walk toward it, a touring car—or what had been a touring car once, for now it was stripped of its fenders and sides and was loaded with crates—drove out and braked. A good-looking man, deeply tanned with thick brown hair so dark it was almost black, climbed out. He appeared to be in his midtwenties. His knee-high leather boots, brown jodhpurs, and open-necked shirt were smudged with black grease. He'd turned his leather cap to shade the back of his neck with the bill, and it gave him a kind of devil-may-care appearance.

He saw her approach, smiled.

"Is that your garage?"

He nodded. "Do you need to hire a car?"

She shook her head. "I was hoping I might stand in the doorway out of the sun for a few moments."

"By all means." He led the way into the garage. "I'd guess you just came in on the train from Tonopah."

She nodded, drew a soggy handkerchief out of her purse, and wiped her face. "Is it always this hot?"

"Seems so. At least it has been since I arrived in May."

She smiled.

"What brings you to Goldfield, Miss . . ."

"Kendall. Meggen Kendall."

Smiling broadly, he wiped his hands with a rag. "Bill Brown. Sole proprietor of Brown Transportation Company."

They shook hands.

"I'm here to visit my father. Jim Kendall. He's a mining engineer for the Mohawk Mines Company. The problem is he doesn't expect me, and the only address I have is a post office."

"Jim Kendall." He scratched his chin in thought. "The name's familiar, but I'm afraid I can't help you out on where he lives. I'll take you over to the company office. They'd probably know where to find him."

She shot a glance at his overloaded automobile, gave a little laugh. He followed her gaze, grinned. "I can make room in no time."

Ten minutes later, the crates removed, the passenger seat dusted off, Bill Brown helped her in, and they started off. The street was clogged with a few other automobiles, a great many rigs and mule teams. Wind swirled dust into miniature twisters around hooves and tires.

Bill turned left at the next corner, and they rolled slowly past tents and more tents—small tents with stovepipes poking through the roofs, large tents with no sides and filled with tables and chairs, as if they were restaurants, tents little more than a canopy to shield rows of lumber and supplies from the elements. In between were board buildings, some two stories high. One corner was occupied by a substantial-looking stone building with rounded front windows. Trash lay half hidden beneath boardwalks and shacks.

Men and a few women of all sorts—rough, dangerous-looking men, dandified men in the showy suits of gamblers, men in obviously expensive boots and new, broad-brimmed hats, gnarled prospectors in dusty canvas work clothes, women plainly dressed, women in elegant hats Meg might have seen in Denver—elbowed their way from wherever they had come to wherever they were going. Occasionally, a small child darted through the maze of legs.

Ahead perhaps a half mile or so, at the far end of the street, a lone, cone-shaped, barren mountain rose out of the desert bordered by mounds of waste dumps and tin-roofed stamp mills where ore was crushed and separated, their chimneys belching black smoke into the cloudless, blue sky. Instead of trees there was a forest of towering right triangles or headframes.

"Quite a place, don't you think?" Bill said, loudly enough to be heard over the noise of the street. He grinned.

She nodded, returned his smile. She felt excitement literally pulse in the hot air.

"Twenty thousand people in this camp," he shouted. "Or so they say."

By now they had gone beyond the main business section of the camp and were heading toward the mines themselves. Meg noted an occasional board shack or tent, but most of the buildings were large, like warehouses. Substantial-looking, with an aura of power.

Bill Brown drew up in front of one and cut the engine. "Well, this is it."

She stared at the large sign over the entrance. MOHAWK MINES COMPANY. For an instant she panicked, not knowing what was going on here, what she should expect. Her father was probably down in a mine somewhere, taking samples of ore in the latest drift.

Bill climbed out, but before he had time to come around to open her door, she got out. "You've been very kind, Mr. Brown."

"Anytime."

"Thank you for everything."

He eyed the door. "Why don't I go in with you?"

"Oh, I'll be quite all right."

"Then I'll wait."

She took a few steps backward toward the door, impatient now to go in. "I'm sure they'll be able to tell me where my father lives."

"I—"

"Truly."

He regarded her closely for a moment, as if trying to decide whether to make an issue of waiting for her, then smiled. "You know where the garage is if I can help."

*   *   *

In the half-light of the Mohawk Mines office, Meg saw she was in a fair-size room, bare of everything but the necessary office equipment: a safe against one wall, several desks, a typewriter, ledgers. Only after her eyes adjusted to the dim light did she notice a clerk standing behind the counter.

She crossed the rough plank floor. "Good afternoon," she said, smiling.

The man's wrinkled white shirt was collarless, open at the neck, the sleeves rolled up. "Somethin' I can do for ya', miss?"

"I'm looking for Mr. James Kendall."

"Kendall?" He stared at her.

Her heart stopped at the alarm in his eyes. "Can you tell me where he lives?"

The clerk continued to stare at her for an instant, then opened a door behind him, leaned through it, and called for someone named Charley.

Meg felt a sense of foreboding as she waited. A man, who looked to be about her age, appeared a few minutes later. He was fairly tall, trim, with light-brown hair combed straight back without a part. He, too, wore an open-necked shirt, khaki breeches, high-laced boots.

"The lady here is after Jim Kendall," said the clerk.

The man frowned. "Charley Thompson," he said as he came toward her. "I was privileged to work with Mr. Kendall."

"Can you direct me to him?"

He gave her a quizzical look.

"Is anything wrong?" she asked.

"I . . ."

Meg's foreboding turned to alarm. "What's happened? Has my father been injured?"

"I thought . . . the fact you're here. I thought the company had sent you a telegram."

Her heart stopped. She forced herself to ask, "About what?"

"Mr. Kendall died as a result of an accident in the Haywood-Mohawk mine two days ago."

Chapter 2

Tess Wallace strode into the Ajax Saloon, her blood boiling. She pushed away the slobbery, eager greetings of Teddy, the Saint Bernard dog maintaining his station at the entrance. She was tempted to crack her ivory-handled parasol over the head of the nearest customer. Today was the sixth day in a row she'd met the train from Tonopah. Still no Jake.

How long could it take for him to arrange the details of a prize-fight? She was counting on the extra business the fight would bring to Goldfield, but waiting around didn't suit her.

Just as she was unpinning her new Italian leghorn straw hat, she felt someone in back of her, then hands encircling her waist. She turned around.

"Do you know how many trains I met?" she asked into Jake's handsome face, the grin showing his perfectly white teeth. "What the hell kept you so long?"

Without bothering to answer, he bent and kissed her on the neck.

She shoved him away, glared at him. "The least you could've done was telegraph."

"Well, I'm here now, and I'm parched. Let's have a drink."

She folded her arms. "What about the fight?"

"I'll tell you all about it over a drink."

Tess glanced past him, saw his Gladstone deposited by the entrance, but no dress box. "Where's the dress for Jenny Lynn?"

His smile wavered.

"You did bring it, didn't ya?"

"The fact is . . . I forgot, Tess. I'm sorry. The business—"

"You're sorry? You forgot?" she said through clenched teeth. "The dress was to be for Jenny Lynn's first day of school."

He reached out to pull her toward him, but she stepped beyond his grasp.

"A kid's first day of school is the most important there is."

"Sure, Tess." His eyes were as innocent and sorrowful as those of a puppy who had wet the carpet and now begged to be forgiven.

She glanced away, seething, sick with disappointment. Nothing in her life had prepared her for the love she felt for Jenny Lynn. With a stone-hearted father, a mother no better, and two brothers who'd left home before she could walk—Tess still had moments when she couldn't believe her daughter was real. Working in Miss Nell's, Tess had known a few whores who'd had kids, had seen the mess, the misery it caused, and she wanted no part of it. She washed herself out proper with boric acid after every customer. If something went wrong, she'd made up her mind to get an abortion and hang the cost. Thank God she'd changed her mind.

From the first moment she'd held Jenny Lynn in her arms, her little face all red, her eyes like tiny blue buttons, Tess had known her daughter was a miracle meant to happen. Somehow they'd managed, the two of them, until last year when her daughter had been five—they were living in Cripple Creek in the mountains above Colorado Springs where Tess had just turned from whoring to tending bar in a saloon—and she'd faced the fact that a saloon wasn't a proper home for a child either.

What Jenny Lynn needed was a decent place to grow up, like a real ranch with horses to ride, plenty of space to run and have fun and be safe. All that took money, more than Tess could make with one eye always out for her daughter. When she heard about Gold-field, she knew that's where she could make it.

Asking around Colorado Springs, Tess had found the Briggles, who had two kids of their own and already cared for two others. They'd seemed kindly, and their house was on North Cascade in a nice enough part of town. Leaving Jenny Lynn with strangers about broke Tess's heart, but it wouldn't be for long. The moment she had her pile, they'd be together again.

"I bet the Bon Ton could order something real pretty, have it sent directly to Jenny Lynn in no time."

"To hell with something from the Bon Ton. Jenny Lynn deserves the best, from San Francisco. Anyway, it might not get to the Springs in time."

"Look. Go over and talk to Mrs. What's-her-name at the Bon Ton this afternoon. She can send a telegram. I'll pay for it. What-ever it costs."

Arms akimbo, Tess felt her fury rise again. Damn Jake's hide for making her lose her temper. She took a deep breath, gave him a frigid stare. "You forgot. You go to the Bon Ton."

"For Christ's sake, Tess. Back off."

A familiar, deep voice suddenly boomed a greeting behind her. "Jake! Welcome back."

Tess glanced over her shoulder and glowered at her partner, Vic Ajax, for deliberately getting Jake off the hook.

Still, Vic occupied a special place in her heart. Slight, gray-haired, no taller than she, he had a hooked nose, a generous mouth, and large, brown eyes that almost always sparkled with humor. Past fifty, to her he was as much an uncle as a business partner. He'd been born Vic Xerxes, but when a mine owner he'd been working for went broke and could only meet payroll through the letter *H*, Vic decided to avoid any future problems of that kind and took the name Ajax.

Jake greeted Vic with a wave, and Vic went behind the grand cherrywood bar they'd ordered all the way from Chicago. "How about a whiskey?"

"Thought you'd never ask," Jake said.

"He'll have a beer," Tess said crisply. She leaned down and stroked Teddy's thick coat, careful to avoid the drool as he panted up at her adoringly. "Unless he's paying."

"Oh, come on, Tess. You know I'm not a beer man." Jake kissed her playfully.

She wished she didn't hanker after him the way she did. Men meant nothing to her unless they were useful, but there was something about the sight of Jake's dark hair, broad shoulders, and flat belly that made her ache with longing. He was the handsomest man she'd ever seen, smooth as silk on the outside, but underneath a crude, tough man who had started his life on the wharves of Seattle. Not worth trusting for a second, and yet—

Vic filled a shot glass and slid it along the bar to Jake.

Tess watched Jake toss it down with a single gulp, heard his sigh of contentment. Maybe now, finally, they could get down to business. "So what about the fight?"

He glanced at her, his eyes serious, with that flat look they assumed when money was discussed. "The San Francisco big boys are coming next week. I promised to fix up special cars for them to travel from Reno the day before the fight. I talked to both Gans's and Nelson's managers."

"I can just hear the clink of those gold pieces now," Vic said.

Tess smiled. Trainloads of men from San Francisco and Los Angeles would flood the saloons and gambling tables before and after the lightweight championship fight. She and Vic would make a nice pile of change. She glanced at Jake, the biggest gambler in a town of gamblers. He'd probably make more money off the fight than anyone, and it wasn't going to be off the price of drinks and the take from poker games. Why couldn't she do the same?

Absently, she twisted a tendril of hair hanging along the back of her neck and let an idea work its way around her head until it came clear to her. "With everybody in town at the fight, the saloons will close for part of the day."

"You think so?" Vic asked as he refilled Jake's shot glass.

"It only makes sense," Tess said.

Jake silently contemplated the glass of whiskey. "I don't know. The boys expect their booze."

"You bet they do. We'll sell beer at the fight."

Jake grinned. "Say now. That's a great idea. I'll get going on it right away."

"Wait a minute. It's my idea. I'll sell the beer."

Jake flashed her a magnificent smile. "Fine. But to sell memorabilia, beer, whatever, it'll cost you."

"In case you hadn't noticed, this is a free country." Her tone was cold. "I aim to make as much money as I can from this fight. I can make a lot extra by peddlin' beer."

He chucked her under the chin. "But I put up the money for this fight."

"You flatter yourself," Tess said tersely. "You put up less than half."

He shrugged, straightened his hat. "Who cares? I leased the land for the fight. I paid to have the ring built, to rent the chairs. As I say, if you want to peddle beer, fine. But it'll cost you."

She glared at him, eyes narrowed. "How much?"

Jake gazed thoughtfully at the ceiling for a moment, then at her. "A thousand. That has a nice ring to it."

"It's highway robbery."

"It's fair."

She pulled in a deep breath, trying to get hold of herself. She wasn't about to let Jake profit from her idea. If she put her mind to it, she'd come up with a way around him. "I won't pay it."

"Suit yourself." He leaned over and kissed the nape of her neck before she could push him away. "Just remember, no one comes on the property without a ticket or a license to sell."

CHAPTER 3

Arms crossed over her ample bosom, Verna Bates stood to one side as the freight men struggled to move another crate inside the one-room shack that was to be the home of the *Goldfield Star*. With disgust, she eyed the banty-rooster-size man who had planted himself on her doorstep. She'd hardly had time to get off the train and follow the freight wagon over here, but this union organizer had known she was in town and was waiting for her.

"I just thought I'd drop by, welcome you to Goldfield," he said with an oily smile. "The name's McGee. Tim McGee."

She gave him an even look.

"You being brand-new, there'd be no way you'd know this is a union town."

"What's your point?"

"Just wanted you to know the papers in town are in our camp."

She cocked an eyebrow. "I don't take kindly to threats, Mr. McGee."

"None intended."

"I think you better get about your business. I've got nothing against unions, but your bunch—"

"The International Workers of the World is all that keeps

the capitalists from raping the miner, stealing his just due."

She stepped aside to let the freight men go past her. "Save it. You know, and I know, you're all a bunch of socialists."

Tim McGee shook his head in mock distress. "That's just the attitude that was the downfall of your predecessor."

"So one paper's gone. Last I knew there were still two."

"Papers that have seen the light."

"Maybe." She turned and stepped into the shack. "Right now, I've got work to do." She slammed the door in his face, pulled in a deep breath to steady herself. She had enough to manage starting up a new paper without trouble from the union.

She went over to check the crates. From all appearances, the Lee press had made the long trip from Creede relatively unscathed, though the type was probably a jumble. She went to the back of the shack, looked around. This would be her living quarters.

As soon as she worked up enough energy, she'd go out and buy the basics: a canvas cot, some bedding, a table, a couple of chairs, a modest set of dishes, a few utensils, an ice chest, maybe a Reliance two-burner oil stove, and a chamber pot. The long move this time had made it too expensive to haul household goods. To replace them now probably would come to at least fifteen dollars. Her pocketbook was already bleeding, and she still had to restock on paper and ink.

She breathed in the stench of offal and rot gut whiskey wafting through the open windows. She was thinking about getting out of her corset and into her wrapper when she heard a banging on the door. Before she could open it, a buff-colored envelope, a telegram, had been slid under the door. She eyed it uneasily, sensing it was from her brother. Never once had Amos sent her good news.

She leaned over, picked it up, worked her thumb under the flap, and pulled out the single sheet. She went to the window for better reading light.

GONE TO BULLFROG STOP JUST TO HAVE A LOOK-
SEE STOP AMOS

She reread it, closed her eyes. The incessant thump from the stamp mills pounded in her head. She was getting too old to start over again. Amos was, too, for that matter. She didn't want to pick up and go to Bullfrog, wherever it was. She'd hoped this time he'd really meant it when he insisted Goldfield was the answer to his dreams.

Lord in heaven, some things never changed. He couldn't stay in a place more than a week before he itched to move on. There were days she couldn't remember the names of all the places they'd lived, her memories a jumble of cabins and false fronts, high hopes, and the routine of packing up, hiring a buckboard, arranging for the treasured Lee press to be trucked over whatever pass lay between them and the next burg.

She sighed, sat on the window ledge. She squeezed her eyes shut for a minute. They'd been blurring a lot lately. She wondered if she was going blind. It happened to old people sometimes, and today she felt old. She straightened her back. A woman alone with no one to lean on didn't have the luxury to be old, much less old and blind.

She'd done for herself since childhood. Her mother, then her father, had died not three weeks after they'd started the trek to California, leaving her and Amos to fend as best they could among the emigrants in Fort Kearney on the godforsaken plains of the Nebraska Territory. They'd been bitsy things, and the sutler's wife had taken them in, watched over them until Verna was old enough to pull her own weight around the store. At sixteen, Amos took off for Pikes Peak. There'd been nothing else to do but go after him. She'd cared for him most of his life. How else would he have survived?

Through the years Verna had fallen in love a few times. Somehow, though, it always seemed to end up being a decision between the man she was in love with or Amos, and Amos always won.

Still, she wasn't sorry. Amos needed her. She made friends easily. True, it wasn't the same as living in the same town all her life where everyone had known her since she was a tyke, but life had its trade-offs. She'd always been a woman of strong beliefs, eager to take up just causes wherever she and Amos lived. As an outsider, she could take an objective view, and it wasn't long before she discovered a newspaper was a power to be reckoned with. The union organizer named McGee who had felt the need to pay her a call obviously agreed. She wondered if she ended up following her brother to Bullfrog whether the union there would be as much of a nuisance.

She leaned out the window and scanned the milling crowd passing the shack. Right now a boy was what she needed. Finally, she spotted one coming out of a store across the street. She put her fingers between her teeth and whistled. The boy looked around. She whistled again and gave a wave. "You, boy. Over here."

He nodded and half-ran, half-hopped across the street, as if one leg was stiff.

"I've got a dollar for you if you help me set up my press."

The boy was thin, ragged-looking, too small to be down in the mines yet. She liked his hustle. "What's your name?"

"Jim. Jim Earnest."

"Are you a hard worker, Jim Earnest?"

"Hard as you'll ever find," he said, jamming his hands into his pants pockets.

"Good," she said. "Come on in and show me."

The boy ducked past her into the shack. She sighed. Lord in heaven, an old woman and a boy to do the work of two men.

CHAPTER 4

$\mathcal{M}$eg's sense of time was all mixed up. She had no idea whether it had been one hour or three since she'd arrived. She was barely aware of the crowds as Charley Thompson guided her along the street toward the mortuary and explained that the accident had happened when an improperly timbered area of the mine had collapsed. Two miners had also been killed. Due to the heat, her father would have to be buried tomorrow. There was no time for Aunt Hilary to make the trip. Still, Meg needed to send her a telegram.

Her mind reeled. It all seemed unreal, a waking dream, a very bad dream. Finally, Charley stopped in front of a board building. A sign identifying it as LITTLE'S FUNERAL PARLOR hung above the door. They went through the open door into a narrow room with piles of lumber scattered about. It occurred to her the boards were probably for coffins, and the realization made her shudder.

A rotund man with a florid complexion, wearing a dusty, high silk hat and a grimy, black cutaway over an equally grimy union suit walked over from the back of the room where boards lay balanced across a series of sawhorses.

"Can I help you?" he asked.

Charley introduced her to the man whose name was Mr. Little. "Miss Kendall is here to view her father's body."

"Jim Kendall," said Mr. Little.

Meg nodded, felt herself tighten, as she might to ward off a blow.

"My condolences. Jim was a fair hand at five-card stud. He'll be missed," Mr. Little said as he removed his hat, drew one arm across his sweaty forehead. "He's . . . The deceased is in the back. Follow me."

A shaft of sunlight streaming through the single window wrapped over the pine box, resting between two sawhorses. Mr. Little went over to the coffin, lifted the lid, and stepped aside. Seized with an urge to flee, Meg felt Charley's hand on her elbow, as if he realized her distress. Like an automaton, she moved to the coffin.

For an instant, before she looked down, she prayed there had been a mistake, that it wasn't her father inside. But there was no doubt. Even with his bruised and battered face, she recognized the man who lay in the pine box, hands folded, eyes closed, as Jim Kendall, mining engineer, wandering but loving father. He wore a suit, obviously new, which was too large for him. Someone had combed his normally unruly sandy hair.

She hadn't seen him much over the years. Yet somehow through the newspapers and the brief notes he'd sent, his occasional visits, she'd always felt they were kindred spirits. She wanted to touch him, perhaps kiss his forehead, say good-bye. But the impatient shuffle of men's feet behind her, the rhythmic sound of lumber being sawed, reminded her she was not alone. Her heart like lead, she took in a deep breath to steady herself and turned away.

As she stood in the entrance of the mortuary in the blinding light and heat of the afternoon, she felt the control she'd held on to so desperately slip from her grasp. The hope her father's death had all been some horrible mistake had faded, then disappeared, like moonlight behind dark clouds. A great wave of grief washed over her and filled her heart with so much pain she wasn't sure whether to scream or cry. Her throat tightened. She caught her breath, squeezed her eyes tight against the tears, but it was no use. Her hands hiding her face, she began to sob.

*   *   *

Meg stood in front of her father's small, flat-roofed house. The only building in sight not built of wood or canvas, it stood in stark contrast with its neighbors. Like Jim Kendall, it was different and seemed to be proud of the fact.

The house appeared to be constructed of speckled concrete. She came closer. The speckles became circles, glass circles, row upon row of them, the bottoms of beer bottles, she realized—hundreds of them laid on their sides, plastered together with adobe.

"Are you sure you want to go in?" asked Charley Thompson from behind her.

"I don't see any way around it." Pulling herself very straight, her heart hammering, she took the key they had recovered from her father's clothing, inserted it into the lock, turned it, and opened the unpainted door.

The room had a stuffy, almost sour, smell to it. But compared with the outside, the air was cool, sending the same delicious shiver down her back as when she used to escape the summer sun in the depths of her aunt's root cellar. Green window shades had been pulled down to block out the sunshine.

Even in the room's dim light, Meg realized at once something was very wrong. Holding back a gasp, she stared at papers, clothes, bed linen, books, and broken dishes strewn across the floor. A cot lay on its side, two chairs overturned. Whoever had broken in had done a thorough job of ransacking the place.

Meg went to the windows, pulled up the shades. As she surveyed the mess, she thought of her father's warning note.

"Miss Kendall . . ."

She looked over her shoulder at Charley Thompson. She'd forgotten he was here. "I need to get the sheriff," she said.

"I'm not sure you'll get much help. Unless it's claim jumping, robbery isn't considered too important around here."

She nodded. "I suppose not."

He righted the cot and the chairs. "Maybe you should let this wait. We could go over to the Casey and rent you a room."

She squatted on her haunches to gather up the papers and books, a photograph album tied shut with pale blue ribbons. "I think I'll stay here."

He didn't reply.

"I'll be quite all right." She glanced at him, strained for a smile. "You've been most kind."

"At least allow me to escort you to dinner later."

She stood, some of the papers and books and the album clutched to her breasts. She put them on the table. "That would be nice. Thank you."

After he left, she surveyed the chaos again and realized she was shaking. She had to get hold of herself. She took off her hat, laid it next to the books and papers. By the time she put some order to the place, her mind would be clearer. She would be able to make more sense of all this.

She picked up the bed linens, put them by the door. She'd find someone to wash them tomorrow. As she stooped to gather the clothes strewn about on the floor, her fingers hit something hard, and she uncovered a long, narrow metal box, its lid open. It was empty. She recalled her father's pleas to hang on to his stocks. Could he have kept the certificates here in the house, in this strongbox? Were they what the robber had been after?

She knew her father had no use for banks. Others must have known that as well, maybe thought he kept the certificates somewhere in his house for safekeeping. Yet her father wasn't stupid. He wouldn't have risked certificates, as easily negotiable as cash, to the chance of a robbery. A broker probably held them.

She pulled in a deep breath, arranged the books on the shelf by the cot, then glanced about the small room. It was as if, in the next instant, her father would walk through the door. A wave of grief washed over her, and she caught in her breath.

Everything that had been her father's was here, everything but the stocks she felt sure, and those she was determined to track down. Until today she'd been a child, the one looked after and protected. Now the tables were turned. He would expect her to do her best, to protect what he had valued.

Glancing about for a broom, she pushed an errant strand of hair off her forehead. She sighed. She must look a mess. She probably ought to try to clean herself up a little before Charley came back to take her to dinner.

*   *   *

The growing dark of early evening was having a cooling effect on the dry air as she and Charley Thompson walked the two blocks to a restaurant called La Parisienne. Yet inside, with the crowd and the noise, it seemed hot as ever. They found an empty table. Charley seated her, and the waiter, a long white apron over his trousers and collarless shirt, handed them each a menu.

Charley ordered a bourbon, then glanced at her. "How about a sherry? The water's not fit to drink."

She smiled. "Actually, that would be nice."

But when it came to ordering food, her father's death had taken away her appetite, and she told him whatever he had would do for her as long as it wasn't too much.

As she toyed with the silverware, she gazed absently around the crowded room at the men, some roughly dressed, others in starched white collars and cravats, all of their faces alive with whatever they were talking about as they shoveled food from plate to mouth with no pretense of manners. The few women with them wore lip rouge and low-necked dresses that showed off their breasts. One of them had an ostrich feather stuck in her coal black hair. Trying not to stare, Meg decided the women must be prostitutes.

After a minute or two she became aware of Charley watching

her. She smiled. "I couldn't have made it through the day without your help, Mr. Thompson."

"Charley. Please. I count myself fortunate to have known your father."

"You were friends, then?"

"I'm only an assistant to an engineer. Mr. Kendall and I didn't actually work in the same mine, but we worked for the same company."

She realized he hadn't answered her question. Still, he was the only person she knew to ask about her father.

"Would you tell me more about the accident?"

"As I say, we didn't work in the same mine, so what I know is only hearsay."

"Which is?"

He looked uncomfortable, glanced away for an instant, then back at her. "Now and again a vein gets wider to form an area of considerable size until it's like a large underground room called a stope."

"I know."

He gave her a small smile. "Anyway, to mine or stope out an area, miners drill upward, load the holes with dynamite, shoot it, muck out the broken ore, and bring it up the shaft." He paused.

"Go on."

"The problem comes in supporting the back of a stope."

"The roof, you mean."

He nodded. "With all the hurry to get out the ore, I'm afraid sometimes it isn't timbered properly, precautions aren't taken."

"You're saying the roof caved in when Dad was there."

"Yes." His eyes darkened with concern. "I'm sorry."

"There were miners with him, you said."

"Two."

"Did they have families living here in Goldfield?"

"I don't know, but I doubt it."

The waiter set their drinks before them. She gazed at the golden sherry in the glass. Mining was a dangerous business. Accidents did happen. Yet her father had managed to go unscathed all these years precisely because he knew the dangers. "Was there an investigation?"

"The superintendent talked to the shift foreman."

She regarded him evenly. "That was all?"

"It's a busy time. With the leasing deadlines—"

"I don't understand."

He took a sip of bourbon. "Leasing's a common practice here. The veins are extremely irregular, so irregular it requires a lot of capital to conduct exploration on a claim. It's a high-risk venture to discover a profitable ore zone. The big money, which is invested through the stock exchanges in San Francisco and New York, was uneasy about that, and refused to put in. So entrepreneurs—like my bosses, George Winters and Chester Nolan—"

Her heart stopped at the mention of the names. "You work for Winters and Nolan?"

"So did your father. They own the Mohawk Mines Company."

She took in a sharp breath.

"Is something wrong? You look pale."

"Just tired." She tried for a smile. "Please go on."

He gave her a quizzical look. "Let's see. About the leasing. Winters and Nolan stepped in and bought a half dozen claims, incorporated, then leased the mines back to the locators for twenty-five percent of what would be produced within a prescribed time limit. Usually six months to a year. For a good many of the richest producers, including the mines within the Mohawk Mines Company, that time limit is December thirty-first."

"All the mines are leased?"

"All but one. So you can see . . ." His eyes seemed to plead for her to understand. "The investigation about your father's accident . . ."

"It took a backseat." She sipped at the sherry, felt its warmth inside her. One man's death in the grand scheme of things didn't matter much. That was what Charley was saying, or what the company had said. She didn't agree.

"Sad to say, I guess it's part of the business."

She couldn't bring herself to reply. For a moment they didn't speak. Finally, more out of politeness than interest, she said, "Tell me about the mine that isn't leased."

"That's the Fourth of July, Pete Eckles's baby."

She stared at him, instantly recalling her father's note. "My father knew a man by that name."

"I guess he did. Now that you mention it, Mr. Kendall told me they went back to the days when they both worked at the Independence in Cripple Creek."

"You say Mr. Eckles owns the Fourth of July?"

"Sure does. He incorporated in Wyoming and capitalized at twenty-five million dollars, issued two and a half million shares. The July has its own ten-stamp mill, its own water source. It's probably the biggest operation in camp."

The waiter brought their plates of trout, riced potatoes, green salad. The meal was beyond anything Meg had expected to find in a mining camp. Charley picked up his fork and knife, ran the tip of the knife down the back of the trout, then skillfully lifted the top layer of the meat away from the backbone. He paused, looked over at her. "I guess you can already see Goldfield isn't your ordinary gold find."

"Apparently not." She took a bite of salad, put down her fork, too distracted to eat.

"Geologists don't even call the ore deposits veins. They say they're irregular masses of dense, flinty quartz. Changes in dip are almost the rule. The pay shoots or pay ore are just as unpredictable. But when a rich vein is found, like in the golden horseshoe, where the Mohawk Mines and the Fourth of July are located, it's Katy-bar-the-door."

Charley talked on, and she listened, picking at her dinner, but feeling a certain comfort in hearing the terms that had sprinkled her father's conversations over the years.

As they left the restaurant and headed back to her father's

house, Meg still had a head full of questions. "Tell me more about the Haywood-Mohawk where father worked, would you?"

He glanced at her, took her arm.

"As I understand it, Jem Haywood was the man who staked the claim. He didn't have enough money to develop it, so Senator Nolan bought him out for a pittance—five thousand dollars, I think—and leased it back to him a year or so ago. Your father was already working for Nolan and Winters at the time. Last April both the Haywood-Mohawk and the mine where I work, which is just next door, the Foster-Girard, hit it big. On one day that month, the seventeenth, taken together, they produced six million dollars."

"In one day?"

He nodded. "Hard to believe, isn't it? As of today, the value is a hundred and fifty dollars a ton, plus a few cents. By any standards, that's rich ore, believe me. Unfortunately, there's a slight problem."

"Which is?"

"Well, the mine that adjoins the Haywood to the south is the Fourth of July, and it's filed a suit for trespass."

"The Fourth of July is just next door? Pete Eckles's mine?"

"Right."

"Is the suit legitimate?"

"I don't think so, though the court seems to think Eckles has sufficient grounds. At this point, my bosses have to produce a survey to show they're in the right. I saw a map your father did that showed pretty clearly the stopes all end on the south along a nearly east-west line, a good one hundred feet north of the Fourth of July claim."

"I should think that would be enough to dismiss the case."

Charley frowned. "It probably would be if the map could be found. Somewhere in the confusion of the accident, it disappeared."

"So there'll be a trial?"

He nodded. "I'm afraid so. It may take months. The court might even shut both parties down until it's settled."

They had reached the bottle house. Meg's mind was swimming

with facts and figures and names, some directly connected with her father's note, some not. She leaned her back against the door, her hands in back of her around the porcelain knob. "The suit brought by the Fourth of July—"

"What about it?"

"Would it prevent Mr. Eckles from coming to my father's funeral tomorrow?"

"I don't see why it should. Unfortunately, he probably doesn't know your father passed away. He left town before the accident."

"Oh." She felt let down. She'd automatically assumed that as a special friend of her father, Mr. Eckles would want to be with her when she buried him.

"There're bound to be others who'll come. Your father was well liked."

She summoned a smile, grateful for his solicitude. He told her he'd rented a rig to take them to the cemetery in the morning, said good night.

*   *   *

Inside, the room was dark. She couldn't remember where the lamp was or whether there were any matches. The tent next door was within a few feet of her open window. Kerosene lamps, suspended from the beam of the tent, swung gently in the steady breeze, their yellow light silhouetting the men inside as they lounged on cots, smoked, played cards. The night was filled with the sounds of their laughter, in the background the pounding from the mills a mile away, across the street a pistol shot.

As her eyes adjusted to the dark, she found her valise, drew out her nightgown. She unbuttoned her suit, took it and her chemise off, unhooked her corset, let it drop to the floor. Finally she stepped out of her drawers, took off her shoes and stockings, and put on her nightgown.

She stretched out on the cot, bare of linens, shaped by her father's body. Her head reeled with what Charley had told her about the Fourth of July mine, about Pete Eckles and his friendship with her father, about the suit and the missing map so crucial to its settlement. Her father had warned her against Winters and Nolan, the men he worked for. Perhaps her father's death hadn't been an accident at all, and they'd had something to do with it. And could it be that it wasn't the stock certificates but the map her father made that the robber had been after?

She stared at the ceiling, her head full of what lay ahead. She had to find the stock certificates. Then, before she confronted Winters and Nolan, she must track down Pete Eckles, wherever he was, to solve the mystery about her father's warning and the map.

In the space of one day, her life had changed.

Forget medical school. Here, not Johns Hopkins, was where she belonged.

Medical school was Aunt Hilary's dream, not hers. It was Aunt Hilary who had interested her friend, Mrs. Philpott, the richest woman in Boulder, in Meg; Mrs. Philpott who had urged Meg to follow in the footsteps of a brilliant, young Colorado woman who had been among the first women to attend Johns Hopkins Medical School. When Meg had quietly questioned the choice of Johns Hopkins, Mrs. Philpott had explained that a little over ten years ago her closest friend and three other enormously wealthy women in Baltimore had been approached by Johns Hopkins University to fund the medical school it hoped—but had no money—to establish. The women had struck a deal with the trustees: admit women to the medical school and the money would be theirs.

By her first year in college, the plan for Meg's future had been set. She had had no objections then. The challenge had intrigued her. She'd even worked in Dr. Mauer's office as a kind of assistant on weekends and in the summers. In due time, Meg had been admitted to medical school. A scholarship was arranged. Everyone presumed she wanted to go into medicine to save mankind, when, in her heart, the real appeal had always been to make a good living.

None of it seemed important now. If she'd grown up living with her father, she would have kept his house, seen to his needs. Her heart ached at the irony that only now she had the chance. She'd stay in Goldfield where she could shepherd whatever it was he'd left her, including his good name, and build on it.

His death was offering her a chance to make something of herself on her own terms, something he would've been proud of.

Closing her eyes, Meg felt the tight emptiness in her chest loosen ever so slightly. The grief was still there and would be for a long time; but in the days to come it would ebb because the kindred spirit she'd felt for her father was a powerful antidote. By honoring him, she would honor herself. She'd be free of the expectations of others. No matter what lay ahead, no matter the risks, her father would be by her side. Once this had been his town. Now it would be hers.

CHAPTER 5

*V*erna sat on the stoop, enjoying the relative cool of the beginning of the business day. A fancy new trap with yellow upholstery and a high-stepping matched pair went by, skirting a twenty-mule team hauling a string of ore wagons. An automobile, the driver in a proper duster, cap, and goggles, wove through the tangle, honking the horn. Horses reared, mules balked. Verna smiled. Not yet 7:00 A.M. and the whole camp was already in a rush, as if there wasn't a second to spare. Every mining town she'd lived in had some of that feel about it. But Goldfield was a step up in spades.

She had to figure out what made the place tick. If she was to make a living, she had to get some kind of an angle to distinguish the *Star* from the two other papers in town. At the moment, none came to mind.

She sighed, stood up, about to go in, when she saw the young woman she'd met on the train. Pale-blond hair beneath a fashionable straw sailor. Her skirt and shirtwaist of good quality. She was a pretty thing, taller than most, with bright, intelligent eyes that sparkled, and a careful, contained way beneath her purposeful stride.

Meggen Kendall. Verna had a knack for names. Meggen Kendall, she was sure that was it. She remembered the girl telling her she'd come to visit her father. As she walked in Verna's direction, straight-backed, head high, ignoring the admiring glances of every man she passed, she looked as out of place as an elegant, yellow tulip in a patch of thistles.

Verna called to her. Meggen Kendall saw her, smiled in recognition as she approached. "Miss Bates, isn't it?"

"Verna."

Meggen Kendall smiled.

"You look like you're in a hurry."

"I'm on my way to the stock exchange."

"Along with every other soul in camp except me." Verna cocked her head, intrigued. "What's the stock exchange got a pretty thing like you needs?"

"My father's stocks, if I can find the broker who holds them."

"So you hitched up with your dad all right then?"

"He died in a mine accident two days before I arrived." Her tone was formal, but her blue eyes glistened with tears. "I buried him *yesterday.*"

Verna ached at the sight of her barely disguised grief. She wanted to reach out and give Meggen Kendall a hug, but instinct told her the young woman would not thank her for it. A sorry was all she decided to offer.

Meggen gave a little nod, pulled in a deep breath, then slowly exhaled. "You're most kind."

"Anything I can do—"

Meggen's smile was polite but distant. She glanced past her down the street. "Someone told me the exchange is in the next block."

The girl obviously had one thing on her mind. No lingering to chat, which would have been nice. All-business.

"They told you right. If you listen close, you can hear the din from here."

Meggen gave a little laugh, thanked her, and went on her way.

With her father dead, there was no reason for the girl to stay in Goldfield. Verna doubted she'd ever see her again. That's the way it was in mining camps. Everybody always on the move, eager for whatever they might find around the next bend. Fine and good for the young who had plenty of time to put down roots later, but hard on the old. She sighed, got up, and went inside.

Surveying the crates that sat in the middle of the floor, she knew she needed a crowbar to open them. Maybe she could borrow one. There sure wasn't any sense wasting the money to buy one just to open four boxes.

She eyed the back of the shack, now her living quarters. The cot and dishes, the two-burner stove, ice chest, and chamber pot had come to more than she'd intended to spend. Add in the cost of the little bit of groceries and slice of beef she'd bought yesterday and it amounted to close to twenty dollars. Plain robbery. A tin of crackers was a quarter compared to fifteen cents in Cripple Creek, a head of cabbage fifteen cents instead of the normal five. She better set up her press and sell some papers or she'd starve in a week.

Someone called her name, and she turned to see framed in the doorway the tall, good-looking young man she'd seen driving around camp, a good-size bundle on one shoulder.

He was grinning at her. "I've got some newsprint for you."

"Bill Brown, isn't it?"

"It is indeed." He stepped inside, put the bundle down on the floor.

She eyed it with a frown. "Shoot, I didn't think it'd come so soon. I haven't even set up the press."

"Why don't I give you a hand?"

"You'd need a crowbar."

"There's one right out in the car."

She tried to smile. "You're nice to offer, but with all the other deliveries you probably have—"

"I'll get those crates open and be out of here in fifteen minutes."

"As I say, you're nice to offer, but I'll manage it later. I've hired a boy to help. He'll be here directly after school."

The young man shoved the bundle of newsprint in one corner. "You're sure? It wouldn't take any time at all."

"Couldn't be surer." She reached into the pocket of her skirt for her change purse. It still held a five-dollar gold piece. "How much do I owe you for that?"

"I'll put it on your bill. You can pay me the next time I come by."

After he'd left, Verna glowered at the crates, cursing herself for turning down his offer of help. What in Sam Hill was wrong with her? She needed those crates opened, and he could have done it with no problem. I can do it myself. She'd said that to herself and the world since she was knee-high, and where had it gotten her? The world didn't care one whit whether she could manage her own life without anyone else's help.

Any reasonably intelligent person would have figured that out by the time she was sixty-five. But not her. Damn. She kicked the nearest crate and hit her right big toe wrong. She sat down on the offending crate and gingerly wiggled the injured toe. It seemed all right.

Enough of this. She'd told the young man she would wait for Jim Earnest, so that's what she'd do. In the meantime, she'd go in search of the local mortician to carve her a new masthead. It was a start.

*   *   *

The heavyset man in the sweat-soaked union suit and filthy top hat had identified himself as Clem Little. Judging from his red face, he was a fair-size drinker. But as long as he could carve her masthead, whether he stank to high heaven, which he did, or drank himself blind was none of her business.

She pulled out the block of wood carved with the name of one of the newspapers she'd put out a few years back from her pocketbook. "I want you to make me a masthead. Like this one, except with *Goldfield Star* as the paper's name. I was thinking maybe a crown of stars over a mountain peak would be appropriate."

"I'm a coffin maker," he said.

"I know, but I thought—"

He studied the piece of wood, turned it over, and examined the back. "Whoever carved this was sloppy."

"I can see you're a man of talent," she said solemnly, playing to his professional pride because she could tell he was reluctant.

He glanced at her. "Ya' gotta like wood if you're gonna do good work."

"I'm sure that's true." She looked around her and spotted the coffins lined up along the opposite wall. "It looks like you're doing quite a business."

He followed her gaze. "That's in case things heat up after the fight."

"The prizefight."

"The same."

He gave her back the wooden block. "Like I say, I'm a coffin maker."

"Mr. Little, you're the only person who can help me on this."

Their glances held for an instant before he beckoned for the block, and she handed it to him.

"Tell you what. Draw me a picture like you want, and bring this thing back for a model."

She smiled. "How soon can you do it?"

"Depends."

She felt a sudden flick of apprehension, anticipating what was coming next. The world revolved around money. "On what?"

"See, if I do this, I'll have to hire another man to do the rest of them coffins the sheriff ordered and—"

"How much?"

He shot her a wounded glance, scowled.

"You do want extra money, don't you?"

"Is that what I said?"

"No. I guess not." She was becoming a cynic in her old age. She wouldn't blame him if he refused to do the work at all. Then how would she put out the paper? "I have to have a masthead for my paper, Mr. Little. I'm sure you see that."

"Like I told ya' already, it depends."

"What if I come back later today? Maybe you'd know by then."

He took off the top hat, reached inside it, drew out a filthy handkerchief, and wiped the sweat from his round face. "Maybe. But I wouldn't count on it if I was you."

CHAPTER 6

*M*eg turned the corner and discovered Verna Bates had been quite right. From the size of the crowd gesturing and shouting in front of the flat-roofed stone building at the end of the block, it looked as if at least half of Goldfield's citizens, men and women, must do business with the stock exchange. Yet that's where she must go.

Once she managed to push past the entrance, she became wedged in the midst of the throng. She couldn't move. The only hope of getting even a glimpse of what was going on was to stand on her tiptoes.

As she strained this way and that around people's heads to gain a better view, she was able to get a glimpse of a large room, maybe thirty feet by thirty feet. A kind of blackboard nearly eight feet high and twice as long occupied most of the far wall. Across its top, in gold lettering, were the words GOLDFIELD MINING STOCK EXCHANGE. Just below were several headings: listed mines, listed prospects, nonlisted. Under each heading were columns divided into small squares with prices written in them.

She scanned the list for the Fourth of July mine. The figures written in the column marked "bid price" were five and a quarter.

The "ask price" was five and three-quarters. Though she was uncertain of the exact meaning of "bid" and "ask," after checking the prices of the other stocks, it was clear the Fourth of July was the leader.

A man in a stiff collar, who looked like a clerk, moved quickly from one column to the next, entering new prices in chalk, erasing old ones. With each change in the figures, fingers shot into the air, waving frantically, and the crowd burst into shouts.

A few feet away from the blackboard, a pot-bellied man stood before a slender podium, a sheaf of papers in one hand, a huge gavel in the other. He was calling out names of mining companies and prices. Occasionally, he would bang the gavel. He and the podium were enclosed by a wooden railing. People were pushing toward four men stationed outside the railing, pressing pieces of paper into their hands.

Even the hot air, thick with cigar and cigarette smoke, couldn't diminish Meg's excitement. She'd read about stock exchanges, but she'd never been inside one before. She wasn't sure what she'd expected, but she knew she wasn't disappointed.

The men standing close to the railing were brokers, she decided, and she pushed her way in that direction. As she drew close, she became aware of the scent of a heady perfume. She glanced around and saw a woman with strawberry-colored hair, stunning in a flamboyant way, standing a few feet away. She wore a stylish deep blue suit with black ruching at the throat and a matching hat trimmed in pheasant feathers. She was laughing with the men standing around her. In that instant, Meg recognized her as the woman with the parasol at the train depot.

When Meg finally reached the railing, she tapped a man in a well-cut, checked suit coat on the shoulder. "Sir, are you a broker?"

The man glanced over his shoulder at her, glared in annoyance. "Say what?" he yelled into the din.

She leaned close enough to catch the mixed smell of whiskey and hair tonic. "Are you a broker?"

"Is this nineteen and ought six? Are we livin' in the great state of Nevada?" He leered at her. "The King Tutt is the best buy you'll find. Guaranteed."

She backed away. "No, thank you." She regarded the other men with slips of paper in their hands, gesturing at the man behind the podium. She tended to judge people by their appearances. A fault, she knew. That these men were a trifle sharp-looking in their dress, some with diamond stickpins as big as fully ripe peas, not quite as she had imagined brokers to look, was incidental. A mining camp was filled with odd types. Brokers clearly were no exception.

She approached each man resolutely, asked him if he held Jim Kendall's stock, only to be summarily ignored. She persisted, but no one had heard of Jim Kendall, much less held his stock. The last man jerked a thumb toward the corner, told her to check with the man in the cage who kept the exchange records. She mouthed a thank-you and pushed her way toward the corner of the room by the blackboard, where a sweating man in a soiled celluloid collar sat at a rolltop desk surrounded by account books.

Shouting, she gave him her father's name and the names of his stock. The accountant flipped through a half dozen ledgers before he told her the exchange had no record of any transactions under her father's name. Her spirits sagged.

"Are there other brokers in camp? Ones who might not be here at the exchange this morning?"

"There's a few trust companies. One's right down the street. Graham Trust Company. Jake Stratton is the man you should talk to."

"Graham Trust Company," she repeated. "Thank you."

* * *

Meg blinked in the blinding sun. The air was like a furnace. She guessed the temperature must be over one hundred degrees. She elbowed her way through the crowd gathered outside the exchange, anxious to find the trust company. Two doors down she found it, a one-story board building with a striped awning. Written in gold lettering on the plate glass window were the words GRAHAM TRUST COMPANY.

She went in. The room was dimly lit. A ceiling fan slowly cir-culated the air smelling of expensive cigars. As her eyes adjusted, she noticed a man in shirtsleeves and suspenders seated at a desk a few feet away. He looked up from a stack of papers and asked if he could help her.

"I'm looking for Mr. Jake Stratton," she said.

"Well now." He leaned back in the swivel chair, smoothing his hands over his balding head, surveyed her figure. He seemed to be trying hard not to smile. "Business or pleasure?"

"Business."

"Sure I can't help you?"

She strained for a smile. "Thank you, but it's important I speak directly with Mr. Stratton. Is he in?"

"Nope."

Her heart sank. "Where might I find him?"

"Could be he's over at the Ajax."

"I'm afraid—"

"The Ajax Saloon. It's on First and Main. Can't miss it."

* * *

By the time Meg stood in front of the Ajax Saloon, her shirtwaist was soaked with sweat and perspiration ran down the sides of her face. She longed for a glass of cold water. Men came in and out, eyed her, grinned. Still, she didn't move. Respectable women didn't go into saloons. She hadn't even ventured into any of the wine rooms sometimes provided for female customers next door to sa-loons' bars and gambling tables.

Still, there was a chance the man who might know about her father's stocks was inside. She had no choice but to go in and ask.

She dabbed her face with her handkerchief, straightened her hat, pulled back her shoulders, walked in.

The sound of a tinny piano music, the click of roulette wheels, and men's boisterous voices filled the big room. A bar lined with customers took up the opposite wall. Men stood behind others, watching, as they played cards at a dozen round tables. A large Saint Bernard, lying by the door, opened an eye, glanced at her, and went back to sleep. Supposedly, Jake Stratton was among the men in this room. Perhaps the bartender would know who he was.

Meg had not gone more than a dozen steps toward the bar when a hand grabbed her arm. Instinctively, she tried to pull free. The hand held her fast. She looked up. The culprit was a heavyset man with a thick, dark beard.

"Let go this instant," she demanded, trying to pull free.

The men seated around nearby tables glanced up from their games and laughed.

The man yanked her toward him. She pushed her free hand against his chest. "I said let me go."

He gave her a drunken grin. "I didn't know this place had girls."

She swung her pocketbook at his head. "Damn you. I said let go of me." She kicked him in the shins.

He only laughed.

By now the card games had stopped. Everyone was watching, most grinning or laughing. No one got up. No one even moved. Not a soul was going to come to her aid.

A pistol shot rang out.

The piano music stopped. The big dog by the door rose to his feet, and growled. Heads swung toward the bar, where a small man wearing a long white apron stood with a revolver in his hand, aimed in Meg's general direction.

Chairs scraped across the wood floor as men got up hastily from tables and moved out of the way.

"Get out, mister. Get out now," said the small man. His voice was low, but there was no mistaking the seriousness of his command.

"You better do it, buster," came a voice from behind Meg. "Vic's a dead shot."

The room had grown completely quiet.

The bearded man's hold tightened on her arm as he stared back at the man with the revolver. "You don't scare me none."

"I said out." The small man's voice was cold now, controlled.

Meg's heart was hammering.

Just then a door next to the bar burst open, and a redheaded woman in a stylish blue suit appeared, pointing a shotgun. The same woman Meg had seen earlier at the exchange.

"You heard the man," the woman said. "Get out, or I'll blow your head off."

"That a girl, Tess," someone called.

His eyes wild and angry, the bearded man shot a glance around the room, hesitated, then thrust Meg away from him. "Goddamn whore," he growled, then lumbered out.

The shotgun cradled in her arms now, the redheaded woman walked toward Meg. "You all right?"

Meg swallowed hard, realized she was shaking. "Fine. Thank you."

"Come on back to the kitchen. You look like you could use a glass of water."

Meg remembered why she'd come in the first place. "I'm look-ing for a Mr. Jake Stratton. A clerk in his office told me I might find him here."

The woman studied Meg for a moment, obviously taking her measure. "He's back there with the water. He's eating one of my pastrami sandwiches. Have one, too, if you want."

Several customers laughed.

"Come on. I'll show you the way." She nodded her head in the direction of the door at the other side of the room.

Still trembling, avoiding the amused stares of customers, Meg followed her. Behind her, conversation started up again. The fid-dle music resumed. Cards were shuffled. Apparently, the brief ex-citement had been forgotten already.

On the other side of the door was a narrow hall, which opened into a sunny kitchen filled with a huge stove, a sink and drainboard, and a large wood table. A tall, broad-shouldered man with thick, black hair was seated at one of the straight-backed chairs and eating a huge sandwich. When Meg and the other woman entered, he looked up and gave a little wave.

"What was the ruckus in there all about?" he mumbled, his mouth full of food.

"This girl came to see you, Jake."

He glanced at Meg. "Do I know you?"

She shook her head, introduced herself. "I think you may be holding my father's stocks."

Jake Stratton put the remains of the sandwich down on the plate and picked up the coffee cup at his elbow. "Who's name is?"

"James Kendall. He was employed as a mining engineer at the Mohawk Mining Company."

"Was?"

"He died a few days ago."

Jake Stratton nodded, as if deaths were a daily occurrence. "I'm afraid to say he wasn't one of my customers." He took a sip of coffee, eyed her. "You might try the banks."

Meg gave a small smile, decided not to explain why she probably wouldn't do that. "That's a good suggestion."

She glanced at Tess, who was holding out a glass of water to her.

"It don't taste like much, but it's okay."

Parched, Meg took it gratefully.

Not until she'd swallowed every drop did she hand back the glass. "Thank you. And thank you again for—"

"You want a sandwich? They're good."

"Oh, I don't think so. Thank you."

The woman called Tess filled Jake Stratton's coffee cup. "I never met a person so big on thanking."

"Habit, I guess." Meg regarded the woman as she moved back to the stove, fascinated by her beauty. Her flawless, pale complexion was a wonder, given this hot, dry air, filled night and day with sand-filled wind. Yet her gray eyes had a sharpness about them that took the measure of a person at first glance. She handled a rifle with ease and ran a saloon. Meg wasn't sure how she would have imagined a woman who owned a saloon to look, but certainly not like Tess. "Especially when someone saves my life."

"You were all right."

"Still—"

"Look. Take some advice. Go teach school somewhere. Gold-field's no place for you."

"So I've been told."

"Pay attention then, and ask around at the banks like Jake said."

Masking her annoyance at the woman's unasked-for advice, Meg offered her hand. Tess eyed it for an instant before she took it in hers. Not surprisingly, her grip was firm, strong.

"It was nice to meet you, Miss— I'm afraid I didn't catch your last name."

"Wallace. The name's Tess Wallace." Their gazes met and held. "And remember, stay the hell out of my saloon."

CHAPTER 7

Tess sniffed the onion, bay leaf, and carrots simmering around the rump roast and replaced the lid of the huge Dutch oven, pleased. She'd done all the cooking herself until last week, when she'd decided to hire Cookie, as she called the Chinaman. He could barely speak English, but he knew his business. That was all that counted.

According to Goldfield tradition, saloons were expected to give out free meals at lunch and sandwiches and cheese at night to customers who gambled and drank. If men came to the Ajax because the food was better, she sure as hell wouldn't object. Any edge she could get over her competition was all that counted.

Wiping the sweat from her face with one of Jake's monogrammed handkerchiefs, she inspected the floor around the flour and cracker barrels for signs of rats. Finding none, she glanced at Cookie, who was cutting thin slices of yellow cheese with the wickedest knife she'd ever seen. She reminded him to sweep the floor again. Cleanliness was next to godliness, the saying went. Though the godliness part was debatable, she'd seen enough cockroaches and rats in her life to know she didn't want them in her kitchen.

Tess opened the door leading to the saloon and stepped inside. Teddy was stretched full length on his back, snoring, under the crap table. She smiled. On first glance, Teddy was just another Saint Bernard. Except for the crazy mess with that schoolteacher type who came in yesterday when all he'd done was growl, he'd fooled many a bad actor who failed to understand how fast a big dog could spring into action, get his teeth around a leg, and chew out a piece of it. The idea of keeping Teddy had been Vic's, but Tess had come to love Teddy nearly as much as she did Jenny Lynn.

She glanced about the saloon as she did every morning. Never once had she tired of admiring the embossed tin ceiling and two rows of lights with their green glass shades hanging low over the crap and poker tables. She sometimes thought about expanding, putting in another bar, making it as big as the Northern with its two thirty-footers.

The outside door was open, and a swirl of sand and trash blew under the swinging doors and across the plank floor. Tess frowned, then shrugged. The choice was dry wind to evaporate the sweat or die of the heat.

Glancing at the watch pinned on her pale green shirtwaist, she saw it was only nine o'clock. Still time to go over the books before the first rush of customers. She went around to the far end of the bar and removed a ledger from its special cubbyhole, which Vic had built for her. Placed neatly next to the ledger were her eyeglasses, pen, inkwell, and several pencils. Her office, she called it.

She heard a thud and knew without looking that Vic had lowered the awning to shade the plate glass front window. In a moment, he'd be back inside to chop ice for drinks.

She and Vic had come into town on the same stage the winter before with the sole purpose of making a lot of money in a hurry. It didn't pay to trust, but the kindness underneath Vic's breezy way appealed to her from the start. She talked about opening a restaurant. His dream was a saloon. She decided to take a chance, and by the end of the week, they'd decided they might make good partners. They'd bought a lot for a hundred dollars at the edge of the red-light district on the west side of town, put up a tent, and started up business. The tent had given way to a solid board edifice. Vic never watered the whiskey, and Tess allowed no cheating at the tables. She'd shoot a man if he tried. The Ajax Saloon was going strong.

Now with the mines spewing out gold like they'd been doing the last six months, Tess was more convinced that she'd made the right decision to trade Cripple Creek for Goldfield to make the money she had to have. The population was about to top the twenty thousand mark, but it wouldn't hold long unless more mines opened up and the number of jobs increased. That's where Jake came in.

Jake was convinced that if he could entice some of the members of the San Francisco stock exchange to Goldfield to see for themselves the ore, the mills, just how big a bonanza the camp was, everything would change. Once Goldfield's stocks were listed on the San Francisco exchange, the New York Curb would give a second look, and others would fall in line. The bait was the lightweight title fight between Joe Gans and Battling Nelson. Every newspaper in the country had covered the story. Most would probably send reporters.

She gazed out the window for an instant, and her thoughts strayed to the girl who had bumbled into the Ajax yesterday, hunting down stock certificates. Funny, someone like her—proper as a school marm—in Goldfield. Yet there'd been fire in her eyes when Tess had warned her not to come back. She liked that in a person.

Tess settled onto the stool. It was past time to get her mind back to the fight and her problem. Just as she knew they would, the other saloons had decided it wasn't worth staying open during tomorrow's fight. So everybody in the world would be there, hot as hell, and willing to sell their souls for something wet. She had to figure a way to sell cold beer and do it without paying Jake a thousand bucks for the privilege.

Placing the ledger and pencil on the bar, Tess put on her glasses and gazed lovingly at the framed photograph prominently displayed at the end of the sideboard. The heart-shaped face smiled back at her. Long, light-brown curls held in place by a huge bow at the back of the head, Jenny Lynn had been five when the photograph was taken last year at a studio in Colorado Springs.

For now, the photograph was all Tess had. But someday soon she'd go to the Briggles' house on Cascade Avenue, pack Jenny Lynn's belongings, take her by the hand, and whisk her away. Someday soon nothing would stop her from reclaiming the one thing that was truly hers.

Subtracting the arm and a leg the Briggles charged for Jenny Lynn's care, Tess still had two thousand dollars saved in the strongbox under the floorboards of the saloon. A tidy sum, but not near enough to buy the place she had her eye on along the Elk River in Colorado and still have money left over to buy a small herd of shorthorn, hire help, and see her through the first few years until she got established. And Jenny Lynn sure wasn't going to wear gunnysack dresses or live in a house no more than a shack with a dirt floor and a tarp as the only door, like she had.

Tess drew a stool close to the bar and sat down. She opened the ledger to where she'd enter last night's receipts. The swinging doors banged together. Teddy growled. Automatically, Tess raised her eyes and peered over the top of the glasses resting on the end of her nose. It was Jake, twirling a silver-headed ebony walking stick.

"Well?" she demanded.

"I'm parched. It's hot as hell out there."

"You're always parched."

"That's because it's always hot." He took the adjoining stool. "Have you seen the railroad cars pulling in? Mahogany paneling. French chefs. I told you I'd get the money in here."

She eyed him. "What about my idea?"

"It's great. I've hired a dozen kids. We're all set. All I need is to see the color of your money."

"You know I can't afford to pay you a thousand bucks. I'm savin' every dime."

"Call it a good investment."

"Call it robbery." The horse trader he was, if she pushed him any more, he'd only jack up the price. There had to be another way.

He shrugged. "Well, gotta go." He started backing out toward the door. "Remember, if you change your mind, give me the high sign. A thousand bucks and the beer concession is yours."

After Jake left, Teddy settled down to sleep again. The two had never been friends. Tess returned to her place at the end of the bar, put on her glasses again, opened the ledger book, but the thought of money to be made wouldn't leave her head. Without ice, under the blazing sun, drinking that beer would be like drinking warm piss. Offer it cold, the world would buy as much as she had for sale.

Jake hadn't leased the whole town, just the area where the fight was to take place. She'd set up a stand just close enough so people wouldn't mind going out to get it. That's what she'd do, and Jake couldn't do a thing about it.

Grinning, she slammed the ledger shut. Goddamn. She hadn't been so taken with an idea for a coon's age.

* * *

Tess lifted her skirts to avoid the horse dung littering the street, stepped up onto the boardwalk, and hurried toward Little's Funeral Parlor in the middle of the block. With lumber scarce, Clem Little was apt to be the only man in town with enough to make the booth she needed by morning.

Though Clem was a steady loser at the crap table, he made enough winning stud poker to balance out. In all the months he'd been coming in the Ajax, she'd never seen him without that filthy top hat, and like most of her customers, he reeked of sweat. She doubted he ever changed his union suit or any other article of clothing, but he was even tempered, a moderate enough drinker. If he had a problem, it was not always paying his tab. She generally let it go for a while. Eventually, he was good for it. Now it could be her ace in the hole.

When she walked in, Clem was shirtless, his galluses over his union suit, sawing a length of board for a coffin. He greeted her with a grin and a wave.

"I need a booth, Clem," she said. "Need it by tomorrow morning. I want to set it up for the fight."

"What kind of a booth?"

"You know. A roof to keep off the sun, a counter, a place to store supplies. Nothin' fancy. Eight by five maybe."

"I'd like to oblige. Sure would," he said, his florid face taking on a soulful look. "But the sheriff put in some advance orders for coffins. Says he wants to be prepared for whatever happens at the fight."

"He thinks the fighters are going to kill each other?"

"The audience might let loose on each other. Never can tell. This is a big one."

"You're right on that score," she said. "Which is why I need this booth."

"Like I say, Tess. I'd do it in a minute if I could."

She smiled, put a hand on a sweat-soaked sleeve of his union suit. "I was doin' books this morning, Clem, and I came across your name. You owe me fifty bucks."

Clem glanced down at her. "I'm good for it. You know that."

"Sure, but I've got a deal for ya. Make me the booth, we'll call it even."

"You're puttin' pressure on me, Tess. With this sheriff's order . . ."

She smiled. "You're a fast worker, Clem. Put your mind to it, and you can do both."

He sighed, shook his head. "I wish I could."

"We're friends, aren't we, Clem?"

His brown eyes reminded her of Teddy's.

"Aren't we?"

"Sure we are."

"So . . ."

"Sorry, Tess, but I've got to turn you down."

Tess left, downhearted but unwilling to give up. She could put up umbrellas for shade. The one thing she had to have was ice. She headed to Bill Brown's garage. He'd know where to get enough blocks to last the afternoon, and he'd get them there in time. There were other freight companies using automobiles, but Brown's was the most reliable. At the moment, that counted more than anything else.

When she strode up to the Brown Transportation Company, she found the place locked up tight. Hands cupped around her eyes, she peered through the fly-specked window and saw only a lone automobile, its wheels off. Damn. What was she going to do? She went next door to the drugstore. An old man behind the counter said he thought Bill was in Tonopah.

Tess went outside, stood in the shade, gazing up and down the street. Without Bill Brown to get the ice, she was in a bind. Then she thought of the other saloons in town. All of them would be shut down during the fight. All of them would have ice. Not a lot, but some. She'd probably have to pay top dollar.

She set off back to the Ajax. Elbowing her way along Columbia, around the corner to Fifth, she wondered what Vic would think of her scheme to get around Jake. The two men got along well enough, though Vic got along well with everyone.

Not high noon yet, the Ajax was already packed when Tess walked in and hailed Vic, who was busy behind the bar. She took off her hat, put it on a shelf in the back room, and returned to give him a hand. In between pouring whiskey and beer, she explained her plan.

"If they supply the ice, the other saloons will want a cut," Vic said in low tones.

"Okay. How about five percent?"

"What's the price of the beer?"

"A dollar."

"You can buy a watch for that much."

"Not much of one. Anyway, they'd only get a nickel a bottle. That's not bad."

Vic shrugged, looked unconvinced.

"Look. We'd be providin' a service to those thirst-crazed folks."

"Stick to what you know. That's what I say, Tess."

"Are you tellin' me no?"

"I am saying to let Jake do it."

"But we can make a lot of money, Vic."

"There are other ways," he said, gently.

"Maybe," she said.

She and Vic returned to waiting on customers, but as the hours passed, she was still reluctant to let go of the idea. Time was running out on her. There had to be a way to get Jenny Lynn back with her before she was full grown. She knew the saloon business, could count on it for a decent income, but it wasn't enough.

They stayed open that night until three. As was their habit, they cleaned up before calling it a day. It wasn't until the gray of dawn that she finally climbed up to her room.

Wearing only her wrapper, Tess gazed morosely out of the window at the street below. The sleeping figures of two men were draped in the doorway of Jedson's barbershop across the street. A few more were stretched out in wagon beds. Every hotel in town was full. All Jake's planning was paying off. For Jake.

It would be hot as the hinges of Hades at the fight. She could have made a fortune selling cold beer. She turned away from the window, untied the wrapper, and tossed it on the end of the bed. The cotton sheet felt rough against her skin as she stretched out on the bed and closed her eyes, then opened them again. In a camp full of money, she had to figure some other way to get her share of it. She'd been saying *soon* for too damn long. It was past time to get off her duff.

CHAPTER 8

*V*erna stood in front of the chest-high type stand, her stubby fingers fitting the last of the type into the stick. In her pocket was a telegram that Amos the Western Union boy had brought an hour ago.

"Red Fox stock to be listed in Frisco exchange at thirteen cents," it had read. "Our big chance. Wire one hundred dollars."

She gave a little snort at the way he always used the words *we* or *our*. She'd never heard of the Red Fox. She doubted if any of the swells attached to the San Francisco Stock Exchange Jake Stratton had brought in for the fight had heard of it either. She felt the familiar ache of disappointment. If nothing else, Amos was predictable.

Every con man in every mining camp where they'd lived had a mark. In her case, Amos was the con man, she the mark, but this time she'd fool him. What he didn't know, and she certainly wasn't going to tell him, was she had been building a little nest egg. Dollar by dollar, fifty cents by fifty cents. The four hundred and seventy-two dollars and thirty-two cents in the Cook Bank wasn't all that much, but it was a start against her old age. The only alternative was a county poorhouse, too grim a reality to think about long.

She glanced at the stick in her hand. Aside from the fight and the full-page ad Jake Stratton had bought to promote the Graham Trust Company, the first few issues of the *Star* had been mostly fill. She was determined that this week there'd be some substance to it.

She put the stick down on the top of the stand, unlocked the stick's clamp, carefully lifted out the type, and carried it over to the galley she'd placed on the large marble slab placed on a high table. Beside it was the chase, a rectangular steel frame big enough to hold the type for both pages.

She squinted at the type set upside down and backward, filling the galley. She looked for errors, found one, and corrected the mistake. She stepped back, surveying the general appearance of the page. This week's editorial was about the poor quality of drinking water. Jake Stratton's ad ballyhooing a new mine took up an entire column on the back fold. The five other ads were interspersed with the copy. It looked pretty good.

Satisfied, she moved the type into the chase, beneath the masthead Clem Little had carved for her, inserted two slugs between each of the seven rows of type on both pages to form the columns. Next she fit finger-length blocks of wood against the type, dropped the metal quoins in next to them. Everything seemed snug as a bug in a rug. She inserted the key in each quoin sequentially and gave it a twist.

She reached up and took down a leather-covered wooden block and the rawhide mallet she kept on the shelf. Moving the block over the type, tapping it firmly with the mallet as she went, evening out the level of the type, she wondered how often she'd done this. Thousands, maybe hundreds of thousands of times, she decided, considering how long she'd been in the business. She took pride in the product she turned out, and the world didn't generally object to a woman running a newspaper as long as it was in a one-horse town.

She put her tools away. Finally, she was set to print.

She picked up the chase and groaned. Lord save her, it seemed to get heavier each week. There was a time hefting twenty plus pounds around was as simple as lifting a carpetbag. No more. Grunting, she lowered the chase into the bed, straightened, rubbed the small of her back.

The paper was stacked along the north wall of the shack. She went over and picked up what her practiced eye told her were about fifty sheets. She placed them on the feed and fanned them out. It was time to run the first sheet. Moving around to the other side of the press, she cranked once. The bed shot forward under the cylinder, and the single sheet flew out into the carton she kept for the printed pages.

She went over, picked it out, and took it to the table by the window to look for irregularities. As she dragged a chair over, she dug in the pocket of her printer's apron for her glasses and felt the telegram next to them. She knew she would send him the money, but at the moment it would have to wait. First, she had to check for type that wasn't taking the ink properly.

She sat down heavily, adjusted the wire frames of her glasses over her ears, ready now to scan the copy. The page was a blur, little more than black streaks. She squinted, but it didn't help. Maybe she had dust in her eyes. She pulled out the handkerchief she kept tucked in her sleeve, poked her fingers beneath the lenses, and wiped her eyes. She blinked a few times. The type looked a little clearer. The page looked all right. The masthead, thanks to Mr. Little, suited her nicely. She was ready to print.

She leaned against the wood of the chair's straight back. Either she was growing soft, or the wood was growing harder. She sighed, straightened, tried to push away the weariness weighing her down. If she was going to report the fight, she better pull herself together.

* * *

The sun was overhead as Verna and Leo Fitz, a reporter from the *Denver Post*, stood in the doorway of the *Star*, watching the crowd as it streamed to the fight.

"Like lemmings running to the sea," Fitz observed cynically.

Verna knew his type. A big-city reporter who got the background the easy way from a local paper. It didn't matter. She was in a perfect position to feed him exactly what she wanted him to write. After the fight, if the promoters were to be believed, money men from all over the country would invest in Goldfield mines. More mines would open up. More people would pour in. There'd be no question about whether the camp could support three newspapers. The *Star* would flourish.

She glanced at the big man in the checked coat and brown derby who stood beside her. He was good-looking in a flashy way, though his belly strained the buttons on his coat. In a few years he would run to fat. She smelled the whiskey on his breath. Every saloon had been closed since daybreak, a first in the camp's brief history, so the man must have a flask in his pocket.

"I've heard Joe Gans won eighteen hundred dollars at a game of dice last night," the reporter said.

"Could be, I suppose. As of this morning, the odds are ten to eight on Gans." She wouldn't have admitted it to a soul, but she'd put two dollars down on Gans herself.

Mr. Fitz shifted the stub of his cigar to the other side of his mouth. "I heard Larry Graham's Trust Company is the backer."

"They put up ten thousand, or at least Jake Stratton, who runs that show, did. The Athletic Association raised the rest."

"Which was how much?"

She glanced at her watch. The fight was scheduled to start at two sharp. Ordinarily, Verna wouldn't have thought twice about going out alone to cover a story, but a prizefight was different, particularly as members of the press sat up close to the ring. An unaccompanied lady in that neck of the woods would be as unwelcome as ticks on a dog. Still, she'd deal with it somehow.

"Ma'am?"

Verna started.

"I say how much was the total pot to promote the fight?"

"Fifty thousand," she said. "As far as I know."

"I heard it was the Graham Trust Company who cooked up the idea in the first place."

"Actually, it was Graham's sidekick, Jake Stratton, the brains of the outfit," she said, convinced it was true. She'd watched Jake Stratton on the train to Goldfield, all teeth and smooth talk. She'd seen his kind in nearly every camp where she'd lived. But this man was smoother, and he seemed smarter. Whether he was a con artist or just a brighter-than-usual gambler—if there was a difference— she hadn't decided.

Even before she'd set up her press, he'd placed full-page ads in the *Star* to the tune of $150. As her best customer so far, he couldn't be all bad.

She'd spent most of her adult life in mining camps, but she'd never witnessed this obsession with mining stock. As far as she could tell, it was just another way to gamble money away.

"I thank you for the background, Miz Bates. I'll stop by on the way back from the fight to let you know the particulars," the reporter said.

"No need." Verna gave him a tight smile, anticipating the shocked look on his face as she pinned on her hat. "Plan to cover it myself."

* * *

The fight was to be held in a bowl-shaped open space west of the railroad depot that, until a few days ago, had served as a sometimes garbage dump, sometimes baseball field. Miraculously, all signs of refuse had been cleared away to make room for banks of makeshift bleachers at the top and rows of chairs, borrowed from every saloon in camp, on the flat ground closer to the ring. In the center was the ring.

The air was still and hot. Verna glanced up at the unrelenting sun. By the end of the fight, if she didn't pass out from heat exhaustion first, it might burn right through her hat and fry her brains. A few of the women scattered through the audience held parasols over their heads. They were the smart ones.

The stands were jammed. Verna couldn't see a single empty chair below them. The noise of the crowd was high-pitched with excited anticipation. Raggedy boys—some so small she wondered how they were able to manage the makeshift boxes packed with beer bottles and hung from straps around their necks—moved up the aisles, hawking their wares. One had a sort of hop to his walk like Jimmy Earnest. There was a carnival atmosphere about the scene.

Apparently wanting to distance himself from a woman too dumb to know where she wasn't wanted, Leo Fritz had left her the moment they'd arrived at the arena. Chin out, shoulders squared, face fixed into a pleasant expression, she pretended she didn't notice or care about the stares as she strode, alone, down the aisle toward the two rows roped off for the press.

A scrawny man, a card printed with the words GOLDFIELD TATTLER stuck in the band of his derby hat, barred her way. "Sorry, ma'am. This section's for the press."

"You're looking at it," Verna said. "The *Goldfield Star*. Verna Bates, publisher."

"Since when?"

"Since a week ago." She went around him.

"Heh, you can't sit there."

Verna glanced over her shoulder at him, tempted to thumb her nose at him. "Says who?"

A ripple of laughter followed her. The upbeat mood of the crowd had helped her out. Maybe she'd get through the afternoon all right after all.

She had no sooner taken her seat than there was a flurry of movement on the other side of the ring. The crowd stilled, as if holding its collective breath, then broke into a roar as two young men, both slender, bare-chested, and dressed in trunks and high-topped, soft leather black shoes, climbed up to the ring and ducked through the ropes. A big man with a round, florid face, wearing a light-colored fedora, climbed in behind them.

She leaned toward the skinny man next to her. "Say, what's the name of the fellow in there with the fighters?"

He looked at her as if she were an exotic animal in a zoo. "The *Goldfield Star* you say?"

She nodded. "And you?"

"*Tonopah Gazette.*" He removed his stained derby, mopped his bald head with a filthy handkerchief. "The fellah is Tex Rickart. One of the promoters."

She smiled. "Much obliged."

They watched as Rickart hailed the crowd. "Gentlemen, we are assembled in this grand areno—"

The audience hooted at the mispronunciation, mocking him for going high tone on them and failing in the attempt. Whatever else he said was drowned in jeers. He left the ring. Another man, thick-set, in a bowler, wearing an open-necked shirt, ducked between the ropes. She supposed he was the referee.

Verna took a sheaf of paper and a pencil from her purse. The sooner this fight began, the sooner it would be over.

The referee introduced the fighters, Gans, a good-looking, young colored man, and Nelson, the challenger, who was white. Each held gloved hands above his head in a kind of greeting. They touched gloves, backed away from each other a few steps, raised their gloves, and set their feet.

A gong sounded. Joe Gans made the first move, a quick, sharp jab to his opponent's chest.

Verna flinched, as if she were the one hit. The men ducked, weaved, jabbed, grappled. She sat, ramrod straight, watching every move so she could give just as accurate an account as the other papers in camp. The crowd roared, cursed. She fanned herself with her pad, amazed how everyone else seemed oblivious of the heat. At times like this, she wondered why she hadn't found another business to go into years ago.

Ordinarily, she wouldn't care who won. Whether her good sense had been swept away by the heat or Goldfield's crazies, as she was beginning to think of the camp's general atmosphere, two of her precious dollars were on Gans. He darned well better win. She needed every dime.

CHAPTER 9

*M*eg strode toward the John Cook Bank, disturbed to see a number of shops already closed. Her father's stock certificates probably weren't there, but the brokers she'd tracked down thus far knew nothing about them. She had no idea where else to look. It was the day of the championship fight, the day the entire camp and half the nation, judging from the crowds of men who had arrived by train and stage in the last few days, had waited for ever since it was announced in the papers. She just hoped the bank was open.

She was within a half block of the stone building that housed the John Cook Bank when she saw two men, one stout, the other a skinny man who looked like a clerk, come out. The skinny man paused, locked the door. Alarmed, she ran toward them. "You aren't closing, are you?"

They looked at her in surprise.

"I need to see Mr. Burlingame, the president."

The stout man smiled. "You are speaking to him, madam."

"Can't ya' see we're closed for the day?" cut in the clerk.

Meg ignored him. "It will just take a few moments."

"I'm sure it will." The stout man kept smiling, adjusted his derby. "Perhaps if you came back—"

"Please. It won't take any time at all. It's simply a matter of look-ing at your safety-deposit records."

Mr. Burlingame studied her for a moment, glanced at the clerk. "Open up, Mike."

"Oh, thank you."

The banker motioned for her to come inside. "I never could turn down a lovely lady, though I must warn you that if it requires more than—"

"It won't, I promise you."

As it turned out, the search of the safety-deposit records took a little less than ten minutes. There was no record her father had ever left stock certificates or anything else in the bank's vault. Mr. Burlingame ushered her out the front door, advising her to check the two other banks in town the next day. She thanked him, and they parted.

Meg paused at the corner to wait for a break in the traffic. She hadn't expected to find the certificates. She doubted she'd find them in any of the other banks either. Still, she couldn't be sure. Ordinarily, she'd have the rest of the day to inquire, but the camp was shutting down for the fight. She'd have to wait until tomor-row.

She thought of the long day stretching before her, alone, doing what? She liked her own company, but that was when she had the option to refuse an invitation to go hiking or sit on the porch with Aunt Hilary. Maybe she'd go back to the house and write her aunt a long letter. She'd meant to do that for days.

Meg had sent Aunt Hilary two telegrams, to notify her of her father's death and about her decision to withdraw from medical school. Aunt Hilary had raised her, nursed her through measles and chicken pox, taught her a woman must have a goal in life. Aunt Hilary had introduced her to Mrs. Philpott, whom she must also write. Meg owed both of them an explanation at the least. She also had to write to the dean of Johns Hopkins Medical School and let him know why she would not be attending.

As she threaded her way through the maze of traffic to the other side of the street and stepped up onto the boardwalk, she ran headlong into Charley Thompson.

"Good heavens. Meg Kendall."

She backed away, smiled as she straightened her hat, more pleased than she wanted to admit to have met someone she knew.

"I thought you'd be on your way back to Boulder by now."

"Did you?" she asked brightly.

Charley studied her for an instant, then turned to two men standing beside him, and introduced her. Doffing their hats, they nodded their hellos.

"I suppose you're on your way to the fight," Meg said for the sake of conversation.

Charley nodded. "Just thank your lucky stars you won't be there. It'll be a scorcher."

"You don't think I should go?"

"I wouldn't advise it. A fight's no place for a lady."

"No women will be there at all?" she asked, intrigued now, certain he was wrong.

"Some, of course, but not—"

"Not ladies."

Their eyes met and he smiled, apparently convinced she understood the situation. "Well, if you will excuse us—"

"Of course."

She watched him disappear into the crowd, then continued on her way to the bottle house. It struck her that he'd been surprised, almost disconcerted at seeing her. He'd been so—stuffy, advising her not to attend the fight. The entire meeting somehow hit her the wrong way.

Once she had closed the door behind her and taken off her hat, she collected pen, paper, and ink, and set them on the table. Pushing Charley firmly out of her thoughts, Meg sat down, ready to begin her letter writing.

Dear Aunt Hilary,

Meg paused, looked up, and noticed the tent across the narrow clearing seemed to be empty. Its regular occupants were miners who worked different shifts, with someone always sleeping or moving about, no matter the time of day. They must all have gone to the fight. She could almost picture them, probably drinking beer, laughing, eager for whatever the day might hold, and she envied them.

Meg returned her gaze to the paper, dipped the pen in the ink well.

I must apologize for the delay in writing you about my decisions.

A train whistle blasted. Again Meg looked up. Maybe it was a signal for the beginning of the fight. She could see the throng of spectators, feel their anticipation, their excitement. Nuts. Who cared what Charley thought? Why should she miss out on it? She put down her pen, stood up. She'd finish the letter when she got home.

* * *

The streets were all but empty as she hurried toward the site of the fight ring that had been under construction all week. From four blocks away, she heard shouts exploding into the dry, desert air. It wasn't until she reached the arena that it occurred to her she'd probably need a ticket to get in.

She approached a man lounging by what appeared to be one of the entrances, smiled at him. "I'm a little late."

"Ticket?"

"Actually, I've misplaced it. I was hoping, what with coming so late—"

"They're goin' strong."

"I'd be willing to buy another ticket at half price then."

"Cheap seats are in the back. Last I looked there wasn't space enough for a bird to sit."

"I could try."

He shrugged. "It'll be a dollar."

"A dollar for a ticket to a fight?"

"A champeen fight, lady. Don't forget it."

She fished a silver dollar out of her pocketbook and handed it to him. She suspected the organizers of the fight would never see it. Still, he'd let her in. She was on her own to find a seat.

Inside, she stood at the back, oddly reluctant to look at the ring and the fighters. She searched for a vacant spot. Even in the open air, she smelled the sweat mixed with beer, and the blood. She was on the verge of deciding her choice to come had been a poor one.

Shielding her eyes against the sun, she scanned the audience again. Charley was here somewhere, probably next to the ring. There were a few women scattered among the sea of men, supposedly none of them ladies. Suddenly, her gaze came to a halt. Verna. Verna Bates. The newspaper lady. She was sitting quite close to the ring, closer than Meg would have liked to be. Still—

Every eye was fixed on the two fighters battling each other in the ring as she walked down the aisle. She saw one empty seat at the very end of the row where Verna sat. Verna was in the center, wedged between two large men. In order to sit next to her, Meg would have to ask everyone else to move down a seat. Seeing no other solution, she decided it couldn't be helped.

When she got to the row, she noticed a sign, tied to the back of the first few seats. RESERVED FOR PRESS. She hesitated for an instant, then leaned across the empty seat, and called to Verna. "Miss Bates—"

Verna looked toward her, stared wide-eyed for only a second or two, then said, all smiles, "Miss Kendall. Glad you could make it." She motioned to her, and Meg squeezed past the man on the end.

"There ain't no room," someone groused in a loud voice.

Verna leaned forward, still motioning to her. "That's it. Come right ahead, Miss Kendall. These gents will be happy to move down one seat to make room for you."

Verna never stopped smiling. Taking her cue, Meg also smiled as she squeezed past the half dozen men. One man cursed her under his breath. She kept smiling. Everyone ended up moving down a seat as Verna had said they would.

As Meg finally sat down and collected herself, Verna patted her on the knee like she'd known her for years. "Meggen Kendall, this is the best thing to happen to me all day."

Looking straight ahead at the fighters grappling in the ring, Meg said, under her breath, "I must apologize. I couldn't see anywhere else to sit. Thank you."

Her eyes twinkling, Verna glanced at her. "You've got it all wrong, dear. It's me that should thank you."

Meg laughed. The day was looking up.

"In fact, I'd say that calls for a beer, wouldn't you?"

Meg stared at her, mildly astonished. "If you think so."

"See that boy there at the end of the aisle, hawking beer? The kid with a bit of a limp. He works for me afternoons. Jimmy Earnest is his name. Contributes to the family coffers as best he can. Wave at him to get his attention, will you?"

The fight went on. For a while Verna made notes for her article about the fight. Meg hadn't realized how close the ring was. She could hear the grunts and groans of the fighters. She finally spotted Charley seated in the front row on the other side of the ring and hoped he'd see her, too. If she caught him looking this way, she might even wave. It would serve him right. She settled back, sipped her beer, and fanned herself with sheets of paper Verna had brought along.

By now she and Verna were carrying on a running conversation about everything from operating a business in Goldfield to the cost of living to their family histories.

"Amos—my brother—is a decent enough man, and I love him," said Verna, casting a sidelong glance at Meg. "The trouble is he's never believed in himself enough to take hold of anything."

Meg nodded, solemnly. "I've never had a brother. Or a sister. I always wished I had."

"They're a curse and a blessing," Verna said.

"I guess so."

They returned their attention to the fight for a moment until Verna asked, "How do you like Goldfield by now?"

Meg glanced at the men seated around them, then down at the ring with its sweating fighters before she looked back at Verna and made a face.

"That bad?"

"That bad."

Verna threw back her head and laughed.

And the fight went on. Ten, twenty, twenty-five, thirty, thirty-five rounds.

The men's bodies gleamed with sweat, transforming their skins into black and white satin. Blood streamed from their lips, their noses puffed into weird distortions of whatever they may have been before. The shadows of the boxers stretched eastward across the crowd as the sun moved toward the horizon. Shouts rose, accusing Nelson of dirty tactics, which was a laugh. The entire performance was dirty and vicious.

A man Verna told her was the promoter separated himself from the men gathered at ringside and climbed up to confer with Joe Gans, then retired to his seat. The men in the front row gathered around him, gesturing angrily. Two rounds later, Joe Gans fell to the floor of the ring, rolled over, and holding his hand under his belt, let out a yell of anguish.

Cries of "foul" sounded. The promoter scrambled into the ring again, said something to the referee, and what seemed less than a moment later, the fight was declared over. Joe Gans had won. A shout of approval went up. The crowd jumped to its feet.

Verna grinned at Meg, announced she'd won four dollars.

The day had faded into twilight. Surrounded by jostling, exuberant men who apparently had placed their bets on the winner, Meg walked slowly with Verna up the aisle toward Elliott Street.

A warm feeling of contentment spread through her. Perhaps it was the beer. Maybe it was Verna's companionship.

Meg recalled that at some time during the interminable after-noon, Verna had offered her a job. She had accepted because she needed the money and she'd enjoy the company. Thinking about it now, Verna probably had been joking. Meg had no skill at writ-ing, so reporting was out. On the other hand, all newspapers car-ried advertisements. Her aunt always said she had a knack for convincing people to do things her way. Why couldn't she sell advertising space? She'd be on her own with time to continue her search for the stock certificates and the map, to find out what re-ally happened to her father. She needed some income if she was to keep eating and posting letters. To rely on Aunt Hilary for money was out of the question. Meg had set out on a new course, which included supporting herself.

Verna paused to catch her breath. Every saloon and store was open for business.

"Let's find someplace for supper," Meg suggested.

"Oh, I don't think so, dear." Verna smiled. "My legs ache and I want to get my feet in some cold water. Most of all, I want to get out of this corset."

Meg gave a little laugh. "I don't blame you," she said, trying to hide her disappointment that the evening was about to end.

"So it's good night," Verna said as they reached the corner.

"I'm so glad I found you today."

The smile on Verna's round face broadened. "It was you who saved the day."

"I'll be at the *Star* first thing in the morning."

"I'm counting on it."

Filled with the joy of having found a friend, Meg gave Verna a quick, little hug, and said good night.

* * *

A whistle blast cut through Meg's sleep. She stirred, turned on her side. For an instant, she wasn't sure whether it was night or day or where she was. Slowly, she opened her eyes and gazed at the green-tinged sunlight, streaming like a patterned scarf across the floor. Her head ached. She remembered the beer and the heat of yesterday.

Blinking, she realized where she was. It was morning. Good Lord, she'd told Verna she'd be on her doorstep first thing. Even without looking at a clock, she knew it must be at least nine. A poor way to begin a job.

She sat up, transfixed by the beam of sunlight, for it wasn't coming from the window but from the row of bottles that served as a kind of wainscoting above the plastered walls. Green ones, brown ones, a few almost clear. She let her gaze travel from one to another until it stopped at the last bottles next to the corner.

There was something about them, something different from the others. It looked like something was inside them. She got up, went over, and peered up at them. This close she saw there was indeed something inside them. Her heart racing, she dragged a chair over, climbed up on it, reached into the first bottle, and carefully removed a tube of paper.

Hardly daring to breathe, she unrolled it and saw it was a stock certificate for a thousand shares of the Genuine Article Mining Company. She'd never heard of the Genuine Article. She pulled out the next tube. One thousand shares of Over the Top. Again, the name was unfamiliar. She couldn't remember having seen either of these mines listed on the board the day she'd visited the stock exchange.

There was one suspicious bottle left. Filled with a mixture of uncertainty and eagerness, she reached in and pulled papers out. There were two sheets. Taking in a deep breath, she opened the first, and her heart stopped. She read the numbers written in a fine Spenserian hand, then reread them. Ten thousand shares of the Fourth of July, the biggest mine in Goldfield, Pete Eckles's mine, the only one not leased, the one that had brought suit against the Mohawk Mines Company for trespass.

The magnitude of the number of shares stunned her. The last

quote she had seen for the Fourth of July was five and a quarter. Five and a quarter times ten thousand was—Suddenly, she couldn't seem to multiply the numbers in her head. She got down off the chair, the roles of paper tucked under one arm, rummaged in her pocketbook for a pencil and a piece of paper, did the calculation. Fifty-two thousand five hundred dollars. My God. For an instant, she felt faint.

Even if her father had bought the shares at a quarter of the present price, or a tenth, it amounted to four thousand dollars. A mining engineer didn't have that kind of money to invest. Her head throbbed. She fought to concentrate. She wished she hadn't had the two beers.

She sat down on the cot, opened the second role. It was a mining map, like those her father used to paste up on the walls of their cabin when she was little. Her hands began to tremble. Across the bottom, written in the neat, block lettering of a draftsman, were the words, Haywood-Mohawk, level 5, August 23, 1906.

This was *the* map. Her heart stopped. She looked at the date again, three days before her father's accident. Besides showing it to Charley Thompson, he may also have taken it to Nolan and Winters. Was that why he had warned her against them? Three people might know he had the map, and someone had come looking for it.

She stood, struggling to understand just how the unfolding pieces to the puzzles fit together, when the obvious occurred to her. Pete Eckles was the key, as he had been from the beginning. As she searched for him, she'd leave the map and the stock certificates in the bottle, the proven safe hiding place, where she'd found it.

CHAPTER 10

*N*estled against him, Tess gazed at Jake's profile in the gray light of dawn. Her hand resting lightly on his hairy chest, she felt it rise and fall with the regular breathing of his sleep.

She thought of the money she and Vic had taken in at the tables and the bar. Jake had made a bundle on the betting. But more important than the fight were the men who had come from San Francisco to watch it, men who saw what a going place Goldfield was, how well the mines were doing.

Jake had explained often enough how the Graham Trust Company made money, how it promoted mining companies, put their stock on the market for ten cents a share, then splashed the country with publicity about the value of the ore, which created a demand and, in turn, drove up the price, the Trust reaping the rewards. Stocks and shares and capitalization and ore values—that's all Jake ever talked about. It was what the entire camp talked about. Buy low, sell high. It sounded so simple.

Her nest egg might grow faster if she handed part of it over to Jake to invest in some of those mining stocks he was always pushing. As soon as he woke up and had his breakfast, she'd talk to him about it. Earlier, their lovemaking had been exuberant, rollicking.

Once screwing had been her business. With Jake, it was fun. She didn't love him. She wasn't sure she even liked him. His love-making, though, was the best she'd known, a tough thing to step away from.

Her pa had beat the hell out of her. Jake knew better than to lay a hand on her. He could be good company when he thought about it, which wasn't often. But they'd had some laughs. That was enough.

A woman was a lot better off without a man. Single, a woman could own property, run things as she saw fit. Married, she was no better than a hired hand. Still, Tess knew a woman alone raising a kid stirred up questions and she planned to use the Mrs. before her name to ward them off.

She lay there, hesitant to move for fear of waking Jake. The night air had cooled the room above the saloon some, but not enough to warrant pulling a sheet over them. As soon as the sun rose, it would be another sizzler. The desert certainly wasn't her choice for a permanent place to live. The heat wore a person out. There had been many a day this summer she'd longed for the cool breezes and icy streams of the Rocky Mountains.

Very carefully, she lifted Jake's arm from around her shoulders onto the pillow and eased off the bed. He roused, then turned on his side, asleep. Relieved, she went behind the screen set at an angle in the opposite corner of the room, took her wrapper off its hook, put it on, and tied it around her. Peeking into the mirror on the wall, she smoothed her hair. Still barefoot, she opened the door, closed it quietly behind her, and tiptoed downstairs.

In the kitchen, Teddy was busy eating leftovers while Cookie prepared lunch for the day. On the table were four loaves of bread covered with tea towels. Tess went to the stove, poured herself a cup of coffee, and sat down. She watched Cookie knead another batch of bread dough.

"As hot as it is, you ought to have a summer kitchen out back, Cookie."

He nodded and said something she didn't understand. Tess gazed out the window at an assortment of work clothes flapping in the wind on a line strung between the neighborhood outhouse and the place next door. The kitchen door opened, and she looked over her shoulder to see Vic. He was holding an envelope in his hand.

"You're up bright and early," she said, smiling. A day didn't go by that she wasn't pleased about their being partners. Vic was one man she could trust.

"Can't make money with the doors closed."

"How about some coffee?"

He shook his head and handed her the envelope. "I went over to the post office for the mail. I thought you'd want to see this."

She glanced at the postmark, instantly apprehensive, then back at Vic. "The Briggles."

"When I saw the Colorado Springs return address, I figured it was from them."

Tess eyed the letter. The Briggles seldom wrote unless it was to demand more money for her daughter's care. It was becoming a frightening pattern, on the edge of getting out a control.

Vic reached for a paring knife on the drainboard and handed it to her. She slid the tip under the sealed flap and slit it open. She pulled out the letter inside, unfolded it, and began to read.

Dear Mrs. Wallace,

Tess smiled bitterly. They knew she wasn't married. The other part of the lie she paid them to perpetuate with Jenny Lynn was that she was an actress with a traveling troupe. She read on.

We read in the papers everyone in Goldfield is striking it rich, which is good news.

Tess grimaced.

Little Jenny Lynn is growing so fast she can't fit in the same pair of shoes for more than a month. Now with winter coming

*on, she will need a new coat. Prices are going up. We know you
do not want to deprive her of the necessities when you are doing
so well.*

"Hah!" Tess exclaimed in disgust. She glanced up at Vic. "Every
letter is the same. Jenny Lynn is growin' out of her clothes. Last
time—I swear it was in June—I sent enough money to feed and
clothe an orphanage. Now this."

"They're bloodsuckers, Tess."

She read the rest of the letter. Jenny Lynn would enter first grade
the next Monday. There would be books to buy. Tess glanced at
the date on the envelope, saw the letter had been sent a week ago.
She closed her eyes, imagining Jenny Lynn, dressed in gingham
with a proper pinafore, her curls brushed back into a huge hair bow,
looking pretty as a picture, probably breathless with excitement,
maybe a little scared, as she set off down the block toward the
schoolhouse.

Tess sighed and folded the letter, slipping it back into the envelope. "God knows what they'll do if I don't pay up."

"Let her come live here, why don't you."

"Not on your life."

"Is it worse for her than with the Briggles?"

"They have kids of their own, Vic. They've boarded other kids
beside Jenny Lynn. I looked into them real careful."

He shrugged his shoulders. "She's your kid, Tess, but if it was—"

She rose, jamming the envelope in the pocket of her wrapper.
"Well, it's not you."

"If you don't pay, then what?"

She glared at him. "They'll tell Jenny Lynn about me. That's
what."

Vic regarded her affectionately. "Is that so bad, to have a mother
who runs a successful business? A mother—"

"You talk like I own a hat shop, Vic."

"What's the matter with a saloon?"

"Ask the women's temperance bunch."

He glanced away for an instant, a disgusted look on his face. "Who cares what a bunch of dried-up old witches say?"

"Don't forget what else."

He cocked an eyebrow.

"Jenny Lynn's mother was a whore."

Vic studied her for a moment. "Do you really think your kid cares about that?"

Their gazes met. Tess wanted to believe him. "I can't risk it, Vic. She's all I've got in the world."

"Not quite," he said, quietly.

She went over, put an arm around his slender shoulders. "You know you're as good a friend as I've ever had, Vic. But Jenny Lynn is family."

He nodded, not looking at her, and stood up. "Sure. It's okay. I understand."

"I'm goin' to get five hundred dollars out of the safe, from my share."

His eyes widened. "Five hundred. You just paid them a hundred last month."

"So?"

"It's for everything, right? For room and board and clothes. Everything."

"The room and board is extra."

"Tess . . ."

She held up a hand to signal the end of the conversation. Placing her coffee cup in the sink, she left the kitchen and entered the saloon. The stink of stale cigar smoke and whiskey hung in the air. She went to the window, opened it. Gazing out at a passing mule train loaded with sacks of ore, she thought about the five hundred dollars. Next month it might be a thousand. By Christmas, the price of silence might be five thousand, or ten. Worse than thieves, the Briggles were extortionists who knew a gold mine—or thought they did—when they saw one.

The minute the San Francisco stock exchange listed Goldfield mining stock, prices would soar. She could continue to squirrel away a dollar here, ten dollars there, let the Briggles suck it away nearly as fast she earned it, or she could use the money she had now to buy some mining stock and make more, a lot more.

She watched men gamble at the Ajax. Most lost their shirts. Yet every once in a while one came along with the smarts and the keen eye who cleaned up. There was no reason she couldn't do the same with the market. She was a quick learner, and Jake could give her tips. If she let Vic pretty much take over the Ajax so she could spend full-time at it, she could make enough profit on trades to be on her way out of here in a month, two at the most.

CHAPTER **11**

*M*eg ran nearly all the way to the *Star*, burst in the door. "I overslept," she said, panting.

Verna glanced up from the papers strewn across the table by the window and smiled, as if there was nothing surprising about Meg's sudden appearance. "It was the beer, I think. It takes getting used to."

"I'm sorry. It certainly isn't the way to start the first day on the job," Meg said, catching her breath. In her embarrassment, she had to force herself to meet Verna's gaze. "That is, if I really do have a job."

"I don't make idle threats." Verna grinned, motioned for Meg to take the chair across from her. "Now then. What can you do?"

Meg breathed a sigh of relief, sat forward, anxious to make a good impression. "I thought I could sell advertising for you."

"You've sold advertising before, have you?"

Meg shook her head, gave a sheepish grin. "Never, but I can learn."

Verna pushed to her feet. "I wouldn't be surprised," she said, drily. "I'll get us some coffee. I think there's enough left in the pot."

Before Meg could protest, Verna disappeared behind the curtain that divided the room. As Meg waited for her return, she thought about Verna's remark. Her direct manner, her grandmotherly appearance, everything about her was so different from Aunt Hilary, tall and stately, who had spent a lifetime weighing every word before she spoke.

A few minutes later Verna reappeared, bearing two cups, and put them on the table. Meg thanked her, took a sip of the bitter coffee.

"Terrible, isn't it?" Verna said with a laugh. "It's the water."

Meg smiled and studied the older woman. Judging from her gray hair caught in a loose bun at the back of her neck, the lines creasing her forehead and the corners of her eyes, she appeared to be about sixty, maybe older. Her neck was so short, it seemed as though her head was sitting directly on her shoulders. There was a solid appearance about Verna, as if nothing would push her off balance. The level look to her blue eyes behind her glasses convinced Meg that here was a person to trust. So she told her about the stock certificates and the map, why she'd put off medical school.

"So now, the way it is," Meg said, finally, "I have to find Mr. Eckles right away."

"From the little I've heard about him, it might be more of a problem than you think."

"Charley Thompson said he was out of town."

Verna cocked an eyebrow. "Charley Thompson?"

"He works for Mohawk Mines, like my father did. He's the one who told me about the lawsuit."

"I take it he doesn't know about the map you found."

"No."

"Good. I'd keep it that way."

Meg downed the last of her coffee, stood. Now that she had revealed her secret, she was even more eager to get on with her search. Yet how could she walk off and leave before she'd done a lick of work? As she wondered how to approach the matter, Verna glanced up at her, a twinkle in her eyes.

"Well?" Verna eyed her. "What are you waiting for? Go. Get out of here. Maybe the Fourth of July office will know where to find this elusive Pimpernel. Then come back and get to work."

* * *

Maybe it was having someone she could talk honestly to about her father's stock. Whatever the reason, Meg entered the large building that held the offices and change rooms of the Fourth of July mine company confident that she'd find Mr. Eckles. Soon all her questions would be answered. As she approached the clerk seated behind a long counter a few yards ahead, she could hear the whir of cables, the sound of a cage exploding past the collar of the shaft. She glanced through the window to the left and saw men move toward it to role off the loaded ore cars.

"I'd like to see Mr. Eckles, please."

The clerk stared at her dumbly.

"Mr. Eckles, the owner of this mine."

"He ain't here."

"Can you tell me where I will find him?"

He shrugged. "Gotta see the super about that."

"The superintendent?"

"That's what I said."

"Might I ask his name?"

"Huh?"

"The superintendent's name. I need to know his name. If you please." Meg was growing angry.

"Mr. Grimble. He's down to town for his dinner."

She glanced at the clock on the opposite wall. Ten-thirty. A little early for the midday meal. Maybe he was also on some kind of business. "Thank you, I'll wait."

It was nearly three o'clock when a thickset man flung open the door and bellowed for the clerk. "Assay reports. Have 'em on my desk in five minutes, Billip."

"Comin' up," the clerk said and dashed into another office.

Meg hurried toward the superintendent, who was riffling through a pile of papers on the clerk's desk. "Mr. Grimble?"

He didn't look up.

She introduced herself. "It's extremely urgent that I get in touch with Mr. Eckles, and I thought you might—"

He glanced up at her, his look flat, disinterested.

"My father was Jim Kendall. He and Mr. Eckles were close friends."

The superintendent returned his attention to the papers. "I can't help you."

"You have no knowledge of Mr. Eckles's whereabouts and you're his superintendent? I find that hard to believe."

He eyed her coldly. "Makes no never-mind to me, lady. I'm busy."

Meg turned away, sick with disappointment. Apparently, Pete Eckles was playing some kind of cat-and-mouse game, making it impossible for Nolan and Winters or their attorney—or anyone else—to reach him. Yet she couldn't believe he'd entrust the total management of the Fourth of July to a superintendent. She knew he was out there somewhere. She simply had to think of another approach. As she went around town selling advertising, she'd have a chance to overhear conversations. Surely, someone in Goldfield had to know where he was.

* * *

Verna made a list of advertising prospects, the costs of ads according to size. Armed with the list, a pad, and freshly sharpened pencils, Meg set out that very afternoon. Her high spirits didn't last long. In a matter of hours, she discovered that except for Swenson's bakery, Voglers' dry goods, and the Imperial Restaurant, business owners were men who either brushed her off or made lewd comments. Not a schoolteacher, someone's wife, or a whore, she obviously confused them, made them uneasy.

The discovery stunned her. She'd been born in a mining camp. She belonged here, or so she'd thought. Perhaps unconsciously, she'd thought that being her father's daughter was enough to be accepted. She realized she was wrong.

She'd grown up pinching pennies, wearing hand-me-downs Mrs. Philpott gave her, pretending not to care she couldn't afford to go to Denver to shop with friends. Money was important. People who said otherwise were rich. Yet until today she'd never actually understood what making one's own living entailed. Some might say that given all her father's stocks, she was making it hard on herself when she didn't have to. Actually, she didn't have that option. Not yet. Not until she talked to Pete Eckles, not until she was convinced she had received the best price. At this point, she knew nothing about stocks. Someday she'd sell her father's stock and make a great deal of money, maybe more than she'd ever dreamed of. Right now she would rely on her earnings, and the reality of what that meant scared her silly.

At the end of four days, she'd sold a total of three ads. Her pay was 10 percent of the amount, or sixty cents. Divided by four, that came to fifteen cents a day. Obviously, she couldn't live on that. She knew without looking in her purse that she was down to the last two dollars she'd brought with her from Boulder. At this rate, she'd have no other choice but to sell some of her stock or starve.

The next week started out no better. It took her half a day to work up enough nerve to go into the Ajax again. Before she'd even finished her pitch, Tess said saloons had no need to advertise and turned her down flat. Humiliated, Meg pasted a smile on her face and left. As she walked along the crowded boardwalk, trying to calm her pounding heart, she heard her stomach rumble so loud she was certain someone might notice. She hadn't eaten since last night. She passed the Continental Restaurant, its doors open to any cooling breezes, smelled the odors of frying steak and baking bread. Her head grew light with hunger. She thought of the Ajax again and its free lunch, and the idea hit her.

Ten minutes later she was back inside the Ajax, meeting Tess Wallace's unreceptive gaze.

"I know you said you didn't need to advertise, Miss Wallace, but I think you're missing a bet."

"You do, do you?" Tess Wallace picked a glass out of a basin of soapy water, gave it a shake, and began to dry it.

Meg tried to ignore the stares of customers. "You're quite right that your regular patrons know the Ajax has the best free lunch in town, but what about the new folks coming to town?"

Tess gave a wry little smile. "What about them?"

"Without some way of learning about the Ajax and its wonderful food, they'll patronize another establishment."

"Could be."

"But if you put a half-page ad in every issue of the *Goldfield Star* with the details about what's to be served for lunch, they'll flock through the doors, and leave your competitors in the dust."

Tess studied the glass she was drying. Finally, she glanced at Meg and asked, "So how much is this half page gonna cost me?"

Meg pulled the sheet with the ad prices out of her pocketbook. She knew she had a sale.

Back out on the street with a promise of a full week of Ajax ads, buoyed with success, Meg remembered Bill Brown, the man who had been so nice to her. She decided his transportation company should place an ad.

When she walked into the garage, he remembered her immediately and offered his condolences over her father's death. "I've meant to come by to see if there was something I could do."

She smiled. "That's kind of you, but I'm doing fine. I'm working for the *Star* now. In fact, that's why I came by this morning."

"Oh?"

"I really think you should place an ad with us."

He leaned against the doorjamb of the garage, wiping his hands on an oil-stained rag. "I wish I could, Miss Kendall, but I already have ads in the other two papers."

"But that's the very reason you should advertise in the *Star*."

He raised an eyebrow and slowly stuffed the rag into a back pocket of his trousers.

"The fact is not everyone reads all three papers."

"I wouldn't think so."

"So to cover the camp, you also need to advertise in the *Star*."

His dark eyes sparked with amusement, he pursed his lips. "I don't know."

"How about trying it out for a few days?"

"Well—"

"In Goldfield, Mr. Brown, time waits for no man."

Bill Brown studied her for an instant, then began to laugh. "You've got me there, Miss Kendall. Put me down for the smallest ad you have."

"For how many issues?"

He grinned. "Two. How's that for a compromise?"

When she returned to the *Star*, Verna heaped on praise for her sales. That night Meg stopped at Greene's butcher shop and paid ten cents for a sausage big enough to make two meals. She could almost taste it, nicely browned, succulent and juicy. She'd need some bread. She ought to have some vegetables. Fresh was out of the question in Goldfield. Canned peas or green beans would have to do. By the time she reached the bottle house, struggling to balance her purchases as she unlocked the door, she calculated she had a dollar and ten cents left.

With difficulty, she managed to grasp the doorknob, turn it, and push the door open with her foot. She put the packages on the wood table, caught her breath. The room was stuffy from being closed up all day. As she unbuttoned the top buttons of her shirtwaist, she was reminded that the few clothes she'd brought with her from Boulder were fast wearing out with the frequent washings. She couldn't afford to buy anything more. Winter would be coming all too soon, and if she stayed in Goldfield much longer, she'd have to send for her coat and probably the suit her aunt had remade for her. There was no other choice but to sell a few shares of her father's stock, either the Genuine Article or the Over the Top, certainly not the Fourth of July. In that case, she should probably put them in the bank for safekeeping and easy access.

Her father's note had pleaded with her to talk to Pete Eckles first. God knows, she'd tried. Yet wherever she went, she was told, and often with a caustic edge she chalked up to envy, that Mr. Eckles was in Hawaii or San Francisco or Chicago—anywhere but in Goldfield.

Then there was her father's warning against his bosses, Senator Nolan and George Winters. In the weeks she'd been in Goldfield, she'd seen them only at a distance, two men in dark suits and soft-brimmed hats, like dozens of other men who swarmed into the camp with money to gamble on stocks. When she'd stopped in mining supply stores to sell advertising, she'd tried to get the owners talking, with the plan that she'd eventually ask them about the circumstances of her father's death. Mostly the conversation was about the latest bonanzas. Not quite as often they talked of mines that had died, a blank wall hit with the rock coming up mostly rhyolite with quartz and no gold worth mentioning. Sometimes, as she listened to them, she could almost imagine her father saying the words, and her heart ached with missing him. Yet in the end, no one had seemed to know anything more about his death.

Meg rolled up her sleeves, got out the lone frying pan in preparation for cooking her treasured sausage. There was no use being discouraged. Even if she hadn't found Pete Eckles, it wouldn't hurt to at least check on the status of her stock.

The next day she started what would be her daily habit of dropping by the exchange after work. She learned some of the terms. The "bid price" was the highest price a buyer was willing to pay. The "ask price" was the lowest amount at which a seller was willing to sell. Bids and asks were made in multiples of an eighth of a dollar or twelve and a half cents. Stocks were traded in what were called "lots." Most transactions were made in "round" lots, meaning one hundred shares or multiples of one hundred. Anything less than one hundred was called an "odd lot." The man at the podium who conducted business was known as the caller.

She went after dark. A few times, on the way home, she felt as if she was being followed, and she stopped in front of a well-lighted store window, glanced over her shoulder, but saw no one. She told herself she was just tired, it was just her imagination. She was foolish to worry. Yet she couldn't quite shrug off her fear.

Then one moonless night, as she turned the corner of Franklin and Crook Streets, just a block from the bottle house, she had a premonition that someone was waiting to harm her. A horse and rig rattled by in the otherwise deserted street. She walked past the oblongs of light that filtered from the windows of the Jump Up Saloon. The stretch of boardwalk beyond was dark, empty.

Uneasy, Meg felt the clutch of foreboding rise in her throat, and she quickened her pace, her senses alert to everything around her. Then, out of the corner of her eye, she thought she saw a figure in a doorway just ahead. She toyed with the idea of crossing the street, but didn't. Telling herself she was being melodramatic, she fought back her fear. With eyes straight ahead, pretending there was no one there, she was nearly parallel to the doorway when a man stepped out and grabbed her.

She fought to wrench free, but the hands only tightened their hold. As she pulled away, one of her heels caught in the cracks of the boardwalk, causing her to trip over her skirts. She screamed, kept screaming. She felt her skirts rip as she stumbled over them. She kicked at the man, clawed at his thick fingers. He was breathing hard, and she smelled the animal odor of him. She could hear her cries echo in the dark as he shoved her down. Her head snapped back sharply against the boardwalk, and her world went black.

She had no idea how long she lay on the dusty street. Somewhere above her, she heard deep, anxious voices. She opened her eyes, and saw several men peering down at her.

"You okay, lady?" a man in a battered soft-brimmed hat asked. "We heard the ruckus and came runnin'."

She stared at the men, not sure for a moment whether to be alarmed until she saw none of them resembled the man in the doorway. As she slowly sat up, the throbbing in the back of her head nearly blinded her. She felt nauseated. "If you don't mind, I'd appreciate a hand up and some assistance to my house. I live at the end of the block."

The man in the soft-brimmed hat took her arm while the others followed, and they walked her slowly to the bottle house. As they reached the door, she felt for her pocketbook that normally dangled from one wrist and contained the door key, and realized it was gone.

"I believe I must have dropped my pocketbook," she said, hearing her shaky voice. "I'll need to go back—My key's in it."

"I'll take a look," one of the men volunteered, and he loped back toward where they had found her. Meg leaned against the door, watching the man search the street and look this way, shaking his head. "No sign of it," he called.

Another man reached past her and tried the doorknob, found it locked. He turned to a companion. "Gimme that penknife of yours, Will. The lady has to get in her house."

A moment later, the lock had been jimmied open, and she was helped inside. One of the men lit the lamp as she was guided to a chair by another. She smelled the whiskey on his breath.

Once seated, she glanced up at the worried faces and gave a weak smile. "Thank you. I think I'll be fine now."

"You're sure?" asked the man in the soft-brimmed hat, obviously still worried.

"Absolutely." She stood up and walked to the door to prove her point. But by the time she closed the door behind the last man to file out into the dark, the room began to spin. She made it to the cot before she fell, and lay down, fully clothed.

With her eyes closed, the dizziness faded. She reached up, gingerly touched the back of her head with a trembling hand, felt her matted hair. She decided the skin must be cut. She was lucky that's all that had happened to her, that and being robbed.

She was disgusted with herself. Besides her key, she'd lost five dollars she couldn't spare. She knew better. She'd been living in Goldfield for a month, had seen the drunks and the hard-looking men among the ordinary miners and prospectors. She'd met up with one of them in the Ajax Saloon. Plainly, walking around the camp at night, alone, was tempting fate. She was lucky to have escaped with a bump on the head, lucky four reasonably sober men had come to her aid. All these weeks she'd been stubbornly living in the dream world of her childhood where grown-ups had protected her from the harsh realities of life as it actually was in mining camps.

It was high time she act with a little more intelligence. The man who had attacked her had meant to rape her. If she knew how to shoot, she'd buy a revolver, one of those little ones, and carry it in her pocketbook. But she didn't. So in the morning, she'd ask Verna to go with her on future evening trips to the exchange.

* * *

In the days that followed, Meg couldn't avoid the reality of the cost of living in Goldfield any longer. Her commissions from advertising sales didn't begin to cover even the essentials. Beyond groceries and water, there was coal oil and the fifty cents a miner's wife charged for laundering Meg's few shirtwaists and underthings. When the Genuine Article hit seventy-five cents, she put aside her resolve to hang on to all her stock, and sold twenty shares.

But before she even had the fifteen dollars in her hands, she watched in dismay as the two-dollar broker who handled small trades took two dollars of it, plus his 10 percent commission, money rightfully hers, for doing almost nothing. She considered the process out-and-out robbery, and vowed to find a way around it.

As she stepped away from the window of the cashier's cage and put the eleven dollars and fifty cents in her pocketbook, she glanced toward the small, cordoned-off area at the back of the exchange where unaccompanied ladies who came to trade were to sit. Not only was the area in the back, but it was off to one side, making it difficult for the auctioneers to see a woman signal her wish to buy or sell.

In her previous visits to the exchange, Meg had come to know the other women who were steady customers. Among them was the saloon owner, Tess Wallace. Another woman, a Mrs. Burlingame, was the wife of the man who had helped her at the John Cook Bank and was a member of the exchange. It was a mixed group. The feeling among them was pleasant, but businesslike. They were all small traders like Meg, who dealt in odd lots, and brokers were largely uninterested in accommodating them. Seeing them as they studied the board, it occurred to her that together they might be able to persuade the exchange to make some adjustments.

She'd talk to them. She had a sixth sense about how best to approach people. Most of the time, they ended up thinking her idea was their own.

*   *   *

In spite of the money Meg lost with every trade, she made enough to convince her that, with or without Pete Eckles's advice, the stock market was where she should be.

Prices changed hourly. Sometimes an overly optimistic promotional advertisement for a mine was enough to whet people's appetites and hope of making a fortune. Usually, it was news of the latest strikes and their ore values which spread like a wildfire across the camp. A mine's stock could soar or plummet simply because the claim happened to be located next door to either a fabulously rich find or a mine that had had the bad luck to hit more rhyolite than gold. Or a miner could come into a saloon and buy drinks all around with a pouch full of gold nuggets roasted out of ore he'd high-graded—stolen—during his shift the previous day. Within the hour, word would be out about which mine he worked in, and another wild trading scramble was on.

Meg knew she should be at the exchange to keep track of the changes in her stock, but Verna relied on her to sell advertising during the day. A week went by without once checking the latest quotes. Finally, Meg couldn't stand it any longer, and she asked Verna to go with her that night after she finished setting type.

It was nearly eight o'clock by the time they set off toward the exchange. The October night air was cool, refreshing. As they approached the entrance, it seemed to Meg the crowd was heavier than usual. She and Verna could barely push their way inside. Finally, Meg was close enough to see the board. The ask price for Fourth of July had jumped to six. She scanned the list. The Genuine Article was up to a dollar, and she kicked herself for selling it at seventy-five. Over the Top was a dollar at the ask price, seventy-five cents bid price.

Meg glanced about, realized Verna had disappeared. Perhaps the heat in the crush of the crowd had been too much for her and she'd gone outside for fresh air. With each change in the figures recorded on the board, each new bid, the crowd shouted at the brokers and waved pieces of paper with their orders in the air. Meg pushed her way into the midst of the crowd standing and sitting behind the railing. She was not surprised to see Tess there. Always beautifully dressed, tonight she was wearing a suit of gray velveteen. To Meg, the outfit looked a little out of place in Goldfield.

Meg shifted her glance to the left, saw a familiar profile. Charley Thompson. An older man, balding and graying at the temples, with pince-nez balanced on the bridge of his patrician nose, stood beside him.

Meg maneuvered through the crush so she could have a better view of the changes to the board. People continued to push through the entrance, wedging themselves along the walls. She wondered if she shouldn't come back tomorrow, then she felt a tap on her shoulder. She looked around and saw Charley. The older man she'd seen him with was behind him.

"My father, Sumner Thompson," Charley said, leaning close to her so she could hear.

Meg nodded, then glanced at Mr. Thompson and smiled.

Charley took her arm. "Would you join us for supper? You can't hear yourself think up here."

"My friend, Miss Bates, is with me."

He smiled, though Meg wasn't sure he'd heard what she'd said.

* * *

Meg and Verna squeezed past other diners in the Mocha Cafe to- toward a vacant table and sat down. Mr. Thompson and Charley fol- lowed.

They ordered the only items listed on the bill of fare: fried steak, fried potatoes, and canned green beans. Once the waitress left, they glanced at one another and smiled politely. The air was stifling, thick with tobacco smoke and the smell of burning grease. Meg wished she'd gone home instead of accepting Charley's invitation.

Sumner Thompson looked across the table at her, smiled as if he could read her mind. "You haven't told me what brought you to Goldfield, Miss Kendall."

"Actually, I read about it when I was living in Boulder, Col- orado," she said, choosing to leave out the rest of the story.

"Boulder. A lovely town. The site of the university."

"I graduated from the university last June."

"My congratulations. I presume you're a teacher then, here in Goldfield."

Meg was struck by his open friendliness, the warmth of his gray eyes framed by the pince-nez. He seemed to have little of his son's stuffy nature. She decided she liked him, and she told him about her father's death and her need to settle his affairs.

He nodded solemnly. "Though your father's passing must be a great loss, I would hope his estate includes some mining stock."

"Oh?"

"It would provide you with a fine dowry indeed."

She smiled. A dowry was the last thing in the world she would have thought of. "Actually, I hope some day to start my own busi- ness."

"A sound idea," he said. Apparently, the notion of a woman in business didn't bother him. "If I were a woman and I lived in a college town like Boulder, I think I'd invest in a bookstore. But that's just a suggestion, you understand."

"Of course."

The waitress came back, bearing a steaming pot of coffee, but Mr. Thompson waved her away. Meg studied the graying man, appreciating the thoughtful way he'd reacted to her idea. Something about him reminded her vaguely of Aunt Hilary. Yet running a bookstore was not what Meg had in mind. Like the hat shop owned by one of her aunt's friends, operating a bookstore was something respectable women could do if they had to make their way in the world. Whatever the business turned out to be, Meg was certain it would be different, new, catering to the needs of today's women.

They continued to sit without speaking for a few more minutes.

Finally, aware she had forgotten her manners, Meg asked, "I suppose I should know, but what is your business in Goldfield, Mr. Thompson?"

Charley and his father exchanged glances.

"I'm counsel for the Mohawk Mines," Sumner Thompson said.

Meg couldn't hide her surprise. "Really?"

"I thought I'd told you," Charley said. "Dad just came in on the morning train."

"Unfortunately, a suit's been filed against my clients," Sumner Thompson said.

Meg searched for a response that wouldn't betray her interest. "Charley mentioned it."

"There's a chance the court may decide to close down both parties during deliberations. Obviously, such a move would be disastrous. I'm here to discuss the problem with Mr. Eckles."

"Mr. Eckles is here in Goldfield?" Meg asked.

"We're to meet tomorrow. That is if he doesn't leave town in the meantime."

It was all Meg could do to keep from jumping up and searching every hotel in town, but Pete Eckles probably would be out to dinner with cronies. Besides, she'd discovered it was a poor idea for her to wander about the camp alone at night. She'd wait until morning to track him down.

* * *

Meg was up at dawn, dressed and ready to call on Mr. Eckles. She wore the serviceable deep blue gabardine suit she'd finally been forced to buy, her hat of the same blue, a pair of white cotton gloves that looked fairly new. Tucked in the bottom of her pocketbook was the map of the Haywood-Mohawk mine.

When she entered the Fourth of July offices, she felt a wave of relief. The clerk she'd talked to before was nowhere in sight. Another man was in his place. She asked to see Mr. Eckles, was told he was with Mr. Grimble, inspecting the new stopes. Meg's spirits soared. She told the clerk she'd wait. She took a chair and sat down. She had a good view of the gallows frame and the hoist beneath it.

An hour, then two went by. A shift came up, the miners' feet banging against the iron floor of the cage, and another shift went down. Meg recalled that at dinner last night Sumner Thompson had mentioned the meeting he was to have today with Mr. Eckles to discuss the lawsuit. She couldn't remember what time Mr. Thompson had said it was to take place. She wondered if there was another hoist in another part of the mine and Pete Eckles had somehow escaped her notice.

She had almost despaired when two bells rang to announce a hoist coming up. She went outside. Beneath the gallows, the cage rattled past the collar of the shaft and stopped. Two men got off.

"Mr. Eckles?" she called.

One of the men, spare with salt-and-pepper hair, turned toward her. "Who wants to know?"

She hurried toward him, blood pounding in her head. "Sir, my name is Meggen Kendall. Jim Kendall was my father, and—"

The man looked startled. "You're Jim's daughter?"

She nodded.

"Come on inside."

She followed him through the door and into an inner office.

He pulled a chair over to the desk, told her to sit down. "I was sorry to hear about old Jim. A good man."

Now that she was actually sitting in front of him, she wasn't sure how to start. "The reason I've come to you, Mr. Eckles, is because of a note my father sent me."

"What kind of a note?" His tone was suspicious.

"I was living in Boulder, Colorado, and it was my father's habit to send me a short note along with the most recent issue of the camp's newspaper. The last one that came just before he died advised me not to sell the stock before I talked to you."

She paused, decided not to mention her father's warning against Nolan and Winters. "At the time, I knew nothing about any stock. Since then, I found stock certificates of three different mines. The largest number of shares—ten thousand, in fact—were the Fourth of July."

Pete Eckles eyed her as he tipped back in his chair. "I gave him that stock."

She found herself smiling. "I must admit I wondered about that. I mean, a mining engineer's salary generally wouldn't allow him to afford that much stock of a mine as valuable as the Fourth of July."

He righted the chair. "Don't misunderstand. Your dad earned 'em, fair and square. Earned 'em for mappin' this mine—mapped it when it was nothin' but a ten-foot shaft. He was like a damn homing pigeon the way he could plot veins."

The backhanded compliment pleased her. She relaxed a little. "I've been watching the price of the Fourth of July mine. As of yesterday the ask price was six dollars. Everyone seems to think it will continue to rise."

"You better believe it will." He rubbed the back of his neck with one hand as he studied her for a moment. Finally, he said, "Tell you what, Meg—" He smiled for the first time. Not a broad smile, but a smile, nevertheless. "You don't mind if I call you Meg, do you?"

She returned his smile. "Of course not."

"Your dad was right to tell you to come to me before you sold that stock. He knew I'd be able to steer you right, and I will."

"I can't tell you how much I appreciate—"

"So what you need to do is sign your shares over to me."

"But—"

He held up a hand. "Hold on. Hear me out. I'll hang on to your stock until I can get you top dollar. Then, and only then, will I put it up for sale."

"I—"

"It's business, Meg. A little lady like yourself— Your dad knew you'd need help."

She pulled in a long breath, pushed aside his implication she was incapable of handling stock that now belonged to her. "Mr. Eckles, I don't want you to misunderstand what I am about to say, but I would need something in writing, some kind of guarantee."

He laughed. "By God, I was wrong about you, missy. You're a regular businesswoman. I see that now. Not like your dad. World's best minin' engineer, no doubt about it, but he didn't know squat about money."

She didn't reply. The man was like a chameleon—one minute telling her she was a mere woman who knew nothing about money, the next applauding her and criticizing her father. She wasn't sure what to make of Pete Eckles. He certainly wasn't the solicitous friend of her father she'd envisioned.

"You're sharp. I like that in a person, man or woman. Investin' in the Fourth is the chance of a lifetime. The Fourth of July is my baby. Nobody knows her better than me. You stick with me, sign over your shares, and you'll have the inside track, make ten times what the suckers out there will make."

"You could be right."

"You know I'm right."

She shifted in her chair. "One thing more."

"Anythin' for one of Jim Kendall's."

Meg pulled the map out of her pocketbook. "I found a map

along with the mining stock. It says on the back that it's of one of the levels in the Haywood-Mohawk." She handed it to him.

Pete Eckles unrolled the heavy sheet, examined the map for a moment before he glanced over at her. "This is Jim's all right."

"I was thinking— That is, it occurred to me there might be some connection between that map and my father's death."

Pete Eckles cocked an eyebrow.

"I've always had the feeling it wasn't an accident."

One side of his mouth pulled into a hard smile. "You think Winters and Nolan—"

"I don't know. That's just it. When I heard about the suit you had filed against the Mohawk Mines Company for trespass—I thought maybe this map might be some kind of evidence, and that my father . . ."

He shrugged. "Could be, but I doubt it. Still . . ." His pale gray eyes darkened. "On the other hand, those two are a nasty pair. With them, anythin's possible."

"So you think the senator and Mr. Winters could have known about the map and realized it proved they were trespassing, just as you'd claimed, then had my father killed?"

"You've got to realize accidents happen every day in mines. There'd be no way in the world to prove otherwise."

She felt her eyes mist, blinked. "I can't let the matter rest."

"Of course, you can't. Wouldn't ask you to." He frowned sympathetically. "You can't send 'em to jail, but you can do somethin' even worse, which gets me back to your stock."

"I don't—"

"If there's one thing Nolan and Winters want more than anythin' else in the world, it's money. They'll do anythin' to get it. They've already proved that."

She waited.

"They want the Fourth of July in the worst way. Which is why we need to stick together, Meg." He paused, leaned forward. "Now, where'd you say the Fourth of July certificates of yours are?"

"In the John Cook Bank safe."

"Fine." He stood up, came around the desk. "You go over there first thing in the mornin' and get 'em out. We'll meet here at— how does ten o'clock sound?"

She rose. "I don't know. Ten o'clock may be rushing it. I appreciate your offer, but right now I really haven't decided whether—"

He put a fatherly arm around her shoulders. "Sure. I understand. It's a big step, missy. But you're smart. That's plain to see. If tomorrow's too soon, we'll do it soon, the next time I come to town."

Almost before Meg realized it, Pete Eckles had wished her a good night, ushered her to the door, closed it behind her, and left her standing outside in the dark. A knot of miners, probably heading for a saloon, passed her. She decided for safety's sake to follow close behind them. As she trudged toward the twinkling lights of the camp, she thought of Pete Eckles's offer.

Though she knew it was often a mistake to judge a person on a first impression, his manner made her uneasy. She tried to remind herself he was a tough prospector, a hardheaded businessman, not a kindly, old uncle. His generous offer had a great deal of appeal. She wouldn't have to concern herself with wondering about the proper time to sell so that she'd get the most money for the stock her father had obviously intended as her inheritance.

Yet, down deep, she guessed she was as stubborn as he'd been. Until his death she hadn't known that about herself. She'd been more willing to follow another's lead. Now she wanted to see if she could manage by herself. As he had. This way, knowing the ways in which she was strongest and most like her father, she could ease the pain of his death and keep him alive in her heart. And along the way she'd find her own dream.

CHAPTER 12

$\mathcal{I}$t was the first of November, surprisingly cold at night, when Verna got another telegram from Amos, extolling the virtues of another mine in Bullfrog, instructing her to send three hundred dollars.

The *Star* was barely holding its own. After the fight, Verna had given her winnings, small as they were, to Meg to invest, and instantly made another few dollars on the stock market. The process both frightened and intrigued her. She was not a betting woman. She couldn't afford to be, and she'd decided not to try her luck at the exchange again. Yet there was something behind the insanity of the Goldfield Stock Exchange that beckoned to her. If she was to offset Amos's voracious appetite for money and avoid the county poorhouse, maybe now was the time to plunge in, headfirst.

Meg had long since become a full-fledged addict. Not a day went by that she didn't stop in the exchange. Though she left the Fourth of July stock in the bank, she used her stock in the Genuine Article and the Over the Top mines judiciously, always trading up. Verna envied her ability. She seemed to have a feel for it that Verna wasn't sure she'd ever master. But Meg pooh-poohed her and said it was time she met other women who traded and saw how well they did.

That afternoon, Verna closed up shop early. If Meg was right, if she could catch on to how it was done, she might be able to keep up with Amos's habit of failure.

* * *

Verna felt a wave of panic as Meg led her toward the fenced-in ladies' gallery and began introductions to the handful of women intently studying the board at the far end of the room. First was a handsome redheaded woman, Tess Wallace, the owner of the Ajax Saloon. Verna nodded in her direction, mumbled something about appreciating their ads. Meg moved on to three other women dressed in natty coat suits with gored skirts, wearing hats so nicely trimmed they couldn't have been bought through a Sears catalog.

Mrs. Burlingame was a small woman with thin, pale-brown hair, who was careful to mention her husband was president of the John Cook Bank as well as a member of the Goldfield Mining Stock Exchange. She reminded Verna of a little, brown sparrow. Next was Mrs. Vogler of Vogler's dry goods store and, last, Mrs. Petticord, who said her husband was an assayer in town.

Verna smiled at everyone, sat down. Normally, she'd never cared much for women's gatherings. Eyes sizing up what everyone wore, talk nothing but gossip. The atmosphere among this bunch was quite different, almost intense. As the group turned its attention to the board at the front of the room, Verna was already intrigued.

"What do you know about the Calumet and Nevada Consolidated Mines Company?" Mrs. Burlingame asked no one in particular.

Verna confessed she'd never heard of it.

Emma Burlingame thrust a sheet, a prospectus, at her. Verna passed it on to Meg who scanned it, then read aloud.

"Act now. Capitalization is two million dollars. Par value of one dollar." Meg glanced up. "It lists officers, directors, and representatives from various cities across the country."

"Where is this Calumet and Nevada anyhow?" Verna asked.

"Esmeralda County, Nevada, is all it says," Meg said.

"Goldfield's in Esmeralda County. Maybe it's in Goldfield," Mrs. Vogler suggested.

Emma Burlingame shook her head. "I don't think so."

"Maybe you could ask your mister," suggested Mrs. Petticord to Mrs. Burlingame.

"I could." Emma Burlingame made a fuss of smoothing the black braid edging of the bodice of her stylish suit. "But I don't see a reason for it."

"Sounds like a brag to me," Tess Wallace said dryly.

"I've got my own nest egg," Emma said, ignoring her. "Why should I ask Mr. Burlingame? It's not his money."

Mrs. Vogler nodded vigorously. "A woman's as smart as a man any day."

"If that's so, Geraldine, why are we sittin' around tryin' to figure the Calumet and Nevada Mining Company?" Sally Petticord asked.

Verna caught a feistiness to the question that might not sit well with the other women, but no one seemed to notice.

"We'll figure it out eventually. No doubt of that," Emma Burlingame said with authority. "What galls me most, though, is how much more money Mr. Burlingame can make when he buys and sells. The price up on that board is what he pays. No commission. Plus he can buy odd lots."

Odd lots made Verna think of property nobody could palm off. Maybe she wasn't too far off.

"It's a case of like it or lump it, ladies," Tess Wallace said. "And sad to say, we gotta lump it."

Mrs. Petticord glanced toward Emma Burlingame, raised her hand as if she was in school. "What we need is a seat on the exchange."

"Sally, you know perfectly well a woman can't get a seat on the exchange, even if she has the money," Mrs. Vogler said.

There were nods of agreement.

"Surely, there's got to be a way around it," Meg suggested.

Verna shot Meg a glance, suspecting she already had an idea to offer.

Tess Wallace snorted in disgust. "Maybe if you live on the moon."

Emma Burlingame cut in. "Actually, Miss Kendall's right."

Meg straightened. All-business. "I think it's time we stop complaining and take matters into our own hands." She let her glance rest on each woman in turn, challenging them.

Verna smiled. Meg was one of the smartest young women she'd ever known. Still, whether Meg realized it or not, she was also in the enviable position of being able to take chances. The Fourth of July stock she owned would someday make her an heiress. With all that money waiting in the background, she could fail at a good many schemes and still make out. It was a nice spot to be in.

"You're so right," Mrs. Burlingame said. "So we must meet. Everyone. You, too, Miss Bates. You're all invited for tea tomorrow. Three o'clock sharp."

Verna eyed the group and wondered how many, beside herself, would show up. She had no intention of joining anything. She'd always been leery of groups. Moving from town to town as she had, being single, she'd felt uncomfortable with women whose talk centered around babies and how best to make soap. It was just that she couldn't miss being in on what was sure to make a front-page story.

*   *   *

The next afternoon as she and Meg walked to the Burlingames on the corner of Fifth and Franklin, Verna decided the cold wind blowing from the north had an unusually damp feel to it. Anywhere else she'd have predicted snow. She wondered if the unusual weather was some kind of omen.

The Burlingames' white clapboard house, considered one of Goldfield's finest, stood out amid the shacks and tents like a swan among common ducks. A bay window bulged out on one side. A stained glass panel of squares of reds and blues and yellows graced the front door. She and Meg climbed the two steps to the front porch, twisted the bell.

A hired girl opened the door, took their coats. The parlor was already filled with ladies. Taking the rocker in the corner, Verna accepted a cup of tea and one of the little cakes Emma Burlingame called petits fours. Verna settled down to scrutinize who of the group she'd met before was here.

There was Tess, the saloon keeper, in her gray velveteen suit trimmed in black silk ribbon with its leg-o'-mutton sleeves and matching hat, black kid gloves, proper and fashionable as if she were the mayor's wife. Geraldine Vogler, the bony woman with big-knuckled hands that had seen their share of work, who Verna knew helped her husband in his hardware store. Bess Archibald, big as a man, ran the Imperial Restaurant. Sally Petticord, a bit prim for Verna's taste. And, of course, there was Meg. Of the seven women, Bess Archibald was the only one who hadn't been at the exchange yesterday.

Verna glanced about the room at the hand-painted china dishes displayed on the what-not shelf, the stuffed elk head over the fireplace. A gilt-framed scene of what she guessed was the English countryside hung on the opposite wall, dark green velour drapes at the windows. But the main attraction, proof positive John Burlingame was a financial success, was the silver tea set on a round table smack dab in the middle of the room.

The undercurrent of high-pitched chatter held a certain anxiety, Verna thought. She was impatient for Emma Burlingame to get down to business. Time passed. More tea was served. It was nearly five when the hostess finally moved to the center of the room and asked for quiet.

"Ladies, I'm going to get right to the point," Emma said. "Everybody in this room was invited because she's bought or sold shares of mining stock. We are all well aware of the problem."

"What problem, Emma?" Mrs. Vogler asked.

"How much the commission fee is costin' us because we can only buy odd lots, for heaven's sake," Mrs. Archibald snapped.

Emma Burlingame held up a hand for silence. "Please, ladies." She turned toward Meg. "Miss Kendall, perhaps you'd like to explain."

Meg smiled, rose. "First of all, you know I'm no expert."

Verna grinned to herself. As the youngest, prettiest woman here, Meg was smart to start out properly humble. Most of the women knew she held some stock; none knew how much.

Mrs. Vogler raised her hand.

"You have a question, Geraldine?" Emma asked.

Mrs. Vogler stood. "Seems like we've talked about all this before. I don't see why—"

"Because we need to talk some more," Emma said, crisply. She turned to Meg. "Go on, dear."

"Well," Meg began, giving the ladies a smile sweet as cake. "We know the chances of me or any other lady in this room being able to buy a seat on the stock exchange are rather slim."

"Slim as a busted straight winnin' the pot," Tess observed, a bite in her tone.

Everyone ignored the remark.

"I'm sure if I spoke to Mr. Petticord about it, he would be willing to give us a cut-rate price on our transactions," Sally Petticord said.

Verna realized she was being pulled into a matter that meant nothing to her personally, but she couldn't keep her mouth shut. "Why in the Sam Hill would he want to do that when he can make money off of us?"

Sally Petticord drew herself up a little straighter. "Because he's the sort of man who is happy to help ladies in need."

"I'm sure he is, Sally," Emma said. "But we're trying to help ourselves here."

Verna watched as everyone looked at one another, as if trying to digest the idea. The front door opened; a man Verna presumed to be Mr. Burlingame came in. "Evening, ladies," he said as he placed his hat on the rack by the door.

"You're back early, Mr. Burlingame," Emma said.

"It's supper time, and I want to be at the exchange by seven," he said.

All eyes were on him. It was as if his appearance had suddenly triggered a new awareness.

"Mr. Burlingame, would it be possible to start a new stock exchange in Goldfield?" Meg asked.

He smiled at her. "I have to admit there are times when a person can hardly get in to place an order."

"That wasn't exactly what I meant."

He regarded her with amusement.

She smiled sweetly, but from where Verna sat the girl's eyes held an unmistakable spark of excitement and determination. "Actually, I was thinking about the ladies of Goldfield starting an exchange. Most of us can only afford to buy less than a hundred shares—odd lots, I think they're called. The fee we pay compared to the number of shares involved is sky-high. If we had our own exchange, think of the money we'd save."

Verna watched the women stare at Meg for an instant, eyes wide, then turn to Mr. Burlingame, who was smiling.

"You're joshing, of course."

His wife stepped forward. "We're in dead earnest."

Mr. Burlingame absently ran a finger underneath the edge of his starched shirt collar, stretched his neck. "We'll talk about this when I get back tonight."

"Fine with me, but we ladies are talking about it now," Emma said, pleasantly.

So, apparently deciding it was safer to stay and guide the conversation than leave, Mr. Burlingame went to the kitchen, returned with a chair, and sat down in the back next to Tess.

"Let's see," Emma said. "We must have seats on our exchange. The question is how much one will cost."

Geraldine Vogler's face clouded. "You're sure this is what we should do?"

"Sounds good to me," Tess said.

"Wait till Jake Stratton hears you won't be trading with him," Sally Petticord said, smirking. "He'll have a fit."

"Are you plannin' to tell him?" Tess asked.

"Of course not," Sally huffed.

"Good. Cause it's none of your damn business."

Emma placed a hand on their shoulders. "Ladies, please. We've got business to conduct."

With a forlorn or maybe more a resigned look, Mr. Burlingame informed them if they wanted to do it right, they'd need a governing committee. In a matter of moments, everyone agreed Emma Burlingame seemed the obvious choice as president and was duly elected. Meg became vice president. To her astonishment, before she could object, Verna found herself elected secretary. Tess was voted in as treasurer, maybe because as the co-owner of a saloon the others presumed she had the largest portfolio of stocks.

They returned to the matter of the cost of a seat. Ten dollars was suggested, then rejected as too low. They'd need money for supplies and rent. They couldn't keep imposing on the Burlingames. Finally, they settled on twenty-five dollars. Those without the full amount could buy a seat on time, Geraldine Vogler ventured.

Mr. Burlingame shook his head, a look of disbelief on his face. "You have to pay cash for the seats."

"Why?" they asked, nearly in unison.

"Because the exchange must have assets to insure trading commitments."

A heated discussion about the meaning of assets followed.

Sally Petticord was quite definite assets were things like tangibles and intangibles. Meg agreed, then expounded. To be a tangible good, it had to have an assigned value, like stocks. It followed, she said, that the assets of the stock exchange would be both cash held by the treasurer and the stock owned by members. Bess Archibald didn't care what assets were and proceeded to plunk down a roll of bills on the table. Verna chuckled to herself, appreciating the gesture. She and Bess were the two oldest women in the room. If youth was impetuous, old age was impatient. It was time to stop the quibbling.

Mr. Burlingame rose. "Ladies, I fear you've put the cart before the horse."

"How's that?" Mrs. Archibald asked.

"According to custom, not just anyone can become a member of the exchange, even if he has the money to buy a seat."

They looked at one another.

"Are you saying there must be some kind of an admissions committee, Mr. Burlingame?" his wife asked.

He shrugged. "Customers must have confidence in the exchange. Thus, only individuals of good character and good credit should hold seats."

"But we're the customers," Emma said. "We're all friends."

Mr. Burlingame stared at her for an instant. "Wait a minute. What do you mean you're the customers?"

"I mean we are the buyers and the sellers, everyone in this room," his wife said.

"You don't intend to let anyone else buy or sell? You won't have any listings except your own stock?"

"Maybe. Maybe not."

Emma's husband looked dumfounded.

Meg raised her hand, and Emma recognized her.

"Madam chairman, may I ask Mr. Burlingame a question?"

Emma gave a solemn nod.

"Sir, do you think we should have other listings and allow others to buy and sell?"

"I don't suppose you have to. But—"

"Who else would want a seat or list stock?" Geraldine Vogler asked.

"Jake might," Tess said.

"I imagine he'd do most anything if it made a dollar," Sally said with that prim smile of hers.

Tess smiled back, in a good-natured way, not letting the remark get to her. "Seems like that's what we're doin' ourselves, Miz Petticord," she said.

Everyone laughed. Verna was taking a liking to Tess. In spite of the smile, the wary look in her eyes was that of a woman who'd had a tough life, yet it hadn't gotten her down.

"Maybe other ladies would want to join us," Mrs. Archibald suggested.

Heads nodded in agreement.

"But how would they know about us?" Sally Petticord asked.

Everyone looked to Mr. Burlingame, but it was Verna who spoke up. "Advertise. I'll write articles, send them out to other papers that carry mining stock quotes."

"When I go around town, I can let people know," Meg added.

It wasn't until well after seven o'clock, Mr. Burlingame still without his supper and still sitting in the back of the room, when the group disbanded.

Mrs. Archibald offered to let them use the room over her restaurant until they found a proper space to rent.

Mr. Burlingame mumbled morosely about their needing a board, a caller, a cashier.

They'd only just started, but as soon as a few things were cleared up, Tess said, they'd be ready to deal the cards.

As they walked out into the dark, laughing, pleased with themselves, each about to head in a different direction, Verna was struck with how the mood of the group had shifted to a kind of giddy excitement. She felt it herself. It was as if they were about to start off on an excursion that held a certain element of danger, which might prove truer than they could know or even imagine.

CHAPTER 13

*T*he following morning, Meg stood at the window of the *Star* and watched the snow that had been falling lightly since dawn, amazed at how pristine it made everything look. White, clean, almost hiding the lumps of manure on the streets, the rusting tin cans tossed between tents and in back of buildings.

Everything was happening almost too fast, going too easily. The first meeting of the Ladies' Goldfield Stock Exchange governing board was scheduled for four o'clock this afternoon at Mrs. Archibald's restaurant. She felt as if she was skating on ice without knowing how thick it was. She had no idea about how to start a business, but it was too late to back out now. She'd just have to learn.

Meg opened the notebook containing the list of regular customers and surveyed the names, pleased to discover that among them were the founding members of the exchange. It was her habit to call on customers every Monday to be certain their copy for the next issue was acceptable. She ran her finger back up the alphabetized list of names. At the top was the Brown Transportation Company.

She smiled. She'd always been attracted to men with his kind of dark good looks and trim figure. If someone had asked her to imagine the owner of an automobile freighting service in a gold mining camp, she wouldn't have described Bill Brown. To be sure, that wild look he had about him fit. The irreverent way he'd stripped down his automobile was what a person might expect. Like her father, always the maverick, but with a gentleness. Yet underneath . . . She couldn't put her finger on it, but there was something about his relaxed manner that reminded her of money and breeding, mostly the latter. She wondered where he'd come from.

She'd better get started if she was going to see everyone before the meeting this afternoon. She took her coat off a hook by the door, put it on, and went outside.

Four blocks later, she stood in front of the Brown Transportation garage, its big doors closed against the weather. She peered through the smudged window, saw no light, but when she tried the door, she found it open. She went in, greeted by the clutter and the smell of oil that typified the cavernous room. An automobile with its wheels removed was obviously under repair. Sticking out from beneath it were two legs.

"Mr. Brown?"

The legs moved until the body attached to them slowly appeared. "Miss Kendall."

"Meg." She smiled. "How did you know who it was?"

"The ankles."

She stole a glance at the hem of her skirts.

He pulled a rag out of the back pocket of his coveralls and tried to wipe the grease from his hands. "The world, seen from under an automobile, takes on an interesting perspective."

She laughed.

"What can I do for you today?"

"It's Monday. I came by to see about your ad."

"It looks great. Keep it just as is."

She drew the pad containing the list of customers out of her pocketbook, made a note of it. She should be getting on her way. Yet there was something about the feel of the place—the smell of the oil and grease, the hulking presence of the machines waiting to be repaired, which seemed to exude a marvelous kind of power—that intrigued her. Someday she would have an automobile of her own. She glanced about. "I'd forgotten what all you have in here."

He grinned. "Not much to see. Tires, tools. The Rambler touring car over there belongs to Phil Petticord. The connecting rod's broken."

"Is that bad?"

"I had to send to Detroit for parts."

"I suppose you're getting ready to pick up some freight or something."

"I thought I'd wait for the snow to stop and the roads to dry a little. When they're wet, they're slick as glass." He grinned at her.

"I hadn't thought of that."

They exchanged glances.

"Can you stay a minute?"

"Well, I—"

"Wait a second." He walked over to a swivel chair next to a battered rolltop desk and carried it to where she stood. "Here we go. Have a seat."

They both glanced at its greasy wooden seat. He whipped out the rag from his back pocket again, rubbed it over the seat, without any visible signs of cleansing.

"I guess I should have a chair reserved for customers."

She smiled. "I really don't have time to sit down." She started to the door, then turned back. "Oh, I nearly forgot."

He grinned expectantly.

"I wanted to tell you about the new stock exchange in town. We call it the Ladies' Goldfield Stock Exchange."

"Well, now. That's quite an idea."

"You think so?"

"Absolutely. More important, though, is what the Goldfield Mining Stock Exchange thinks."

She stared at him. The thought the established exchange would object had never occurred to her. The possibility was alarming.

"But, heh. There's certainly enough business to go around." His smile made her believe him.

She let out her breath, calm now. "Our listings will be limited at first, mostly the stock we each bring, but we intend to expand soon."

His smile held.

"Mrs. Burlingame is our president. She also happens to be the wife of John Burlingame of the John Cook Bank." As she talked, the exchange slowly took clear shape in her mind as it hadn't until now. "You do invest, don't you?"

"Who doesn't?"

"Well, you must trade at our exchange. For a while, until we can rent more permanent quarters, it's on the second floor of the Imperial Restaurant."

He laughed. "What a whale of an idea."

She tilted her head, eyeing him, still a little wary about how seriously he was taking her, uncertain what he meant.

"Tempt the palate, tempt the pocketbook, all at the same time."

She chuckled. Until this instant, she'd never thought of the idea, though likely Mrs. Archibald had. Bill Brown's reaction to the exchange seemed to be a good omen.

*   *   *

It was nearly five o'clock when Meg hurried up the stairs of the Imperial Restaurant. The sound of women's voices told her she was late.

She entered the long room, saw the rest of the board of directors standing by a table and four chairs, waiting for her. She smiled, apologized. As she pulled off her gloves, she glanced about and tried to visualize how the room would look once it was transformed into the Ladies' Goldfield Stock Exchange.

Along one side were three narrow windows, bare of curtains for now, offering a view of the street below. Packing boxes and cartons were stacked at the far end. The board could be mounted there. They'd get some long tables and chairs where the board members could sit. The room was dark. They'd need lots of lamps.

"Meg, pop out of that trance and come sit down."

The voice was Verna's. Meg shifted her gaze back to the group. "Sorry. I was just thinking how to arrange the room."

She took off her coat and they all sat down. She decided not to mention the matter of whether the Mining Stock Exchange would sanction the newcomer. Surely, Mr. Burlingame would have mentioned it if there was some question. Anyway, the ladies had every right to start a new business if they chose.

A blue enamel coffeepot, four cups and plates, and a plate covered with a sparkling white dish towel sat on the table. Verna folded back the towel, revealing a layer of something that looked like a deep cookie large enough to fill the plate, cut in quarters. "Mrs. Archibald sent these up. Scones, she says they are. Says she baked them on a griddle. Never had them myself." She selected one, took a bite, nodded her approval.

Emma poured the coffee. The plate of scones went around. They ate and drank in silence for a minute or two, then Emma Burlingame pushed her plate aside, and called the meeting to order. Verna called the roll. They looked at one another expectantly.

"I guess we have to organize," Meg said.

Emma pulled a pamphlet with official-looking gold lettering on it from her purse, held it up. "The Goldfield Consolidated Mining Stock Exchange constitution. It won't hurt to see what it says."

The sound of footsteps came from the stairway. A frazzled-looking girl in an apron, carrying a kerosene lamp appeared. "Miz Archibald says this is for you ladies." She placed the lamp in the center of the table and headed for the stairs.

"Tell her thanks," Tess called as everyone pulled their chairs closer to the table and the circle of light from the lamp.

"As you can see when I pass this around," Emma said, handing the booklet to Meg, "we will need rules about membership, initiation fees, purchase of memberships by the exchange, dues."

Meg gave the booklet to Verna, who leafed through it, whistled softly. "Not including the list of members and the index in the back, this thing is thirty-nine pages long. Do we really want to do this?"

Meg had no intention of letting Verna discourage the others from accomplishing their purpose. "Ours can be a lot shorter."

Verna flipped a few more pages. "Ladies, listen to this. Memberships shall be limited to three hundred. Every applicant must be a male person and at least twenty-one years of age."

Tess hooted.

Verna glanced around at them. "Don't we want it open to both men and women? Let's just say every applicant must be at least twenty-one."

Emma looked doubtful. "I don't know. Maybe it would be better if we confined the exchange to ladies."

"We won't make as much money if we do," Tess said.

Meg eyed her. Tess might be a saloon keeper, maybe an ex-whore if rumors were to be believed, but she had a way of cutting through to the heart of matters. "That's a good point."

They settled on open membership, confirmed the twenty-five dollars for the initiation fee, decided on ten dollars a month for dues.

"With those prices, half the camp will join up," Verna said.

"Ladies—" Emma cleared her throat to get their attention. "May I remind you, we do not accept just anyone. Members must be of good character and credit."

Verna made a wry face. "In Goldfield?"

Emma gave her a level look. "Just what are you insinuating, Miss Bates?"

"Not insinuating a thing, Emma. Just asking a question."

Emma frowned, turned to Meg. "Turn to page six and the listing requirements, dear. Look at the paragraphs about a listing committee."

Tess broke in. "I thought we were just going to list our own stock."

"Well, sure," Meg said. "But don't we want to get some of the new mining companies to list their stock with us? They seem to spring up every day."

"Come on. Face facts," Tess said. "Any straight-up outfit would list with the gents' exchange. At least until we get ourselves a reputation."

Meg dodged past the issue. She wanted to keep things moving. "Here on page twenty it talks about a clearing house that seems to handle the delivery of stock and money." She turned the page. "It's supposed to take an offer or bid of a board lot to make an exchange quotation." She looked up, hoping one of the others could explain what it meant.

"Does it say what constitutes a board lot?" Emma asked.

Meg skimmed the rest of the page for the answer. "Here. I'll read it. 'The following number of shares shall constitute a board lot: a thousand shares of stock selling up to a dollar per share; five hundred shares in stocks selling one to two dollars per share; a hundred shares in stocks selling two dollars or more per share.'"

Tess huffed, "What kind of help is that?"

Meg glanced over at her, thrust the book at her. "You figure it out then."

Tess gave her a cool look. "Wouldn't touch it with a ten-foot pole. You're doin' fine."

Meg gave a stiff smile at the backhanded apology. They'd never get anywhere if they started fighting. She returned her gaze to the page. "Here it is. No bid or offer of less than one-fourth of one cent from last bid or offer on stock selling over one cent per share up to twenty-five cents per share and one-half cents from twenty-five cents to one dollar—"

"Hold on a minute." Verna stood up, surveyed the small group. "Does anyone in this room really understand a word of this gibberish?"

Meg gazed at the stolid figure, the serious face, and realized how fond she was growing of her. "Not now. Not this minute. We have to read up on it, think about it. The main thing is we want to make it cheaper and easier for people to buy odd lots. Once the little in-

vestors, like us, find out what we've done, they'll come running."
She looked at Emma. "Do you think you can get us each a copy of
that constitution by tomorrow?"

"Maybe. This one came from Mr. Burlingame's desk at home."

Tess looked disgusted. "No guts?"

"I beg your pardon," said Emma, her tone ice cold.

"You swiped it without askin'. Am I right?"

Emma gave her a withering glance. "Though I'm sure you would
not appreciate the problem, a married woman has to work around
things sometimes."

Tess smiled at Emma, poured herself what was left of the coffee.
"I thought you were independently wealthy."

Emma's bosom seemed to expand with indignation. "As I say, a
married woman has limitations she must work within, but then you
wouldn't know about that."

Tess sat back, crossed her legs, smiled as if unaware of the not-
so-subtle innuendos. "Emma, you don't have to be nasty. I know
what women can and can't do with money and property better than
you. All I'm sayin' is go up to Mr. Burlingame and say you want
three more constitutions. For God's sake, he's no big bad boogey-
man."

Emma gave a humph.

"So how about meeting again tomorrow?" Meg said. "Same
time, same place. In the meantime, Emma get us copies of the constitution. We'll read them, then bring them with us. How does that
sound?"

She had anticipated complete agreement. Instead Emma said
she didn't want to miss seeing to Mr. Burlingame's supper two
nights in a row. Tess had the Ajax to tend. Verna mumbled something about putting the paper to bed.

Fed up, Meg pushed to her feet, looking at each woman in turn.
"Either we're going to have a stock exchange, or we aren't. If we
are, we'll meet here tomorrow at four o'clock, just like today."

CHAPTER 14

$\mathcal{T}$ess arranged her Persian lamb-trimmed cape about her shoulders, pulled on her gloves. "Meg's right," she said. She was damned if she'd let this chance to make some real money slip away.

The corners of Emma's thin mouth puckered into something like a smile. "Four o'clock then. Tomorrow."

The strain between them loosened. Tess was glad. She depended on these women, and for the first time in her life, she felt as if she was halfway accepted in polite society. She still couldn't believe the ladies who had gathered at Emma Burlingame's yesterday had made her one of the leaders of the exchange. Her knowledge of running a business could account for most of it. Her clothes helped. She knew that. Once she'd tended toward bright colors and flashy style, but she'd studied *Vogue* magazine, paid attention to the dress of the women who appeared in the society pages of the *Colorado Springs Telegraph Gazette* and the *Denver Post*. She dressed like a lady.

Yet, when it was all said and done, she guessed it was just because it was Goldfield. Freewheeling, anything-goes Goldfield. Rich swells shared hotel beds with down-at-the-heels prospectors. The madam of the Blue Parrot whorehouse waltzed into the Palm

Restaurant on the arm of the owner of the biggest mine in town. Now a ladies' stock exchange. None of it would last, but who cared? The ladies' exchange would give her a way out of the box she'd been in, and she'd have a little respect in the bargain. It was more than she'd expected.

As she followed Emma down the stairs and out onto the boardwalk, Tess knew that by now Vic would be wondering where in the Sam Hill she was, but at the moment she didn't want to think about serving drinks. For days, she'd been trying to decide whether to have Jake buy her one hundred shares of the Red Fox in Bullfrog or of Goldfield's Florence. He had assured her both were no-lose propositions. Until the Ladies' Exchange was on its feet, she still had to go through a broker. She decided to stop in at the exchange. She'd cover for Vic another night.

As always the place was crowded, but she managed to find herself a seat in the ladies' gallery from where she could see the board. She glanced at the list of stocks again, saw the Rescue mining company. Jake's Graham Trust Company listed it in their number one category, a best buy. According to him, the price was destined to go nowhere but up. She remembered Meg had bought ten shares the other day. Tess decided to go down the street to Jake's office and ask him about the Rescue before she went back to the Ajax.

Pulling her cape tight against the cold, Tess went outside and down the block to the entrance to the Graham Trust Company. The lights were on. She tapped on the door, called Jake's name.

A few minutes later, he pulled the door open. "What's the occasion? I thought you were over at the Ajax, keeping Vic honest."

She swept past him. "I was at a meetin' of the Ladies' Goldfield Stock Exchange."

He glanced at her. "Say again."

"You heard me."

"What're they exchanging, recipes?"

"Recipes for makin' money so we won't have to pay bandits like you in the process."

He grinned at her. "You've been smoking that sweet stuff over in Hop Fiend's Gulch."

"Make fun. That's okay. You'll see." She undid the clasp of her cloak, tossed it over the chair in the corner. "In the meantime, I want you to buy me some stock. Trouble is I can't decide between the Red Fox and the Rescue."

Jake went around his oversize mahogany desk and sat down in the high-backed chair. He waved her toward the black leather chair in front of him. "Sit. I'll be through with this in a minute, then we can talk about it."

Tess arranged the skirts of her plum-colored faille suit as she leaned back in the comfort of the overstuffed chair, watched Jake scan the latest batch of telegrams from his contacts around the country. She crossed her legs, twisted a tendril of hair hanging along the back of her neck. "What does all that telegraphin' cost you?"

"Twelve, fifteen thousand, give or take."

"A year or a month?"

"A week."

She straightened. "That's enough to buy my ranch."

He gave a derisive grunt and glanced up. "Your ranch in the sky."

"You wish," she retorted. They'd been over the subject dozens of times. The day she packed up and headed east to Colorado, fancy Mr. Jake Stratton would be up a creek, and he knew it. She was his eyes and ears. There wasn't a week that went by she didn't pass on a tip about a would-be investor at the Ajax or some other saloon in town.

Jake straightened the pile and put it in a wire basket on his desk. "The Florence is going like hot cakes," he said as he stood up. "Most of these telegrams are buy orders."

"That settles it. Buy me a hundred shares of Red Fox."

"Always the maverick, eh, Tess?"

"You said they were both good."

He shrugged. "Someday you should stop investing by the seat of your pants."

"Someday you'll be glad I didn't."

He removed his overcoat and soft brimmed hat hanging on the rack in the corner. "Be like me, babe. I base my decisions on the best mining engineers' advice."

She helped him on with his coat. "Now who's dreamin'?"

He turned, pulled her into his arms, ducked his face beneath the wide brim of her hat to give her a kiss. As he slowly released her, he studied her face with an admiring gaze. "You're the most gorgeous alley cat in the world."

She stepped back, gave his face a brisk slap. "That makes you a sewer rat, buster."

He grinned, rubbing his face. "Just two peas in a pod. Isn't that the expression?"

She decided for once she wouldn't rise to the bait and let herself get sucked into a fight. It was time to leave.

Outside, the air was raw, but the streets and boardwalks were as full as if it was a balmy summer night. She elbowed past men with half-crazed looks in their eyes, as if they had only a few days to live and by God they were going to make the most of the time left. Goldfield was on a roll. The sky was the only limit, and even that might give way. The entire country believed it and bought whatever stock was offered, few questions asked.

It was democracy in action, the only way the little man can hope to make any money, Jake had told her dozens of times. Never mind the old way of writing stuffy letters to potential investors about good prospects. Go after the man on the street through newspaper ads to every city of any size. It worked. The orders poured in.

True, there'd been a few times the issue was oversold before the ads reached the newspapers, but Jake just refunded the money. He was a go-getter, up with the times. If she was to put her faith in a broker, he would be it. But in a few days, a week at the most, she wouldn't need a broker. She'd have a seat on the Ladies' Goldfield

Stock Exchange and make her own market *if* she and three other women, who didn't know each other from Eve and had nothing in common except the itch to make money, could agree on a constitution and settle on all the rest of the details. It was a helluva a big *if*.

CHAPTER 15

The other women had gone on their way an hour ago. Meg sat alone in the yellow pool of light from the kerosene lamp on the middle of the table, rereading each page of the constitution Emma Burlingame had left with her. Tomorrow they'd have to make some crucial decisions that could make the difference between success and failure. She came to Article VI, Annual Election, and paused.

This time next year, the Ladies' Goldfield Stock Exchange would have its own annual meeting. With the money she would have made, she'd be running some kind of business of her own. Would Verna still be running the *Star?* Emma and her husband might have moved to a big city. Los Angeles maybe. As to Tess, Goldfield would always have saloons. She'd probably still be operating the Ajax.

Men's voices and the odors of good food cooking drifted up from the restaurant downstairs. She thought of what she had in her cooler at home, remembered the slab of cheese. It would be enough. The scones she'd eaten earlier had taken the edge off her hunger.

She sat back, idly rolling her pencil between the palms of her hands, thinking about the women she'd joined forces with, how little she knew about them.

Emma was a woman careful to have the world know she had a say about what went on in the Burlingame household when she really didn't. The law said what was hers was his. Up to this point, John Burlingame probably had been happy enough his wife had found a harmless pastime to keep her out of his hair. But once Emma began to make some real money, would he claim it as his own?

Then there was Tess. The stock she'd bring to the exchange was vital to its initial success. Yet Meg didn't know what to make of her. She'd never known anyone who ran a saloon and had been a whore. Tess was no ordinary woman. She stood out. When she walked down the street gazes followed where she went. A person couldn't ignore Tess—not her looks, not her tongue, certainly not her elegant clothes. The exchange might lead to new paths for Tess as it might for her. Yet there were times when Meg caught a look in Tess's eyes so sad it nearly broke her heart.

And Verna. She'd already become part mother, part aunt, a friend. It was evident Verna's health wasn't the best. Likely her no-good brother would plague her for the rest of her days. Whatever money Verna made from the exchange was bound to go straight into his pockets and down the drain. Yet the few times Verna had talked about Amos, their growing up as orphans at Fort Kearney, following him to Colorado, Verna had made it all sound like an adventure rather than experiences to be endured. Verna Bates was a remarkable women.

Meg closed the constitution. She'd take it home with her tonight and study it more. It occurred to her she was the only one among the governing board who'd been to college, though she never intended to mention the fact. Who you were didn't count in Goldfield. Tomorrow was literally tomorrow, not next year. Maybe when they considered the constitution again tomorrow afternoon, fussing about the annual meeting would be a waste of time. The exchange simply had to work.

She was stiff from sitting. The lamp was beginning to smoke. It was time to go home. She put on her coat and hat, blew out the lamp, and went downstairs. She paused to tell Mrs. Archibald the board would like to come back again tomorrow afternoon. Meg turned to go, found the door blocked by a group of men waiting to sit down. She squeezed past them. A man's voice behind her called her name. She glanced over her shoulder, and saw Bill Brown.

Working his way through the crowd, he smiled. "Miss Kendall, hold up a minute."

She answered his smile, not really surprised by how glad she was to see him again.

"Have dinner with me."

"I'm on my way home. But thank you."

"I'll walk with you then." The men around him, who were taking in their conversation, exchanged knowing grins. She could tell they were waiting to see how Bill would fare. "Actually, I'd like that," she said. "Thanks."

Outside, his hand on her elbow, he said, "You saved my good name in there."

She suppressed a grin, kept her eyes straight ahead. "You must be quite a ladies' man."

"You bet. Beautiful women are one of life's pleasures."

"Like Cuban cigars."

He gave her a sidelong glance, grinned. "I had that coming."

They walked in silence for a few yards before he said, "If I dare ask, what were you doing at the Imperial?"

She glanced up at him, weighing how much detail to share. Most men became easily bored when women talked about serious matters, but Bill Brown wasn't most men. That much was obvious. She'd noticed it before, and each time she'd been impressed. "We were having the first board meeting of the ladies' exchange and it definitely wasn't smooth sailing."

"How so?"

She gave a rueful chuckle. "It seems organizing a mining exchange isn't as easy as we might have thought. There's so much to consider. The cost of a seat, the rules for listing . . ."

"Just keep at it." Bill steered her out of the way of two drunks stumbling out of the door of the corner saloon. Ahead was her father's bottle house. "Giving the Goldfield Mining Stock Exchange a little competition has real appeal. As I said before, there's business to go around."

They stopped at her door, and she thanked him for seeing her home.

"My pleasure," he said. "You know I've been thinking . . ."

"Oh?"

"We should go for a drive next Sunday."

She felt a little let down. She'd been so sure he was going to say something more about the exchange. "I'm not sure about Sunday. Miss Bates had mentioned—"

He cut in, smiling, his eyes bright. "There's a fellow near Montezuma you should meet. He has a mine he's talking about capitalizing. It might be something you'd want to list."

She gazed at him, realizing he was one step ahead of her. The board had never tackled the matter of how to get additional listings.

"We'll have a picnic on the way." His smile spread. He was obviously pleased with his idea. "I'll come by for you at eleven."

With a wave of his hand and a see-you-then, he wheeled, strode away, leaving her standing in the doorway. She hadn't even agreed to go.

Chapter 16

*V*erna stepped out of the *Star*, locked the door. The sky was gray with a flat, heavy look that reminded Verna of Nebraska winters. Gone was the bright sun that had warmed her aching bones the last few days. She was on her way to find Jimmy Earnest. He hadn't come in for days, which wasn't like him. She'd come to depend on him, more than she liked to admit. He was smart, and he caught mistakes her blurry eyes sometimes missed. Besides, she'd grown right fond of him.

After she found him, she'd write up an article about the ladies' exchange to send to the *Los Angeles Times* and still make it to the Imperial by four for the governing board meeting.

Striding down Main Street, she could see her breath. As she passed the two-story Union Hall, she was tempted to thumb her nose at the damned socialists. The last straw had been two weeks ago on election day. She had been gathering information for a story about the election, the polls conveniently next door in an empty store, and when the lunch hour arrived, she went over to check the voter turnout.

She'd no sooner stepped inside the store than a big, mean-looking so-and-so, who seemed to be in charge, got up from the table where he'd been sitting, picked up the ballot box and registration book, and muscled past her out the door.

She'd followed him, explained she was with the *Star*, asked how the vote was going. The man had merely shrugged. "I'm on my way to lunch, lady. Follow along if you want."

In the restaurant, the man had set the box on a chair beside him, put the registration book on top of it, and crowned the whole shebang with his big slouch hat. He ordered. The meal came, and he proceeded as if he had nothing else in the world to do but eat. Verna had decided to park herself by the entrance to see if any voters would show up.

Voting had become a habit with her the last twelve years in Colorado since they'd granted women suffrage. She resented not being able to do so in Nevada. But so be it. Suffrage was contagious. Sooner than later, women across the country would get the vote.

That day as she had waited in the restaurant, a few men did come and demand to vote. The polling judge told them to go right ahead. He'd given them a ballot to mark. Once he finished eating, he'd take the ballots back to the polls, check them out. If they appeared to pass muster—

"Muster?" a puzzled would-be voter had asked.

The man had looked genuinely surprised at the question. "If you vote for the union candidates, I'll put them in the ballot box."

Verna had waited for a reaction, but none came. No one seemed to give a hoot. It was no surprise, then, when Wobbly candidates were elected as sheriff, county judge, jury commissioner, and to the majority of seats on the town board.

With the sheriff in their control, it was obvious Vincent St. John, the union leader, and the rest of his followers would have the run of the camp. Verna was sick of it.

Mincing no words, she'd said as much in her last editorial, placing as much blame on the companies and the apathy of the general citizens as she did on the union. She was almost disappointed Tim McGee, the ugly little man from the union who'd first paid

her a call, hadn't come by again so she could give him a piece of
her mind, face-to-face. Maybe no one had read the editorial.

But at the moment she had to put her mind on finding out if
Jimmy was all right. She knew his dad mucked ore at the January.
His mother took in laundry. He had a sister Mary Lou, a baby
brother named Mikey. He'd told her they lived in a tent on High
Grade Hill across from Sundog Avenue, over on the west part of
town.

Not knowing the neighborhood, Verna had to stop people twice
and ask directions. Finally, out of breath, she stopped in front of a
tent covered with tar paper. A neighbor had said it was rented by
the Earnests.

She knocked on the unpainted door, waited for a response.
When none came, she knocked again. "Jimmy. Jimmy Earnest," she
called, her mouth against the door.

She could hear someone moving about. The door opened a
crack, and the small face of a little girl with large, frightened eyes
appeared.

"Mary Lou, it's Miss Bates from the newspaper," Verna said,
"I'm looking for Jimmy."

The door opened a little wider. "Ma's sick, so he had to deliver
the wash."

Verna wasn't one to butt into others' business, but here was a
case where help was needed. "May I come in?"

The door closed. Verna stared at it for a moment before she decided it was time to take matters in hand. She opened the door,
went inside.

The small space was almost totally taken up by three beds made
of bedsprings covered with blankets. Lying on one of them under
a pile of quilts was a gaunt woman with pale brown hair. Mary Lou
stood next to her like a little watchdog. In one corner was a tiny
inkstand stove. The air was almost as cold inside as out. Verna
glanced about, saw no sign of a heater.

Between two of the beds was a trunk. A large box, draped with a piece of velour curtain, apparently served as a dresser, a small mirror above it. A few pictures that looked as if they'd been cut out from magazines hung on the canvas walls. Hemstitched sheeting served as curtains for the two windows.

"Mrs. Earnest, we haven't met. I'm Miss Bates. I don't mean to interfere, but I've been worried about Jimmy, and now I find you in bed."

The woman tried to smile. Her eyes looked unnaturally bright, feverish. "I'm sorry we put you out, Miss Bates. Jimmy was supposed to come by to let you know." She coughed. "You needn't worry. Little Mary Lou here is a good help to me. I thank you anyway."

Verna glanced about. "The baby, Mikey?"

"Mikey's with Jimmy," said the solemn little girl.

"I see." Try as she might, Verna couldn't visualize how Jimmy would be able to manage caring for a baby as he delivered wash.

"Looks like I've got the flu." Mrs. Earnest coughed again. "It's goin' around I hear."

"Has a doctor been by?"

"I wouldn't trust a one of 'em."

"Maybe there's a tonic I could go for."

"Costs money."

Verna nodded, glanced about at the brave attempts to make the tent a home. She understood all about pride. Mrs. Earnest wasn't about to accept help. Still, with the temperature outside close to freezing and the sickness, they had to have heat in this place.

"As a neighbor I'd surely like to bring over something for your supper, Mrs. Earnest."

Verna saw the spark in the woman's fevered eyes. "Earnests don't take favors, Miss Bates."

"I understand, but I'm fond of Jimmy. I'd feel much better knowing you were on the mend."

The woman's gaze held a stubbornness not even sickness could soften. "You mean well, Miss Bates, but we're already beholden to you."

"Because I hired Jimmy? Nonsense. He's worth twice what I pay him." Verna patted the little girl on the head. "Mary Lou, you take good care of your mother. I'll be back."

*   *   *

Verna hurried down the hill to the Billings Butcher Shop, picked out a four-pound pinbone roast. The price was seventy cents. At Greenberg's General Store she bought a dozen potatoes, a head of cabbage, milk. After some searching, she found the shelf where tonics were displayed, chose a bottle of Seidlitz Homeopathic Cure for Chronic Congestion and Headache. She fished the ninety cents out of her change purse.

Just as she handed the money to the clerk, she spied the big tins of hard candy on the shelf by the cash register. Fifty cents. A lot to satisfy three kids' sweet tooths. But why not? She decided on a five-pound can of lemon drops.

Her final stop was Pitt's hardware and supply. The heaters were in the rear. Most were big, weighing over a hundred pounds from the look of them. But a few were small enough for a tent. She inspected these with an eye to price and size, whether they used coal or wood. A brand called the Iron Ace seemed to fit the purpose exactly. Three feet high, it took coal and had a draft ring that would offer heat on all sides. If it hadn't been for the four-dollar price tag she'd have bought it without another thought.

Until she'd started to lose her sight, money hadn't meant much to her. Now every penny counted. Still, how could a person weigh the cost of a stove against the lives of a family of five?

Zeb Pitts came back to wait on her.

"This Iron Ace heater is about what I'm looking for, Mr. Pitts, but I'm afraid there's a problem."

"Is that so?"

"The price."

"Supply and demand, Miss Bates."

"Two-fifty seems a fairer price."

He scowled. "Oh, now."

"Two seventy-five then."

He shook his head.

"Tell you what. I'll give you three dollars if you throw in the pipe and enough coal for a week."

Zeb Pitts looked thoroughly aggrieved at her proposal.

"How about a nice ad on the front page of the next issue of the *Star?*"

He brightened.

"Excellent," she said, pleased at her solution. "You can deliver right away, can't you?"

"I—"

"Fine. I'll write down the directions."

* * *

As Verna retraced her steps to the Earnests' tent, her arms loaded with her purchases, she caught sight of Jimmy just ahead. He was carrying a wash basket. She called to him. He turned, gave an embarrassed smile, stopped to wait for her.

"Jimmy Earnest, shame on you for not telling me your mother's sick," she said, half-scolding as she caught her breath.

"I stopped by the paper just now, Miss Bates. You wasn't there."

"Weren't there," she corrected.

"Weren't."

"I did a little shopping to tide you over."

Jimmy's thin face sobered. "It's good of you, Miss Bates, but I don't—"

"Earnests don't take favors. Your mother told me." Out of the corner of her eye, she noticed the clothes in the basket move. Jimmy followed her glance, squatted, folded back the dirty laundry, revealing a dark-haired child with a sweet, open face who looked about six months old. He was wrapped in a blanket.

"Meet Mikey," Jimmy said, gently tickling the child. "He's warm as a bug in a rug in there."

She laughed. "I'll bet he is." She leaned closer, cooed at him. The child gave her a toothless smile.

"Mikey likes you," Jimmy said in a serious tone.

"Does he like lemon drops though?"

"What kid don't."

"Doesn't"

Jimmy grinned. "But he might be too little yet."

"I suspect you're right." Verna sighed. "I should have thought of that. Oh, well."

Jimmy's smile disappeared. "Did I say somethin' outa turn?"

"Not a thing. Come on. Let's get to your house. My arms are getting tired holding these packages."

* * *

Over Mrs. Earnest's protests, Verna started up the stove, put the roast and potatoes on, sliced up half the cabbage, made a fresh pot of coffee in readiness for Mr. Earnest's return from work at the January mine. By the time she left, Mrs. Earnest was close to tears, said she'd never been paid such kindness.

Verna patted her hand, told her she'd be back to see how she was faring. It was growing dark, nearly five o'clock. Verna had missed the start of the ladies' stock exchange meeting, but she felt obliged to stop by the *Star* first to see if anyone had dropped by an order for an ad.

Outside, she hurried along, intent on getting to the meeting of the exchange before everything was decided. People who went by her were hunched into their coats, hands on their hats against the icy wind coming out of the north. There might be more snow tonight. She drew her coat collar up to protect the tips of her ears.

By now the lamps and electric lights were turned on in the stores and saloons. Through windows she saw customers moving about, talking and laughing among themselves. A wave of loneliness rolled over her as it always did this time of night. How little some things changed in her life. As a child in Fort Kearney, she'd stood at the edge of the wagons stopped for provisions and a brief rest on their way west and sometimes felt nearly overwhelmed with longing as she'd watched the families gather for their evening meals. Now, as then, the rest of the world was tucked in, cozy, together, and she stood on the outside, looking in.

She began to shiver, decided to take a shortcut to the *Star*. Leaving the crowded boardwalk, she ducked behind a half-finished building, stepped over debris strewn on the ground. She turned left, passed an outhouse, and was just coming around the back of a saloon when she tripped over a pile of rusting cans. She fell headlong to the ground.

Stunned, it was several minutes before she could get to her feet. She'd been an old fool to venture off the beaten path in the dark. As she picked her way around the rotting garbage strewn in the space between two tents, she caught sight of the electric light above the red and black sign of Goldberg's Grocers, next door to the *Star*. She was almost home.

Once out on the boardwalk again, she hurried across the street. The light from the sign cast an eerie shadow. For a second, she thought something was tacked to the door of her shack. As she came closer, she saw it was an owl, or what was left of an owl. Through the years, she'd seen other owls nailed to doors, always intended as death threats.

This poor little creature with its long legs and earth brown feathers spotted with white was a burrowing owl. Its home was the prairie, not the alkaline flats around Goldfield. Someone had gone to considerable trouble to try to frighten her. She knew this was the work of the Wobblies. If they intended to upset her, they had.

Until now she'd been able to drive off fear by acting in the face of it, not letting it take charge of what she did or didn't do. Now, losing her sight, getting old—as much as she fought against both—she found herself caught up in the fear. She trembled, found herself looking up and down the street, afraid of what she might find, afraid of what she had found. Even the irony of the poor, dead owl didn't quiet her.

CHAPTER 17

By Sunday the only snow left was bunched up against the north sides of the shacks and tents. The air was crisp, invigorating. The wind, for once, was calm; the blue sky cloudless. Meg's spirits soared.

She'd thought about Bill's invitation to take her on a drive all week, one moment deciding he wouldn't remember, the next sure he would. Just to be on the safe side, she'd stopped by the Bon Ton yesterday and bought a veil to tie around her hat. She was anxious to see the mine Bill had mentioned might be about to capitalize because a list of new stocks was essential if the exchange was to attract customers.

Once the wording of the constitution had been worked out, the opening had been set for this Friday. All three Goldfield newspapers would be carrying the story. She'd arranged for fresh flowers to be shipped in. Tess said the fiddle player from the Ajax could come over to play. The Imperial would serve cakes. There was some debate about whether champagne was appropriate before they decided it was. It would be a grand affair.

Meg dressed with particular care, all the while telling herself there was no earthly reason to count on Bill showing up. She went

over to the *Star* to have breakfast with Verna and check on how
she was doing after the dead owl incident, then came back and read
the day's issue of the competition, the *Goldfield Tattler*. It was only
ten-thirty.

She paced. She swept the linoleum rug, poured lye down the
hole in the privy. She had just settled herself at the table with
paper, pen, and ink to write to her aunt when she heard someone
knock. Her heart skipped a beat. She jumped up, took a deep
breath to calm herself, slowly opened the door, and looked into the
broadest grin she'd ever seen.

* * *

A few minutes later, wearing a duster he'd brought her, the veil tied
over her hat and under her chin, she climbed in the Franklin and
they were off.

Bill steered down Crook, took a right onto Ramsey, then north
again on Main. It seemed to Meg that every mule skinner, every
driver of a rig, every man on horseback hailed him, took in her presence beside him and grinned.

She glanced at him, laughed. "It must get a little awkward, getting this much attention every time you go out driving?"

He shrugged. "Goldfield's a friendly place."

The rows of shacks and tents had thinned. The endless acres of
bleak, gray desert edged by barren hills off to the east and the flat-
topped Malapai mesa to the west stretched before them. They had
reached the outskirts of town.

Bill handed her a pair of goggles, put on his own. He glanced at
her hat. "Better batten down the hatches there. As soon as we get
onto the turnpike, I'm going to step on the gas. The boys do their
best to keep it up. The T-rail clears the brush and chains smooths
it out some. But it still has its share of potholes, so you better hang
on."

Minutes later they were careening along the road set aside for
autos. The cold wind against her face, Meg gripped the side of the

auto with her right hand and whooped with the sheer joy of it all. "I bet we're going twenty miles an hour," she shouted at Bill.

"Say what?" He did a sharp turn to avoid a Joshua tree.

"We're going twenty miles an hour," she repeated with difficulty. The speed nearly took her breath away.

Bill glanced down at a gage on the dashboard. "Twenty-five, to be exact."

"It's marvelous."

He grinned at her. "Want to try it?"

"You mean me drive?"

"Sure."

"When?"

Bill let his foot off the accelerator, applied the brakes. "How about now?"

Meg stared at him. "You're serious, aren't you?"

"Why wouldn't I be? You've driven an automobile, haven't you?"

Meg thought of her friend and his yellow Rambler, of one wild ride they'd taken between Denver and Boulder, her sitting on his lap, steering. Though she'd wanted to, she'd never actually sat behind the wheel by herself. "Well, in a way."

"Great."

Bill nodded to the north. "That's where we're headed. Montezuma's behind those hills. Maybe ten miles from here."

They exchanged seats. Meg pretended a casualness she didn't feel. She placed her hands on the steering wheel, glanced at him.

He smiled. "Are you ready for a quick review?"

She nodded, drew back to get out of his way as he leaned across her, reaching for the controls. The feel of his body pressed against her breasts and lap sent a pulse of energy through her.

"You'll be using these pedals down here on the floor. The one on the left is the service brake. The one in the middle is the clutch. That one on the right is the throttle accelerator. This box here next to you is what's called the 'H' plate."

He drew back, met her eyes with his green ones, and smiled. "Clear so far?"

"Absolutely." She was sure her hands were shaking as she reached out to release the brake.

*   *   *

A half hour later, Meg drew to a stop, dizzy with exhilaration from the power of this machine that could tear across space. The trip hadn't been without its down side. She had killed the engine three times and nearly collided with a Joshua tree. Though she'd never admit it to Bill, she thanked God they hadn't met another machine. Still, she was pleased with herself.

Bill stretched his arms to the sky, grinned at her, climbed out. "Nothing to it. Am I right?"

She laughed. "I thought I'd tip us over for sure when I made that turn back there."

"You just took it a little fast."

She smiled as she untied the veil and lifted it off her hat. "There's nothing like it."

He leaned against a fender, eyed her.

"You know what I like the most?"

He crossed his arms, waited.

"The speed. Whizzing along, the wind in my face. It makes me feel so—free."

He threw his head back and laughed.

"And you know what else?"

He shook his head.

"I'm going to buy an automobile of my own."

"Great!"

"In fact, I think I'll buy a dozen and sell them."

He cocked his head, grinning at her.

"What do you think of that?"

"I think it's time for some Mumm's extra dry."

"Marvelous," she said exuberantly, only barely aware of what he'd said. "Automobiles are so—liberating."

"You said that."

She laughed. "A woman can just get in and go without having to depend on anyone to take her."

"That she can." His eyes were dancing. "How do truffles sound?"

"Truffles?" She realized she'd been off, concocting a dream out of the dry, desert air. She collected herself. "Truffles in Goldfield? Champagne, of course. But truffles?"

"Maybe I exaggerate about the truffles. How do canned salmon sandwiches sound?"

Her heart was unexpectedly full. She thought of her selling automobiles. Possibilities were out there, with no limits in sight. Everything was coming together. "Wonderful. I'm hungry as a bear."

From the backseat, Bill lifted out the basket prepared by the Palm Restaurant. He put it on the ground next to the running board where they decided to sit. Meg lifted the lid. Inside were the salmon sandwiches carefully wrapped in linen napkins, more napkins, silverware, a corkscrew, ramekins of crème brûlée, and, of course, Mumm's extra dry champagne.

She handed Bill the bottle of champagne. With a certain gusto, he worked out the cork, which promptly shot into the blue sky. The golden champagne fizzed, spilled out onto the sand. They laughed as Meg hurried to hold out glasses to catch what remained.

They toasted, sipped, ate the sandwiches, which were mostly bread and very little salmon, finished off the crème brûlée. If Bill's intention was to impress her, he had succeeded.

Doubting she'd have another chance to drive anymore today, she sat back, relaxed, let the champagne take hold. Her eyelids felt heavy. She longed to crawl in the backseat and take a nap.

"Are you still game to go see my friend?"

She blinked. In the haze of champagne, she'd almost forgotten they'd come on business. "Of course."

* * *

The Franklin bumped and bounced off the turnpike onto a road that was no more than wagon tracks.

"How big is this mine your friend owns?" she asked as the machine crawled along.

"They're down about fifty feet. He's got four men working, all that can fit at the moment. The last assay run looked good."

"What did you say his name was?

"Slim Pattison. We met when I was roaming around out here one day and got stuck in the sand. He and his burros pulled me out. When he came into town for supplies, I tried to pay him back."

"You grubstaked him."

"You could say that."

Ahead was a lone headframe, two neat rows of bulging ore bags nearby, and tailings mounded along a barren hillside. Four burros and several horses munched hay from a makeshift feeder in a small corral. Beyond were two tents and a shack. A tall, gaunt man with his sleeves rolled up climbed out from a hole beneath the headframe.

Bill slowed to a stop, set the brake, and cut the engine. The steady throb of a gasoline engine filled the air.

"Wait here a minute." He got out and gave a wave of greeting to the man by the headframe.

"Heh, there, Slim. It's Bill Brown," he called, walking toward him.

The man, who wore work shoes and canvas trousers, pushed his soft-brimmed hat off his forehead and shielded his eyes against the sun. When Bill reached him, they shook hands, talked for a minute or two. Bill motioned toward the car and Meg. She could see he was smiling. They talked a little longer. Meg grew tired of waiting. She decided to see what was going on.

Slim Pattison's pale blue eyes studied her as Bill introduced her, explained a little about Meg's interest in the mine.

"Bill said you're kin to Jim Kendall. He was a good man."

"Thank you," she said.

"Never could figure how he and Eckles were pals."

"They'd known each other in Colorado."

He nodded. "Seems I heard that."

"I've been told Dad's death was an accident. Do you think it's true?"

"Hard sayin'."

The look in his eyes told her the subject was closed. The realization disappointed her. She glanced past him to the headframe. "So this is the Montezuma Queen."

He nodded, glanced at Bill. "I took in a sample day before yesterday."

"Good value, is it?" Bill asked.

Slim shot a glance at Meg, as if uncertain how much he could trust her. "Another few days of blasting, some more mucking, we'll be opening up another drift. We'll need more men. On shares. Like the others." He looked back toward the headframe.

Bill said, "Last I knew you were about to incorporate."

"Thought I would. Yeah. I talked to Dick Little, the lawyer over by Ramsey Street you mentioned. He said he'd draw up the papers."

Meg decided it was time to step into the conversation. "Will you be incorporating in Delaware?"

Slim Pattison squinted at her, kicked the toe of his boot into the sand. "Maybe."

"I suppose you'll organize with the usual capital of a million, the usual par value of a dollar a share."

Slim Pattison glanced up at her, obviously uncomfortable. Meg decided there was no point in beating around the bush. "The fact is, Mr. Pattison, the Ladies' Goldfield Stock Exchange is looking for new listings. Your company sounds like a fine prospect."

Slim Pattison's forehead knit into a frown. He looked to Bill, who explained more about the Ladies' Goldfield Stock Exchange, but the frown held.

Meg pressed on. "As you're probably aware, most of the ladies in Goldfield do a great deal of trading. We expect they will be coming into our exchange regularly."

He gazed at her with a look she couldn't decipher.

"Of course, you could try to sell stock on the street," Meg said. "Though I doubt you'd realize the best price for it."

Slim shot Bill a helpless kind of look.

"I realize you have the option of listing with the Goldfield Mining Stock Exchange, although I understand they do an extensive search about value per ton, that kind of thing. Send a well-respected engineer down to inspect the drifts." Meg smiled. As she listened to her own words, she thought they had a certain ring of authority.

"On the other hand, you could hire your own engineer, well-respected, of course, though I suspect that would take a good deal of money."

Bill had folded his arms across his chest. His lips pursed in all seriousness, he slid her a glance. She saw his eyes dance.

"So, taken altogether, Mr. Pattison, I think your company, once it's incorporated, and the ladies' exchange can come to a mutually satisfactory arrangement. I'd like you to give serious thought to listing with us."

She paused, then went on. "As far as our governing board giving its stamp of approval, I'm sure once they know of Mr. Brown's backing that will be quite enough. Of course, as an officer of the exchange, I must put the listing of your company to a vote before the entire board. But now, thanks to this visit, I can personally verify yours is a reputable operation."

Slim Pattison whistled softly through his teeth, gazed around at the headframe as if he longed to escape from all this talk of business with a woman and get back down to dig out more gold.

"Well, I guess we should let you get back to work," she said cheerily. "The next time you're in town to talk to your attorney, I hope you'll stop by. Our temporary headquarters are above the Imperial Restaurant."

* * *

Meg tied the veil back over her hat, drew the duster around her as Bill started up the engine, and climbed in. They and the Franklin cast a long shadow out across the sand, almost like an apparition in the eerie, treeless landscape where only the gray leaves of low-lying saltbush, frowsy and unkempt like gnarled old ladies in tattered cloaks, fluttered in the wind. To the west, the last of the fiery sun hung on the crest of the barren mountains for an instant, bathing the horizon in shades of magenta and peach, then plunged out of sight. Not until that instant had Meg realized how late in the day it was.

"It looks like it'll be dark before we get back to Goldfield," Bill observed in a casual tone as he steered the machine along the high side of the wagon ruts.

"How will you see to drive?"

"No problem there. I've got the new Prest-O-Lite acetylene lamps."

"Oh. Good." She'd never heard of Presto-O-Lite acetylene lamps, but she'd heard just enough horror stories about being lost in the desert to make her uneasy. Still, Bill traveled this way often. He could probably find the way with his eyes shut.

"In fact, I think I'll take a little shortcut to get us back in better time."

Meg's uneasiness grew ever so slightly.

"See there ahead. That dry streambed, off there at an angle?"

Meg squinted into the growing dark and thought she saw what looked like a road. "How much will that cut off?"

"As much as four miles."

She hung on tight as the car bucked like a horse, teetered but stayed upright as Bill drove down a slight incline of an arroyo to the sand-filled streambed.

"Couldn't you get stuck in this?"

He nodded, his hands gripped on the steering wheel. "Could, but won't. Trust me." Just then the car hit something. Bill gunned the engine. Meg held her breath, hoping against hope that whatever they had collided with wasn't anything major enough to stop them. But a few yards later, the automobile slowed, stopped, sagged to the right.

"Damn," Bill said under his breath.

She gave him an inquiring look.

"All bets are on a puncture."

Meg glanced about. "It's almost dark."

Bill nodded, pulled on the hand brake, cut the engine, climbed out of the car. Meg followed him as he went to the back to inspect the extent of the problem.

Bill sank to his haunches, surveyed the flat tire in the dimming light.

"Is it bad?"

Bill ran a hand over the tire casing. "One of the unfortunate hazards of modern transportation."

"Can you fix it?"

He glanced up at her. "If I can't, I'm in the wrong business."

Meg felt a little chagrined by her question. "How long will it take, do you think?"

"An hour or so." He stood, walked to the front of the car, reached under the dash, and pulled out a toolbox.

Meg sat on the running board, watching as he put it down on the sand by the errant tire and opened it.

He glanced behind him. "I need some rocks for blocks. They shouldn't be too hard to find in this streambed. I'd guess it was a rock we hit. Wait here."

"I'll come."

"You wouldn't want to twist an ankle."

"I'll take your arm. If we fall, we fall together."

He laughed, offered his arm, and they set out.

It took a while to find four rocks large enough to qualify as blocks, but find them they did. Meg carried one, Bill the others. A rat scurried across their path, and she tried to ignore it. Finally, each of the rocks in place against the wheels, Bill got down to the matter of removing the tire.

The night air was already cool, and Meg hugged herself against the chill as she watched Bill jack up the car, pry off the casing. He sat back on his heels. "Tell you what. I think I'll take the front headlamps off and bring them back here for more light."

He rummaged in the toolbox, drew out a screwdriver, and went up to the right front headlamp, clamped in place ahead of the fender. By touch, he unscrewed it from the metal bracket. He brought it back and put it down at a safe distance from the left rear wheel.

"Meg, there's a water bag under the dash. Could you bring it over?"

She remembered seeing the water bag. A moment later she handed it to him. He dug a match out of his back pocket, reached for the water bag.

"What are you going to do?"

"I need to add a drop or two of water to the acetylene in the bottom of this lamp, then I'll light it." He unscrewed the top of the water bag, deftly added a few drops to the bottom of the lamp, struck the match, and held it to the gas. Instantly, a beam of light flooded the rear of the automobile.

Meg clapped her hands. "You're a wonder, Bill Brown."

He grinned at her. "Just a bit of magic. I do it every day."

With practiced movements, he pried off the casing, pulled out the inner tube. He got the pump out of the toolbox, attached the hose to the valve stem of the casing, pumped with one hand while feeling for the leak with the other. "Ah, found it. Now it's just a matter of a patch, time for it to dry, and we'll be on our way."

Meg glanced at the running board. "I guess I'd knock the jack off if I sat down. Would it be all right to use the robe we sat on for the picnic?"

"Sounds good to me."

She pulled it out of the backseat, spread it across a patch of sand, sat down.

"Do you like poetry?" he asked as he peeled off the backing from the patch, applied glue, and pressed it in place over the hole in the casing.

"Some. We memorized the usual stuff when I was in high school. I translated the *Odyssey* in college if that counts."

"Kipling's my favorite." In the light from the acetylene lamp, Bill's face had a chiseled look to it, his skin very dark, almost ruddy. His nose was straight. Engrossed with patching the tire, he had a funny way of working his mouth.

He glanced over at her. "Ever hear the one about Adam and the devil?"

She shook her head, and he began, still working,

> "When the flush of a new-born sun fell first on Eden's
>   green and gold,
> Our father Adam sat under the Tree and scratched with
>   a stick in the mould—"

He stood. "Well, now that that's finished, enough of poetry, even Kipling, for the moment." He came over to the robe where she was sitting. "Mind if I join you?"

She patted the space next to her. "I saved this seat just for you."

He lay back, leaning on his elbows, stretching his legs out in front of him, gazed up at the sky. "A bunch of stars up there."

She looked up at the dark dome strewn with chips of diamonds. "There are indeed."

For a moment, they contemplated the sky in silence.

"Where'd you learn Kipling?"

"At a saloon in Cambridge when I was supposed to be studying."

"You went to Harvard?"

"For a while."

"Is Boston your home?"

He glanced at her. "It was once. My father and I came to a parting of the ways over automobiles."

"Automobiles?"

"Well, not automobiles per se." He gave a rueful chuckle.

"Browns are expected to go into banking, after Harvard, of course, and marry the right young lady. Right meaning having the proper pedigree. One day, as I started my last year at school, I thought about all that and decided no thank you."

She pulled her legs up, hugged her arms around them. "You left?"

"That I did. Took the money Gram left me, chucked school, went to New York, and found the Vanderbilt Cup."

She laughed. "That's an automobile racing cup."

"You bet it is."

"Did you win it?"

He let out a hoot of laughter. "Not exactly. I'd driven my father's Cadillac. But until that day on Long Island, I'd never even seen a race, much less been in one."

She leaned a cheek on her knees, watching him. "So what happened?"

"A friend had an Olds, and we decided to enter the race. It was to be run over a two-hundred-eighty-four mile course on Long Island." He glanced at her. "God what a day it was—pennants fluttering in the breeze—like a sailboat race almost. Spectators dressed to the nines. The roar of engines enough to stir the soul of a dead man."

She smiled, picturing the day, sharing the excitement she heard in his voice.

"The Olds came in last."

"And you came out here."

He grinned up at her. "Eventually. In the meantime, I went back to New York, joined the American Automobile Association. They have a garage in midtown. I learned what I know about engines from the mechanics there. About float-feed spraying carburetors that could be throttled and choked to adjust the amount of fuel, magneto generators, why the three-point suspension axle was good." He paused. "But I get carried away."

She shook her head.

"I went back to Boston, told Dad I wanted to buy a machine of my own and race it. To say he didn't like the idea is to put it mildly."

She gazed past him, thinking of her decision to take a different course than her aunt had planned. Unlike with Bill, no one had put a foot down, refused to let her do it. If she failed, she had no one to blame but herself. But she wouldn't fail. They might not all realize it now, but the women of Goldfield depended on her to make a path for them they'd never had open to them before.

He sat up so their shoulders were touching. "Anyway, without his blessing, I bought a car with the rest of the money I'd inherited and headed west to San Francisco, got there just in time for the fire. After the excitement died down, I worked my way south, and here I am. End of story."

He stood up.

"Do you think the patch is dry yet?"

"Let's give it another few minutes. I think I'll turn off the lamp." He frowned. "You look frozen. Why don't you put the robe around you?"

After a brief debate, they both sat on one half of the robe, the other draped over their shoulders as they waited for the patch to dry. Out in the dark somewhere, a coyote howled. They talked about dreams and automobiles. He intended to test-drive the latest models. In her head, she saw them—shiny, fast. Her heart quickened. Maybe automobiles were in her future, too. She turned to look at him, imagined how it would be to work with him when she sold those late models to women. They talked on. Meg couldn't remember ever before having quite the same kind of a conversation with anyone.

* * *

Meg smiled, inordinately pleased with herself and the others as she surveyed the low-ceilinged room that had been transformed into the Ladies' Goldfield Stock Exchange. Today was the grand opening.

Blackboards lining the far wall displayed more than a dozen

stock offerings, bid and ask prices neatly written in. Most of the issues belonged to the founding members, but the Montezuma Queen was there, too.

Mr. Linton, whom the board had hired as the caller, stood at the podium. A short, muscular man with a carefully waxed handlebar mustache, he had a military bearing that gave the impression he could handle any situation that presented itself.

Meg edged around the room toward a dozen women standing expectantly in the section reserved for exchange members, which was just to one side of the blackboard. They were talking to one another earnestly, studying the board. In their midst was Tess Wallace, today in a black faille suit trimmed in velvet scrolls. The magnificent hat she wore was set off with black ostrich feathers. Meg adjusted the sleeve of her own conservative gray wool suit and regretted the choice she'd been so pleased with only minutes ago. In comparison to Tess's stylish black outfit, hers was not dowdy exactly, for the suit was new and expensive, but more like one meant for a slightly prim schoolmarm.

Halfway back, Emma Burlingame stood talking to her husband and Slim Pattison, who had made the trip into camp especially for the occasion.

The air was filled with anticipation and hope. Surveying the anxious faces of her fellow exchange members, Meg was reminded of wedding guests at a church, breathlessly awaiting the entrance of the bride. She walked to the far wall where a long table covered with a sparkling white cloth had been set up. Plates of cookies and little cakes had been arranged around the magnificent bouquet of lilies that had arrived in the nick of time on the morning train. Champagne glasses were artfully arranged on either end. At the appropriate time, after the governing board of the Goldfield Mining Stock Exchange arrived, which Meg was certain it would in spite of the threatened boycott, Mrs. Archibald was going to send up two of her waiters with bottles of Mumm.

Mr. Burlingame had explained it was the custom for an established exchange to be on hand for the opening of a new one. The president, George Barker, was sure to give a fine speech about the health of Goldfield's economy. Emma Burlingame, as president of the new exchange, would make a gracious reply. Meg could hardly wait.

She glanced at the clock next to the board. Four-thirty. The articles in the newspapers had said four. Maybe they should have set the opening for six, but it was too late now.

She and Emma exchanged glances, smiled uneasily. Meg went over and made small talk with the other ladies. Verna put an arm around her shoulders. "They'll be here. It's early yet. People will come. You'll see."

But by seven o'clock only a handful of men had arrived. Vic, Bill Brown, Mr. Vogler, and Mr. Petticord. A few others straggled in, apparently after the advertised free food and drink. None, of course, were members of the Goldfield Mining Exchange.

It was plain the Ladies' Goldfield Stock Exchange had been stood up.

Chapter 18

Tess stood outside the Imperial and glanced up at the darkened windows of the exchange. To all appearances, the ladies' exchange was dead before it even had a chance at life. But, shoot, more than one corpse had sat up in the coffin just as the lid was about to be shut and surprised the hell out of everyone.

Back at the Ajax, she went about the business of serving drinks and watching the games, eyeing every customer as someone who should be trading at the exchange. The question was how to get them there. She could use her stash to bribe men into coming, but that wouldn't work. Verna should definitely print up more handbills, advertising the exchange, and hire boys to plaster the camp with them. At that point, Tess ran out of ideas.

The next morning the ladies' exchange opened right on time. Emma, Meg, Verna, the women who had bought seats, put on smiling faces. But after four days, only eleven trades had been made. Sally Petticord suggested the exchange might have been a mistake. Two women sitting with her, whose names Tess didn't catch, agreed. Talk like that was dangerous. Something had to give, and soon. That night the solution came to her.

*   *   *

Tess smiled at the sound of Mr. Linton's brusk voice calling out asks and bids as she climbed the narrow stairs, careful to hold her skirts around her so the wool wouldn't snag on the splinters of the rough-cut walls.

"Come on, boys. We're almost there," she said over her shoulder to the line of Ajax customers trudging up behind her. The next batch was going to be from the Great Northern. She and Vic had covered every saloon in camp, explained the problem. At first, there'd been some grumbling over the idea of trading at an exchange run by women. It was unnatural. But after she'd told them about the new listings they wouldn't find at the other exchange, the chance to buy at rock bottom prices and sell high, plus the good eats, they'd given in, said they'd give it a try.

At the top of the stairs, Tess unhooked the clasp of her Persian lamb cloak. The morning had warmed up, and the fur was too hot. She walked into the long room, filled with the odors of strong coffee and cigar smoke, and glanced around. On the table next to the door were a pot of coffee, cups, and three plates holding Mrs. Archibald's crumb cakes.

Tess motioned to the assortment of off-shift miners and general floaters she'd brought. "Help yourself, boys. Then make yourselves some money."

She surveyed the others in the room. Not counting Mr. Linton, the cashier, Meg, and Emma, she guessed there were about fifteen customers. One of them was Jake, absorbed in calculating something on the back of what looked like a Graham Trust flyer touting a hot new prospect. She hadn't seen him for over a week.

"Where were you openin' night?" she asked as she approached him.

He glanced up, smiled.

"You said you'd be there."

"Babe, when did I ever miss a meeting of the Montezuma Club?"

"When you play poker," Tess said coolly.

"You have me there."

"Mr. Burlingame managed to get here."

Jake's smile faded. "He doesn't have Winters and Nolan trying to ruin him."

"Oh, sure. Winters and Nolan are tryin' to ruin you. Tell me another story."

"It's true. They're trying to wipe me out of business, and I'm not going to let them do it."

"I don't get it."

He pulled her to the side of the room. "The senator and his pal are calling for more collateral for the loans my customers have taken out."

"So?"

"So it'll force the little men to sell at a loss to cover."

"And Mohawk Mines will be able to step in and buy cheap. Correct?"

Jake gave a hard, cynical smile. "Sometimes you're pretty smart."

"You're not goin' to let them get away with it, are you?"

"Not if I can help it, believe me." He glanced away, looked around the room, as if wanting to change the subject. "You know, this place looks pretty good."

"What'd you expect?"

"I might even buy a seat."

"If you get past the membership committee."

"My, a membership committee. Aren't you the swells? Just like the big boys."

She gave him a level look. "You make me tired, Jake."

He grinned, gave her cheek a brisk pat. "Well, nice seeing you. Gotta go."

Someone touched Tess's arm. From the faint scent of lily of the valley, she knew it was Meg.

"Is he going to buy a seat?" Meg asked, her eyes on Jake as he left the room.

"As soon as he decides people want to trade here he will."

"Thanks for dragging in all those customers," Meg said.

"There's more where they came from." Tess moved toward the front of the room. "Let's take a look at how our companies are doin' today."

As she stood next to Meg in front of the board, Tess studied the listings, amazed. Yesterday the only stocks listed were their own, and now there were half a dozen more. "What's goin' on with these new companies? How'd they get approved? I thought I was head of the listin' committee."

"You are, but—"

Tess shot her an angry look.

"The opportunity came up this morning and you weren't here. They paid the listing fee we agreed upon, and—"

"So you decided to list them without checkin' to see if whether they were an up-and-up operation. Just listed them."

Meg colored. "An exchange has to have listings to bring in customers, Tess. Face it."

Tess didn't want to fight with Meg, but she wasn't about to be walked on. She took in a deep breath, scanned the new listings. Meg had a point. With a shrug, Tess said, "Okay. Just don't do it again."

For a split second, Meg's expression went ice cold, then shifted into that stubborn little half-smile of hers. "I wouldn't think of it. I wouldn't dare."

Neither of them moved as they stood facing each other like two kids after the same toy until finally Tess couldn't hold back any longer, and she burst out laughing. "You wouldn't dare? That'll be the day."

Meg's tight smile loosened, broke into a full grin. "I'm sorry, Tess. I should have asked you first."

"Oh, forget it. We're all just learnin' the ropes." Tess slipped a hand through Meg's arm. "Let's go over and talk some of those gents into buyin' some stock."

* * *

A month went by. The exchange was crammed with customers. Tess was making good money from her trades. The listing committee met twice a week. Thanks to Mr. Burlingame, who advised them to set up two classifications—preferred prospects and prospects—the customers knew immediately whether a company owned property favorably located with ore values verified by an engineer or whether the location still was unimproved.

Verna ran daily articles in the *Star* about the potential of the recent listings and sent copies to newspapers that published mining stock quotes in every town in which she'd ever worked and a lot she hadn't. Sally Petticord picked up information from her husband's assay office about rich assays of ore samples brought in and where they came from. Then Meg, who had made an arrangement with Bill Brown, drove out to the mine in question and attempted to persuade the owner to apply for a listing on the new exchange.

The *Los Angeles Times* did a little article on the ladies' exchange that raised a good bit of local stir. Some folks said the success was just because an exchange run by ladies was a curiosity. Others claimed it was the bargain-counter price to buy a seat. Still others pointed to the brokers—who made a profit from the differences in prices between the two exchanges—pushing it. Whatever the reason, Tess was getting closer to her ranch.

* * *

To Tess's annoyance, though the ladies' exchange grew more crowded by the day, Jake still hadn't plunked down his money for a seat. There was no further news on the progress of Pete Eckles's suit against the Mohawk Mines. The three mines in question continued to operate twenty-four hours a day. She and Meg decided that to be on the safe side, in case the district court shut the whole operation down, they should know more about the best-producing mines fringing the Mohawk Mines–leased properties, particularly the Jumbo, the Red Top, and the Genuine Article.

Not to their surprise, they discovered Winters and Nolan had taken out options to buy the Jumbo and the Red Top three months earlier with the intention of an eventual merger. All they needed to do was find a lender with the cash to clinch their deal. If the court closed two of their mines temporarily, they'd have others.

Winters and Nolan could do no wrong. The camp's infatuation with whatever they owned kept boosting the prices. Once the merger went through—and Tess was sure it would—the price of the Jumbo and Red Top would be out of sight. Neither she nor Meg owned any Red Top. Only Tess held any Jumbo stock. Meg still had five hundred shares of Genuine Article. Though it wasn't part of the Mohawk Mines merger, the Genuine Article was right next door. They both knew the minute the merger went through, its value would skyrocket.

Over supper one night in the kitchen of the Ajax, they decided a plan of action.

"This is what we should do," Meg said, helping herself to another slice of Tess's fresh sour dough bread. "The Red Top stock is already over-priced, so let's concentrate on the Jumbo and the Genuine Article."

"Sounds okay." Tess went to the stove, picked up the coffeepot. "More coffee?"

Meg nodded, savoring the smell of the bread as much as the subtle bite of its flavor.

"We'll spread the word around camp that we'll buy whatever anyone has to sell," Tess said, replacing the blackened pot on the back of the stove.

Meg swallowed, grinned. "There's something downright satisfying about being able to control a market."

"What about Verna?" Tess asked. "She should be in on it, don't you think?"

"She's apt to resist. Both the Jumbo and the Genuine Article are over five and a quarter, and you know how stuck she is on never buying anything over a dollar a share." Meg took a tentative sip of the steaming coffee.

Tess sat down. "Don't worry. I'll talk to her."

* * *

On November thirteenth, just as the entire camp had predicted, the Mohawk Mine merger became final, and the Goldfield Consolidated Mines Company was created. The price of the three mines reached an all-time high. Investors became madmen to buy, and Verna was eager to sell every share she owned. Only Tess and Meg's pleadings convinced her the price would keep going up. And it did.

In the dark of night, on the edge of sleep, Tess couldn't help feeling proud of how fast she'd learned the stock market game. With a reasonable sense of timing and a little savvy, she'd made money, a lot of money. She was riding high.

* * *

Tess sat at the end of the bar, enjoying the feel of the morning sun soaking through the back of her shirtwaist. By Christmas she'd be out of here. In the meantime, there was Thanksgiving to celebrate, and she'd asked Bill Brown and the entire board of directors over to the Ajax for a feast.

Tonight she and Jake were going to see Nat Goodwin in the *Gilded Cage*, playing at the Hippodrome. It was because of Jake, who was a personal friend of the star, that the troupe had agreed to stop in Goldfield on its way to San Francisco. After the show, in honor of the occasion, Jake was throwing a cast party with oysters and champagne in the private dining room of the Palm Grill. She'd been looking forward to it for weeks, but before then she had business to do.

Her account books at her elbow, her checkbook in front of her, she dipped her pen in the inkwell, drew it out carefully, and wrote a check for two hundred dollars in care of the First National Bank of Steamboat Springs, Colorado, then signed her name. Next, she drew out a sheet of paper and wrote a short letter to Ezra Block, the president, explaining the amount was intended as earnest money against the final purchase of her ranch. She found an envelope, slipped the check and the letter inside, and sealed it shut. She strode to the post office, her heart pounding with excitement over what she'd done. She knew eventually she'd have to tell Vic. They'd talked about the ranch before, and his reaction had always been the same.

"What do you know about running a ranch, Tess Wallace?" he'd said. "Just because you grew up on a scrub farm don't mean you know cattle."

He'd scowled and scolded her, and she'd wished he hadn't. Vic was as good a man as she'd ever known. She wanted him to wish her well, to approve of what she was doing.

* * *

Dressed in her pale yellow silk, her hair dressed over pads the way they showed it done in *Vogue* magazine, and wearing her new white kid gloves, Tess peered out the front window of the saloon for some sign of Jake. Behind her was the usual din of customers' laughter and talk. For the millionth time, she glanced at the clock hung at one end of the bar. It was seven-thirty. The performance was to start at eight. If Jake stood her up, the galoots lined up at the bar would never let her live it down.

Then there he was, elegant in his evening suit, gleaming black silk top hat, and white gloves. At the sight of her, he grinned, swept off his hat and gave a little bow. In spite of herself, she felt her heart lurch.

"You'll knock 'em dead, babe."

"You're not bad yourself," she said and handed him her cloak to put around her shoulders.

Her arm through his, they hurried down Crook Street, rounded the corner, and crossed Fifth. In the dark, it was hard to see the horse dung. One misstep and her silk slippers would be ruined. The cold worked under the cape. She almost wished she'd chosen a dress with a high neck.

As they neared the Hippodrome, Jake slowed his pace. "Babe, I've got a favor to ask."

She eyed him, leery of the "babe" he'd used twice now.

"There's a man named Ed Bryant who has the office next to mine. He's a San Francisco stockbroker whose firm holds an option from the Graham Trust on a hundred thousand shares of Red Fox."

"He ought to have a seat on our exchange."

Jake scowled, as usual annoyed at the mention of the ladies' exchange. "Anyway, his firm has oversubscribed its allotment. He's desperate to get his hands on twenty-five thousand shares. We've got them. But he doesn't know it."

"What does this have to do with me?" she said, glancing at the crowd streaming into the theater. She wanted to stop talking and go in.

"I want him to pay through the nose for those shares, Tess. Through the nose." His voice was low, angry.

Tess glanced at him, paying attention now. Jake wasn't the excitable type. "I still don't see where I come in. What's he done that's got you so steamed up?"

"The rat listens into my calls."

"What do you mean, 'listens into your calls'?"

"His office is next door. Every time I get a call, he picks up his telephone and listens in. He gets the news as soon as I do. It's not bad enough that I have to battle Winters and Nolan. Now I have a neighbor, passing himself off as a reputable broker who—"

"He's a cheat," she said, suddenly as indignant as he was.

"Damn right."

The crowd outside the theater was thinning. She caught sight of Meg and Bill Brown as they hurried inside. "Jake, can't you tell me about this later?"

He ignored her. "Here's where you come in. He knows you have a seat on the ladies' exchange. He also knows you're thick with Verna Bates, whose brother in Bullfrog supposedly has an inside track to the Red Dog. This afternoon, I let it slip that you and Verna just got back from a visit."

"But that's a lie. I've never been in Bullfrog. You hardly know Verna, and she hasn't seen her brother for months."

"Now here's the important part," he said, ignoring her.

Only a handful of men stood outside the theater.

"We're goin' to miss the first act."

"They'll hold the curtain till I get here," he said.

Jake was prone to exaggeration. Normally, she wouldn't have believed him. But he and Nat Goodwin apparently were thick as thieves.

"Now listen carefully." His expression took on a dreamy look as it always did when he was about to work a con. "Our seats are right in front of Bryant's. I arranged it that way."

She waited.

"When we go in, I want you to look all excited. We sit down, you tell me that just as you were getting on the stagecoach in Bullfrog, Verna's brother came rushing up with big news about the Red Dog. He swore you to secrecy, but the news was so big . . . Well, you've got the idea."

She nodded, smiling ruefully. "What's the news I'm goin' to blab?"

"That they struck six feet of two-thousand-dollar ore at the Red Dog, that Verna is to hold on to her shares and not sell for under five dollars."

"I don't get it."

"It's simple. Bryant is going to overhear this news. He's going to get me aside at intermission and beg me to sell him more shares. I won't do it. But when he gets to the cast party, I'll reconsider, see?"

"The Red Dog is still a loser, Jake. Even with all your hype."

"It has potential," he said, taking her face in his hands and kissing her lightly on the lips. "What do you say?"

She drew back, wanting to steer clear of his touch, which never failed to rouse her. "I'll do it on one condition."

"Anything, babe. You name it."

"List the Red Dog on our exchange. Since you don't have a seat, I'll get the commission."

"Now, Tess. Be reasonable."

She caught the shift from "babe" to "Tess." Her terms had scratched the real Jake. "I'm dead serious."

"We'll work all that out later." He took her arm, propelling her toward the theater entrance.

"I mean it," she said, glancing up at him as they went inside.

"I know you do, babe."

"So it's a deal?"

Before Jake could answer, several other latecomers joined them, and the moment had passed.

CHAPTER 19

$\mathcal{V}$erna sat next to Jimmy Earnest, wide-eyed and wiggling, in the front row of the Lyric Theater, jammed to the gunnels with stinking bodies that probably hadn't known a bath for months. The air was choked with smoke. Flasks were being passed around. The noise level was close to intolerable.

Last week, when Jimmy had let it slip that his birthday was the following Sunday, she'd wondered what to do for him. When she'd spied the advertisement for the camp's latest moving pictures, *Scene in the Philippines* and *Life under the Circus*, two for the price of one, she knew that's where they'd go.

They'd been waiting for what seemed hours for the show to begin. Just as she was about to give up hope, the piano player suddenly struck a series of thunderous chords. A hush fell over the theater. She glanced at Jimmy, not moving a hair now. The overhead light went off, a wide beam from the arc light focused on the screen in front of her. She held her breath.

Verna had seen only one other moving picture show in her life. To actually be able to watch people walking about on a screen as if they were right in the same room was still nearly unbelievable to her.

The title "Scenes from the Philippines and Our New Possessions" appeared in black lettering big enough for Verna to see
clearly. Soldiers marched across the screen. "Our boys defending
the Philippines," read the caption. Cheers broke out. The piano
player played a Sousa march. She clapped her hands to her mouth,
amazed.

A pompous-looking, gray-haired man, decked out in a naval
uniform with a chestful of medals, strutted in front of rows of
sailors. Admiral Dewey. Clapping broke out, but Verna wasn't
taken with the man. Another scene flashed up on the screen. A
sad collection of short, brown-skinned men in white pants and
shirts, barefoot and wearing straw hats, lined up against an adobe
wall. The caption said they were insurgent prisoners. Boos erupted
from the audience, but from the sorry looks of them, Verna didn't
see how they could hurt a flea. The light flicked and other peas-
ants in hats that looked like umbrellas appeared, trudging through
water behind the skinniest cows she'd ever seen. Finally, more soldiers and sailors, a warship, and "The End."

The light came on, and she glanced at Jimmy for his reaction.

"It's swell, ain't it?" he said, grinning at her.

She smiled back, let the *ain't* pass. People stood, stretched, some
watching the operator as he prepared for what was still to come.
A few minutes passed, the lights went off again. Quiet.

The words "Life under the Circus Tent" appeared on the screen.
A line of elephants, each of their trunks linked to the tail of the
animal immediately in front, appeared. Trapeze artists swung by
their knees, somersaulted in midair. Verna's heart stopped. Girls
in tights inched across a wire strung high over spectators' heads.
Then, suddenly, long before she'd seen enough, it was over.

Light filled the room again. The audience, talking and laughing, got to its feet, shrugged on coats, thumped outside. In a few
minutes, except for the man dressed in the rumpled evening suit
who was rewinding the reel, she and Jimmy were alone.

"Well?" she asked, smiling fondly at him.

"When do they show it again?"

"When we buy some more tickets."

He frowned, glanced at her. "I wish Ma and Pa could've seen it."

"They've never seen a picture show?"

He shook his head, stood up, hands in his pockets, and watched the man removing the reel of film from the moving picture machine. "Which show did you like the best, Miss Bates?"

"The circus, I think; I got tired of the soldiers."

He nodded. "I kind of felt sorry for those men in the straw hats."

"The ones by the wall or with the cows?"

"The ones by the wall." His expression was thoughtful. "Do you think they were shot?"

"I suspect they were. It said they were insurgents, remember?" She gave his arm a brisk pat, glanced behind her at the moving picture operator, who had picked up his coat. "I guess we better get out of here before they throw us out."

As they walked through the dark toward the *Star*, they talked about Thanksgiving. He told her his mother planned to bake a chicken if they could get one. They paused to inspect the window display of a mining supply store. Jimmy pointed out which lamps, which picks, which shovels were the best. Standing next to him, watching his serious young face, she felt such a sense of contentment she hardly dared to breathe for fear of breaking the spell.

In her heart, she knew it was only a matter of time before the Goldfield balloon would burst. The ore wouldn't last forever, and once it was gone the camp wouldn't either. Jimmy's father would have to find work somewhere else, taking Jimmy with him. She shoved the thought aside.

She'd read about the new-fangled machinery in the stamp mills that extracted smaller amounts of gold from the rock so that a good profit could still be made. God knows, technology had its place. But what made Goldfield throb with life had nothing to do with chemicals and engines and all to do with the tantalizing hope as old as the first gold strike thousands of years ago. Anybody who could get himself here might strike it rich. If he didn't make it prospecting, he could high-grade a tidy sum, even parlay it into a small fortune at the stock exchange.

But with the merger the Mohawk Mines Company had pushed through and the approaching leasing deadline, all that would change. How soon the effects would be felt was hard to say. First off, the mine owners would clamp down on the high-grading. Then the union would step in and flex its muscle. The easy money would dry up, and before long the mining stiffs—Jimmy's dad among them—the gamblers, the whores, even the tradesmen would move on to another camp. The ladies' stock exchange might hang on for a year, but not much longer, which would be a shame because Meg put such store in it.

A mining camp was not the place for putting down roots or making friends. Verna was safe on the roots part. Any day now Amos might telegraph for her to follow him to Arizona or God knows where else. But for the first time in her life she'd made some friends. Meg and Tess, in particular, who filled a big hole in her life. Most of all there was the boy. She felt downright tender toward him, like she might toward a grandson. He had changed her life.

*   *   *

The daytime temperatures were holding at a steady thirty degrees, lower for late November than any old-timer could remember. Verna was as settled in as she'd ever been in a mining camp. Her little shack was cozy enough, but no matter how hard she tried, she couldn't seem to get the heater she'd bought at Vogler's Supplies to do right. Either the air in the office grew so hot she couldn't breathe or it was so cold her fingers numbed as she set the type.

Whenever the wind let up, she liked to walk past the outskirts of town for a bit of exercise. With the cold, there was no cause to worry about snakes. She searched for something to admire—the colors of the sand and rocks, the shapes—but all she saw was the endless gray, the barren hills, the silly-looking Joshua trees that were actually just cactus, all scattered with trash that had blown out from town. There were days when she would have given her eyeteeth to see just one pine tree. She was beginning to think that whether Amos got Bullfrog out of his system or not, she would pull up stakes and go back to Colorado the second after she sold her stock.

* * *

The Tuesday after Thanksgiving Verna was setting up the next day's issue when Jimmy came bursting in, his cheeks red, his nose running.

"Wait till you hear the story I got for you, Miss Bates." He wiped his nose with the sleeve of his coat.

"Have."

"Have." Jimmy came over to the type table where she was working. "They're collectin' license fees over in the tenderloin."

"Who is?"

Jimmy shrugged. "The sheriff, I guess."

"Collecting city license fees isn't a story."

"Even when the ladies are paradin' up and down in front of the houses and the dance halls with signs?"

She felt a prick of interest. "What kind of signs?"

"They say 'unfair,' things like that," Jimmy said. "There's a big ruckus. A real crowd is gatherin'."

Verna grinned at the sight of his eager face.

"We don't want the *Tattler* to scoop us, do we?"

She laughed. Jimmy had the makings of a first-rate reporter. If only he could stay in Goldfield a little longer.

"Hold on a minute," she said. "I'll get my hat."

* * *

Verna heard angry shouts and cheers blocks before they reached Myers Street, where Jimmy had seen the whores with signs. The street was filled with men. Traffic was at a standstill. As they rounded the corner, Verna spotted the placards bobbing over the heads of the crowd.

She stood on tiptoe. "Jimmy, I can't make out what they say."

The boy took her hand. "Come on, I'll get you through."

They inched their way to the front of the throng, milling in front of a whorehouse and the dance hall next door. Three young women, smiling and looking pleased with the attention, held signs affixed to broomsticks. Verna still couldn't read them.

"I left my glasses, Jimmy. Read those things to me, will you?"

"It says that 'Miss Lizzie's and the Unique Concert Hall are unfair houses.' "

"What else?"

"That 'We request all Union men not to patronize these places. The unfair girl workers are Millie Alfred, Little Fay, Skiddo Babe, Kittie La Belle, Mazie, Fay, and Rosie.' "

Jimmy glanced at Verna. She turned to the man next to her. "What's all that mean, mister?"

"The girls at Miss Lizzie's are cuttin' their prices."

"There's a standard price?" She found the idea funny. She knew the Wobblies, the IWW, had tried to organize every working man and woman in the camp, but whorehouses seemed to be stretching it a bit.

"Is the union paying those girls while they're picketing?"

He shrugged. "Couldn't say."

She and Jimmy watched the goings-on for a moment more before she said to the man, "So they're not really on strike."

He eyed her warily. "Lady, what's your game, anyway?"

She broke out her sweet-little-old-lady smile. "Just curious, that's all."

The man moved away from her. Verna instructed Jimmy to stay put while she interviewed the picketers. It was easy enough to laugh at the goings-on if she let herself forget what past experience told her. As sure as the sun came up every day, the union was gearing up for a strike soon, and it wanted no stragglers.

Taking the pad and pencil out of her pocketbook, she approached one of the girls. "Pardon me, miss, I'm with the *Goldfield Star*, and I'd like to ask you a few questions."

The girl wore no hat. Her henna red hair was caught up in a

loose knot on the top of her head. She'd put a man's coat over her dress. She smiled broadly at Verna, revealing a mouth full of yellow, crooked teeth. "My name's Millie. Spelled with an *i-e*."

Verna noted the name. "Why are you girls picketing?"

The girl looked indignant. "Miss Lizzie's and the Unique cut prices. It says on the sign. Can't you read?"

"All the houses are unionized?"

"What are ya', some troublemaker, grandma?"

Verna only smiled at what was obviously meant to be a slur. "So there are some houses like Miss Lizzie's the IWW couldn't rope in. Is that it?"

Out of the corner of her eye, Verna caught sight of the dwarflike union man, Tim McGee. The whore with the dyed red hair also saw him. "Leave me alone. I ain't sayin' nothin' to ya," she said loudly, then trounced off, waving the placard as she went.

Verna turned toward the union man, nodded in recognition.

"Didn't expect to see you here, Miss Bates," he said, casting a sidelong glance at Jimmy. "Who's the kid?"

A warning alarm sounded in her head. "He works for me."

Tim McGee's eyes narrowed as he took a closer look at Jimmy. "Your old man's a Wobbly, ain't he?"

But before Jimmy could answer, Verna took him by the arm. She'd been a fool to let him get involved. "Come on. Let's get on back to the paper."

CHAPTER 20

*M*eg inspected the engraved invitation requesting the pleasure of her company at the Petticords' open house from two to five
o'clock on Sunday, December first. It smelled of money, as fine an
advertisement for the exchange's success as a full-page ad in every
paper in camp.

Sally Petticord claimed she'd deliberately set the party for the
first of December to get a headstart on the other holiday festivi-
ties. Privately, Meg suspected the principle reason for the occasion
was to show off the "suit," as she called it, of living room furniture
Sally had ordered from Grand Rapids, Michigan, with money she'd
made trading at the exchange.

The Petticords' house was kitty-corner from the Burlingames',
in what was considered to be the best part of town. Its clapboard
siding was painted white, and its second story, by Goldfield's standards, made it quite grand. Since greasewood and cactus were all
that would grow in the sand, there'd been no attempt at land-
scaping. A porch ran around the two sides facing the street. A sub-
stantial shed that served as a carriage house occupied the back of
the lot.

Meg joined the guests filing up the front walk and onto the

porch where Sally Petticord and her husband stood by the front door, shaking hands. A girl in a serviceable black, cotton dress and starched white apron and cap took people's coats.

Inside, Meg craned her neck, looking for Verna or Tess. She knew Bill wouldn't be here. When she'd mentioned the party last week on their way to the ladies' night musicale at the Montezuma Club, she hadn't been surprised at his reaction. Rubbing elbows with Goldfield's so-called high society was not something he enjoyed.

"There are people in Goldfield who would kill for the invitation," she'd said, teasing.

He'd grinned. "Then if I don't go, someone else will have the chance."

"Oh, Bill," she'd said in mock disapproval, enjoying the feel of his hand on her arm. For weeks, she'd told herself they were just friends, two people who enjoyed each other's company. They often had dinner together. Bill let her drive his automobile when he wasn't making deliveries. But Goldfield wasn't a place where people settled down. He'd said more than once he intended to buy half of an automobile with his cousin in San Francisco and drive it in a cross-country tour this spring. He'd be gone and she'd stay in Goldfield. Both of them had broken loose of earlier ties to shape their lives as it suited them. Why not now? Yet for weeks, she'd felt as if there was something, like an invisible chord wrapping around them, gradually binding them together.

When they'd reached the Montezuma Club above the Palace, all Meg could remember of the endless program was a pianist, supposedly from Italy, playing two Chopin etudes and a shift boss from the Jumping Jack mine who sang Irish ballads in a magnificent baritone voice. As Bill had taken her home, he had held her hand. She had held hands with dozens of men, kissed nearly as many, wrestled amorously with a few. Yet the first instant his fingers had wrapped around hers, she'd felt such a jolt of electricity course through her she'd had to catch her breath.

On the way back to the bottle house, dodging the traffic, making their way around knots of men gathered outside saloons, she'd been like a sleepwalker, unconscious of her surroundings. At the door, he had kissed her lightly, and she had looked up at him without speaking, the feel of his lips still on hers. He'd smiled, said something about dinner at La Parisienne when he returned from Reno. A moment later, he'd been gone. As she'd stretched out on the cot, she'd touched a finger to her lips. It was hours before she'd fallen asleep.

Now in the crush of the Petticords' small parlor, Meg forced herself to stop thinking about him. There wasn't any point in it. As she squeezed past the Burlingames, she caught sight of someone watching her. Looking more closely, she saw it was Charley Thompson.

Her glance met his. They exchanged smiles. In their chance meetings on the street, he always made a point of telling her how busy he was, about all his added responsibilities since the Mohawk merger. He obviously thrived in the reflected glory of his bosses. She still suspected he knew more about her father's death than he'd told her. But after the chance meeting that night at the Goldfield Mining Exchange, when she'd met his father and had dinner with them, she'd realized the extent of both their connections with Winters and Nolan. She'd decided then that Charley would never tell her any more than he already had.

Charley started to walk in her direction when a man she didn't recognize came up to him, said something, diverting Charley's attention. Meg moved past people, relieved she had escaped a conversation with him, and accepted a cut-glass cup filled with something that looked like strawberry crush from the hired girl.

Suddenly, there was a flurry of activity by the front door. She craned her neck to discover what was going on, and saw Sally Petticord, all smiles, enter on the arm of a man who appeared to be in his twenties. Meg had never seen him before.

"Ladies and gentlemen," Sally called to her guests.

Conversation ebbed, died.

"We have a wonderful surprise."

Meg glanced across the room at Tess, dressed in her magnificent peach-colored watered silk, and winked. Tess and Sally Petticord had carried on a friendly sparing match from that first afternoon at the Burlingames. Meg could hardly wait to hear what Tess would say later about Sally and her grand ways.

"Let me introduce you all to Reverend Emmett Good." She said his name slowly, as if introducing someone of great importance. She turned to the smallish man and beamed.

Reverend Good gave a suitably grave nod to acknowledge the introduction. His appearance was starched, clean, everything exactly in place. As he surveyed the guests, his expression was a perfect deadpan. Meg was certain he'd never doubted or questioned anything in his life.

His light hair was carefully combed back with a neat part down the middle. His apple cheeks shone. He wore a proper brown three-button single-breasted worsted suit, white shirt and high collar with a black tie.

Sally stepped aside. "Now then, Reverend, you must know who we are."

His mouth worked into a strained smile.

"Let's see." She turned to Verna standing next to her. "Let me start with Miss Bates, owner and publisher of one of our newspapers, *The Goldfield Star*, and the secretary of the Ladies' Goldfield Stock Exchange, which I told you about."

He gave the barest nod.

Sally went around the room, one by one, until only Tess remained to be introduced. With a stiff smile, Sally said, "And Miss Wallace."

The minister gave her an inquiring look, as if wanting to know more.

"Miss Wallace is the co-owner of a saloon." Sally said nothing about her being the treasurer of the exchange.

Instantly, his smile froze. "A saloon?"

"You betcha. The Ajax, named after my partner, Vic Ajax," Tess said pleasantly, as if unaware anything was amiss.

No one moved. An automobile's backfire outside reverberated in the silence. It was as if the entire gathering was holding its collective breath.

Sally Petticord appeared on the edge of tears when her husband stepped forward, cleared his throat. "Yes, indeed, Reverend, our ladies in Goldfield are amazing the way they've taken to this exchange of theirs. Thought it up themselves, by golly. It even made the Los Angeles papers. Keep a woman busy, I always say, and you'll keep her out of the store."

"My." The minister's tone was sour.

Meg glared across the room at Phil Petticord, felt her insides clamp tight. *Our ladies*, indeed. She, for one, was not any man's lady, never would be if she could help it. And the way Sally tried to ignore Tess . . . Meg forced a cool smile. "You must come on over to see the exchange, Mr. Good. We offer a fine variety of listings."

"I fear I will be otherwise engaged," said the minister gravely, and he swung his gaze in Tess's direction, shook his head. "The sinners of Goldfield will require my full attention."

Every person in the room tensed.

Tess slipped a hand through Jake's arm in a proprietary way, smiled as if oblivious to the minister's meaning. "Even money you'd find half of those sinners at our exchange, Reverend. You should do like Meg says and come over."

The minister visibly recoiled. Most of the guests affected looks of outrage. An awkward silence held the room until, once again, Phil Petticord stepped forward. "Well, Reverend—"

The eyes fastened on Tess turned almost reluctantly in Phil's direction.

"You must be thirsty, sir. Let's go into the dining room and get you some punch."

A look of pure relief spread over Sally Petticord's face. The guests parted, and she guided the minister toward the punch table, away from Tess.

Conversation slowly rallied. As Charley turned to talk to John

Burlingame, who was standing next to him, Meg watched the Petticords and Reverend Good sipping punch. Aside from an itinerant Catholic priest, men of God had not frequented Goldfield. Apparently, that was no longer to be the case.

Meg felt a desperate urge for a breath of fresh air. She edged past guests, stepped outside to the porch.

Tess and Verna were sitting on the top step, seemingly unaware of the cold as they gazed westward toward the sun as it hung balanced on the barren top of the Malapai. They looked over their shoulders at her as she closed the front door.

"I thought that might be you coming out," Verna said.

Meg leaned against the door. "Can you really believe that in there?"

Tess gave a wry smile. "I guess the reverend's goin' to civilize us and close us down in the doin'."

Meg glanced at her, chose to let the observation pass for now. "And Phil Petticord. 'Our ladies are having a wonderful time.' As if we were playing cards or having a tea party."

"Face it, Meg. That's how most of the gents see us," Verna said dryly.

Tess looked over at her. "It's me, a saloon keeper and an ex-whore, rubbin' shoulders with that bunch in there, that's the fly in the ointment."

"You're the treasurer of the exchange," Meg said, trying to control her anger.

"What does that count for?"

Meg and Verna looked at her.

"Listen, with the boom times around here, it was bound to happen."

Meg ran her hands briskly up and down her arms and strode to the end of the porch and back, trying to figure out what was going on. "You're both wrong. It doesn't have anything to do with the reverend or with you, Tess."

Her friends eyed her.

"Every man in there is jealous of the success we've had, and it's finally coming out in the open. Clem Vogler, Phil Petticord, the lot of them. Even John Burlingame. Not to mention Jake Stratton. It galls them we've made money with our brains. That little minister is just an excuse to close us up."

"That's half true." Tess stood up, dusted off her skirts. "But I'm tellin' you, Meg, once folks make their pile, they get the urge to hide the rough edges as quick as they can. They start puttin' on airs. The gents quit gamblin' and whorin'. Some even go to church." She gave them a wicked smile. "So here I am, bold as brass, mixin' with them as if they haven't stepped up in the world. They want to be high society, Meg, and they can't be until I'm back where I belong, so I'm quittin' the exchange."

"You can't."

"I'm ruinin' its reputation, Meg. I was a whore. That's fact. And don't pretend you didn't know that."

Meg looked into the honest, gray eyes of her friend who had such an unerring way of cutting through the sham in life. Most of the women in the camp were whores, but Meg didn't know them. Tess was a friend who had put that life behind her. She had a daughter she adored, and she ran an honest business. "There isn't a woman inside this house who can hold a candle to you. If you quit, we all quit."

Tess shook her head, gave a small smile. "You don't get it. Tomorrow those good ladies in there and the gents, too, will pick up their marbles and start tradin' at the other exchange."

"No, they won't. It was just the minister. Once Sally and the others come in tomorrow, and we have a chance for a good talk—"

"To hell with talk," Tess cut in.

Out of the corner of her eye, Meg saw Verna watching Tess in that steady way of hers.

"I don't know, Tess. Talk has its points. I need the Vogler and Petticord ads."

Meg looked from one friend to the other, intent that nothing come between them. "Of course you do. Anyway, when those biddies come to their senses tonight and remember how they don't have to pay commissions anymore, they'll stay put. So no one on our board is resigning. No one." She fixed her glance on Tess. "That includes you."

CHAPTER 21

$\mathcal{T}$ess lay awake all night, the bitterness over the turn of events at the Petticords' eating at her. She was tempted to carry out her threat to quit, but her pride wouldn't let her. She'd show up like usual, head high.

The next morning, she waltzed into the exchange, not surprised to see the room was nearly empty of customers. She told herself she couldn't care less. She still had her seat, didn't have to pay commission. That's what counted. She took her usual place among the front row of chairs facing the board, shrugged off her cape. A moment later, Emma Burlingame came in and sat next to her.

Friendly as could be, Tess smiled over her anger and said, "Lord, can you believe this weather?"

Emma Burlingame glanced at her.

"Cold as a nun's tits draggin' in the snow."

For a split second, shock or surprise, maybe a little of both, flashed across Emma's placid face then vanished as the thinnest hint of a smile twitched at the corners of her mouth. "Well, not quite that cold."

Chagrined, Tess shifted her gaze and pretended to study the board. She hadn't expected Emma's matter-of-fact reaction to her raw remark about the weather, made to test Emma, to see where she stood. She deserved better. Ashamed, Tess swallowed her pride and apologized.

Emma gave her a level look. "You're a good woman, Tess Wallace. If it'd been me, I'd never have invited Mr. Good, and I'd of thrown those prissy do-gooders out on their ears."

Tess regarded her warily, not sure she quite believed her.

"Meg and Verna and I talked about it before you came in. If we could make amends, we'd do it. As it is, we'll just pretend it never happened." She reached out and took one of Tess's hands, gave it a reassuring squeeze.

Her eyes stinging, Tess smiled. The treatment she'd received at the Petticords hadn't surprised her. She'd been a fool to hope for more, yet the humiliation continued to lie heavy at the pit of her stomach, like a meal of beans and tough meat with too much gristle. Emma's gesture of friendship helped ease the ache.

*   *   *

Two weeks went by. The women who had stopped trading began gradually to filter back in. The drive to make as much money as they could off the frenzy of new strikes was too much to resist. The board of directors decided to keep the exchange open until eleven. Even Sally Petticord couldn't stay away. Tess felt her spirits take a turn for the better.

Some of the stores had already put up displays to remind people that Christmas was coming up. But as Tess listened to the throb of the stamp mills, felt the tension in the camp as the lease deadline loomed, she doubted anyone cared if Christmas came or went.

*   *   *

The morning was bright and clear as Tess came down to the kitchen for her first cup of coffee. Outside, men's shouts rose above the usual din, and she wondered what the commotion was about. Cookie returned her "good morning" with a grunt, handed her a plate of eggs and bacon. Taking the chair closest to the window, she breathed in the aroma of the fresh brewed coffee and fried bacon. She hadn't realized how hungry she was. Just as she filled her mouth with a forkful of fried egg, she heard the front door burst open, and Vic calling her.

"They've called a strike!" His face flushed from the cold as he rushed into the kitchen. "The union wants a raise from four to five dollars for an eight-hour day. The operators say no dice."

She swallowed the egg, frowned at the news. Strikes seldom did anything except slow business. "Does that mean everythin' is shut down, even the leases?"

Vic shrugged, accepted a cup of coffee from Cookie. "I'd guess the owners will have to give them an extension."

Tess picked up a strip of bacon, bit off the end. It was crisp, just the way she liked it. Savoring the salty flavor as she chewed, she stared out the window at the snow drifting over the trash piled behind the building next door. Once word of the strike was out, the market was bound to be affected. Investors would get nervous, prices would fall. She and Jenny Lynn couldn't afford to have that happen.

It occurred to her that for the first time in all the years she'd lived in mining camps she was in the same boat as the owners. The strike couldn't have come at a worse time.

* * *

The snow was still falling at midnight. Downstairs, the saloon was noisier than usual, filled with men trying to stay warm and pretending the strike called this morning would have no effect on them. Faking a headache, Tess had come up supposedly to lie down for a while. She wanted to have one last peek at Jenny Lynn's presents she'd ordered from San Francisco before Bill Brown picked them up in time to make the morning train. Barring more snow, he had assured her they'd be in Colorado Springs in time for Christmas.

As breathless as if the contents were meant for her, she opened the first of the two dress boxes on her bed, removed the red velveteen dress with puffed sleeves, its collar trimmed in Valencienne lace. It had its own petticoat and bloomers, hemmed with the same lace of the dress. As gently as she'd stroke a baby bird's feathers, she ran her hands over the fabric, touched the collar, imagining Jenny Lynn wearing it, holding out the skirt, oohing over the lace.

Tess put the dress back in the box, arranging it carefully so it wouldn't muss, replaced the top. She reached for the bigger box, pulled the lid off, folded back the layers of snowy tissue. The rabbit fur coat she'd ordered was lined with pale-blue satin as was the matching tam. Jenny Lynn would look like a princess in it.

Satisfied, she eyed the sturdy wood box Vic had set by the door. It contained the Red Rover sled she'd ordered. To get a look at it, she'd have to pry off the boards to see inside, and she didn't want to do that. She decided it was enough to know it was in there. They wouldn't be together, but Jenny Lynn would have nice presents to open and know they were from her ma.

Tess went to the mirror above the dresser to check her hair before she went downstairs again. She pulled out some of the hairpins, brushed her hair smooth, replaced the pins. Satisfied with the results, she was about to turn away when she noticed the crow's-feet around her eyes. Maybe it was the poor light. She leaned closer to the mirror.

Sure enough. Crow's-feet. She was no spring chicken anymore. The desert wind and dust were hard on her skin, no matter how much cold cream she slathered on. Well, according to her plan, she'd cash in her stocks right after Christmas, sell her half of the saloon to Vic, and be headed to Colorado before New Year's.

Her spirits raised, she went to the door and nearly collided with Jake.

"I've been looking all over for you, babe. We need to talk."

Tess tried to move past him. "I've got to get back to work. Can't it wait till later?"

"I don't think so." He came into the room, closed the door. "How much can you lend me?"

"You know my policy, Jake. I don't lend money to anybody."

He put his hands on her shoulders, smiled into her eyes. The familiar electricity she felt at his touch ran through her. "Would I ask you for anything if it wasn't urgent?"

She tried for a stony look, but he'd peaked her curiosity.

He must have seen her weakening because he said, "Winters has been spreading rumors about the Graham Trust Company, impugned our good name."

"What'd they say you don't like?"

"Do you want to see the list?"

Tess sat down on the end of the bed, motioned for Jake to have a chair.

"First and foremost, they claim our books are under inspection by the post office department."

"Are they?"

"Do you even need to ask that question?"

Tess wasn't moved. "Well?"

"Do you know what being inspected by the post office department implies?"

Tess shrugged.

"It says to the public the Graham Trust Company has been sending fraudulent claims about mining stocks through the U.S. mails."

She leaned back on her elbows. "Has it?"

Jake came over, sat on the edge of the bed next to her. This close, she found it hard to resist him.

"You, of all people in the world, you ask that question?" He looked truly wounded.

"I didn't say I doubted you, Jake."

He moved closer, kissed her deeply. "Of course you didn't, babe."

She struggled to free herself from his grasp.

"Tess . . ."

"I've gotta get back to work."

He kissed her again, pushed her back, and his hands cupped her breasts. "God, but you've got you a body."

His touch, the smell of him on her was too much. She shoved him away from her, sat up.

"A quarter of a million's what I need."

"Oh, come on. Does anybody around here look like John D. Rockefeller?"

"You could raise it. Burlingame would lend it to you for the asking."

She inspected the pupils of his eyes. "Have you been drinkin'?"

"Cold sober." He gave her an ingratiating smile. "Fifty thousand then."

"Forget it."

"How about Vic?"

"Leave Vic out of this."

"What about the exchange?"

"What about it?"

"You and Meg and Verna could sign over your stock to me—"

"What in the hell are you talkin' about?"

"It'd just be temporary, for collateral against our loans at the State Bank and Trust."

She stared at him.

"Tess—"

"No."

"Tess—"

"I said 'no,' Jake. My money's for Jenny Lynn."

"You're willing to stand by and let me get dragged off to jail?"

"Even if I was willin' to give it to you, what's in the safe is chicken feed."

Stone-faced, he studied her for a moment, before a hint of smile appeared at one corner of his mouth. She could almost see the wheels turning inside his head as he reached for another scheme. The pleading look in his dark eyes a moment earlier had turned steel hard, like an animal's backed into a corner. "Don't worry about it, Tess. Forget I asked."

There was nothing more to say. Heavyhearted, Tess followed him downstairs and into the saloon, where he immediately joined a table of men playing five-card stud. Vic was behind the bar pouring drinks, talking to customers. Several regular customers saw her come in and greeted her. Giving them an absent wave, she went up to Vic, said she wanted to talk to him for a minute.

"You look grim as death," Vic said, his eyes dark with concern. "What's going on?"

She led him to the end of the bar near the kitchen. Careful to keep her voice low, she said, "Jake asked me for money."

"Are you going to give it to him?" His tone was disgusted.

Vic had never approved of Jake. She just hadn't wanted to admit it to herself.

She shook her head. "He says he needs fifty thousand. It's somethin' to do with the postal inspectors."

"I'm not surprised."

"Nolan and Winters are tryin' to force him out of business."

Vic gave a rueful snort. "Do you believe that?"

"He wouldn't lie about it."

A customer called for a beer. Automatically, Vic gave a nod in his direction. "Be right with you."

Vic turned his gaze, regarded her with solemn eyes. "Don't trust him, Tess. He'll break your heart."

CHAPTER 22

$\mathcal{M}$eg smiled at Phil Steiner, a broker from a San Francisco house who had bought a seat on the ladies' exchange ten days earlier. From that day on, she'd noticed that whenever any Fourth of July stock came up, he'd handled the trade. Curious, she'd kept an eye on him. Last night, the tall, white-haired broker, old enough to be her father, had sent her an invitation by messenger to accompany him to a Christmas Eve party hosted by Senator Nolan and Mr. Winters at the Palm Grill.

"I received your kind invitation, Mr. Steiner," she said, nearly shouting over the din of frenzied investors. Most were margin buyers, trading at 90 percent of par value. Not even the strike nor the shutdown of the major mines could keep them away. And, judging from the number of women she saw around the room who owned seats, the momentary yearnings for respectability had completely disappeared. Reverend Good had never shown his face. In fact, she hadn't even seen him around town. Perhaps the enormity of his task to save Goldfield sinners had overwhelmed him.

"Then you will accompany me?" Mr. Steiner asked.

She'd been waiting for the right opportunity to meet Nolan and Winters face-to-face. Shysters, thieves, con men were everywhere in Goldfield. But these two could be murderers. To even contemplate spending Christmas Eve, of all nights, with them was ridiculous. Yet it was an opportunity she couldn't pass up. Phil Steiner was her entrée. Besides, she wanted to find out why his firm had such an interest in the Fourth of July.

"I'd love to," she said.

He beamed. "Splendid. I will come by for you at seven."

* * *

Meg smiled as she moved past Phil Steiner, who held open the front door of the Palm Grill. The sign in the window said CLOSED TO PUBLIC CHRISTMAS EVE: PRIVATE PARTY. She wondered if the senator and George Winters owned an interest in the restaurant, too.

As she stepped inside, she was greeted by fake palm trees draped with ropes of red tinsel, strains of a carol being played by a tinny piano and violin. By Goldfield's standards, the Palm Grill had gone all out in honor of the season.

Ahead, to her left, she saw the senator and George Winters, standing next to the bar among guests in an assortment of evening dress. The regular dining room, off to the side, had been set up to resemble a cabaret with small tables grouped about and candles in their centers. It was nearly empty.

Phil collapsed his silk hat with a snap, handed it to the girl taking wraps. Meg unhooked the evening cloak Tess had loaned her and handed it to him. She caught her reflection in the mirror on the opposite wall, pleased with what she saw. The elegant dusty-rose chiffon evening dress, trimmed in seed pearls and lace, fit so well it might have been made for her instead of Tess. The elbow-length ivory kid gloves emphasized her slim, well-shaped arms. A tiny, delicate beaded evening bag hung by a gold chain from one wrist. The pearl earbobs completed the picture of a woman of beauty, taste, and means she had deliberately constructed.

"Shall we go in and say hello to our hosts?" Phil offered his arm, and she felt his eyes on the swell of her breasts revealed by the low-cut gown. She hoped George Winters and the senator would be equally taken with her.

* * *

As Meg watched Senator Nolan, suitably decked out in full evening dress, holding court before a dozen fawning admirers, she decided he looked for all the world like a bottom-heavy penguin instead of the shrewd gambler he was. George Winters—small, compact, with heavy dark brows and the pasty complexion of the sick—stood beside him. There was a look of evil about him that made her shiver.

"Merry Christmas to you, sir," Phil Steiner said to George Winters. "May I introduce Miss Kendall?"

Winters shot her a strange glance.

"A festive occasion," she said smoothly, offering the barest of smiles.

"The drinks are on the house," he said, then turned to the man next to him.

The man's rudeness was legendary, yet Phil Steiner was obviously taken aback for a moment before he gathered himself together again, took her arm, and introduced her to the senator.

His washed-out blue eyes had the deceptively cheerful squint of a man who would sell tickets to a hanging. "Ah, yes. Miss Kendall of the ladies' stock exchange, if I'm not mistaken."

Meg hid her astonishment with a smile. "I'm honored to serve as the vice president of the executive committee."

"Mr. Winters and I have been meaning to talk to you ladies."

"Really?" She kept smiling.

"But this is no time for business. Make yourself at home," he said expansively, and beckoned to a waiter with a tray full of champagne glasses.

Meg took a glass. Phil Steiner ordered a double bourbon and started up a conversation with a man who was unfamiliar to her. As she sipped the Mumm's, feeling the faint tickle of the bubbles

along her lips, she wondered what business the senator could possibly have with the exchange. Whatever it was, it would surely be
to his benefit.

The front door opened, and more guests streamed in, some she
recognized—the Burlingames, the Petticords, the Voglers, Charley
Thompson, a dozen merchants who'd bought advertising space.

She found herself standing with Emma and Sally, talking about
nothing in particular. Out of the corner of her eyes, she saw Phil
Steiner, a glass of bourbon in hand, frowning as he huddled with
John Burlingame at the far end of the bar, undoubtedly talking
stocks. But there was something grimly urgent in their expres-
sions. Was the strike about to be settled? Had the senator and Winters agreed to extend the leases? In either case, the price of stocks
would be affected drastically. She was tempted to go over to them
and ask, then thought better of it.

After what seemed a very long time, the guests were herded upstairs to dinner. Place cards had been set out on the tables. For a
few moments, she looked for place cards to indicate where she and
Phil Steiner were to sit, but soon gave it up when she realized the
other guests seemed to be sitting wherever they pleased. She
glanced about for Phil, found him already seated at a table with
their hosts and carrying on a heated conversation.

"Here you are, Mr. Steiner," she said brightly as she came up to
the table. Gazes turned to her for an instant, then to Phil Steiner.
She could see him fight through the cloud of alcohol for an instant
to recall who she was before he slowly pushed to his feet, held her
chair. "Miss Kendall. I do apologize. Business, you see."

"Of course." She settled her skirts, wishing she knew what business.

Waiters came with plates of sirloin steak, fried potatoes, and
canned green beans. The talk ceased as everyone concentrated on
the meal before them. Phil Steiner attacked his steak with vigor
for a moment or so, then apparently forgot about it and ordered
another bourbon. Meg glanced around the table to see if anyone

noticed, but the other men were debating the last value of the Red Top before the strike.

Plates were removed. Coffee was poured. Slabs of fruit cake were brought in. More champagne was passed, and the senator rose to propose a toast to Christmas. Expectant quiet spread across the room.

A forced smile on her face, Meg raised her glass, fearful the champagne might be more than Phil Steiner could handle. But before he even reached for the glass, he fell quietly across her lap, and passed out. The man on her right gave a low, derisive chuckle. Leaning close to her, he said, "Poor slob, can't take the heat of the kitchen, I guess."

She swung a steely glance toward him. Oddly, she felt a need to defend Phil Steiner, but his dead weight was crushing her gown. She wanted him off her and was quite prepared to remedy the situation herself. Just as she started to push back her chair, the senator put down his glass, came around the table to where she sat, grabbed Phil by one arm, picked him up, and shoved him at a waiter. In one deft motion, the waiter slung Phil over one shoulder like a side of beef and disappeared down the stairs.

Nervous laughter spread across the room, edging out the silence. The senator signaled the piano player and the man with the violin, who struck up a fox-trot. Meg smoothed her skirts, took a deep breath. Given the circumstances, it occurred to her she should make arrangements to go home, but she wasn't ready to leave.

Her thick-necked dinner companion who had commented on Phil Steiner's behavior shoved back his chair and asked her dance.

"I don't think so. Thanks," she said, forcing herself to use a pleasant tone. She glanced across the table at the senator. "I was saving the first dance for the senator."

* * *

"I fear Mr. Steiner's not used to our whiskey," said the senator, propelling her around the small space set aside as the dance floor.

She smiled at him. "So it would seem."

"One man's misfortune is another man's advantage."

"So they say," she said, still smiling. "Nonetheless, it's a lovely party."

"Mr. Winters and I thought it was only fitting, given the season."

She looked into the friendly, blue eyes and thought how they must have looked at her father when he showed the senator the map, trusting that his boss would see his miners were trespassing and stop operations along that drift. How like him, and how wrong he'd been. Senator Nolan and George Winters would steal another man's children if it would make them a profit.

"It's a shame though—" His smile switched to a deep frown.

"What is?"

"It reminds me of the money changers in the temple."

"I beg your pardon?"

"The talk here tonight. Stocks. Prices."

"It's Goldfield's passion, Senator."

He nodded, soberly. "Exactly my point."

"Which is?"

Beads of perspiration rimmed the senator's broad forehead. "If you don't mind, perhaps we should take a little rest, catch our breath." He led her to the corner of the room by the windows overlooking the nearly empty street below. She could feel the cold seeping through the panes.

"You were saying, Senator?"

"Ah, yes." He dabbed his brow with a snowy handkerchief. "Mr. Winters and I believe that it would be most appropriate to shut down the exchanges. Including the ladies', of course."

She stared at him. "Why?"

"As I said, the anxiety of the working man caught in this horrible strike."

"I don't see how—"

"The season, dear lady. Peace and goodwill toward men. Yet we go on without surcease, worshiping the coin of the realm instead of the Son of God."

Meg couldn't believe what she was hearing. To close down the exchanges would be disastrous. Once the word was out, the prices would plunge. Margin buyers would automatically be forced out of the market. They'd lose everything.

"It would be temporary, of course. We've already talked to the Goldfield Mining Stock Exchange."

"What did they say?"

"They will have a board meeting later this evening to consider the matter. But they agree to the wisdom of our suggestion."

"You know that for a fact, do you?"

He nodded.

She studied the senator's grave expression. He oozed sincerity. Her father had believed this man and the other men he'd worked for were as ethical as he was. That faith had led to years of being cheated out of wages and finally being killed. Meg was no such believer. This man and his partner had a hold over the men's exchange, and he was counting on the women being too stupid to realize the consequences. "Our exchange would want to consider the matter before giving you our answer."

"I don't see the problem, Miss Kendall."

"The leasing deadline is only a week off. Our customers rely on us."

He reddened for an instant, then produced a crooked smile. " Come now, Miss Kendall. You can't be serious. A proposal to pause from the nonstop pursuit of the almighty dollar in observance of the true spirit of Christmas is a perfectly legitimate request. As to your customers—"

She gave him a level look.

He glanced down and flicked a bit of food from his vest. "I believe Mrs. Burlingame is on your board, and she is in this very room."

"However, two other members of the board are not."

"So?"

"As I said, such a serious decision must be made by a vote of the entire executive committee."

He rolled his eyes with impatience. "Why, for heaven's sake? You are the vice president. Mrs. Burlingame is the president."

"We have the interests of all those owning seats on the exchange to consider, not to mention our customers, who trade with us in good faith."

"I will send a messenger for your affirmative answer by noon."

"And if the answer is in the negative, which it is sure to be, what then, Senator?"

He shrugged, his eyes ice cold now, and walked away.

*　*　*

"Had you heard about the proposal to close down the exchanges before tonight?" Meg asked Charley, who had been instructed by the senator to escort her home.

The night was cold and dry, the air still. Instead of panicking over the senator's decree, she had been filled with such energy by the challenge that it was as if she were riding on the crest of a great wave across the ocean, sure she would never topple off. Every sense—her hearing, sight, smell—was razor sharp. The two men who she was certain were responsible for her father's death wanted something from her, something, for once, they couldn't buy. She was the one the senator had come to. Now it was up to her to measure up to the challenge, to defeat him at his own game.

"I had no idea till you told me yourself," Charley said.

She glanced at him, uncertain he was telling her the truth. "If both exchanges closed, the price of stocks would go down like a rock."

"I expect they would at that."

"People would lose thousands. The banks would cut the margin percentage. It could be disastrous."

"The prices are overheated. You'll have to admit that much."

She wasn't surprised at his defense of his bosses' proposal. "The senator claims the other exchange has agreed to it, but—"

He eyed her. "You don't believe him?"

"Let's say I'm suspicious."

They had reached the bottle house, and she handed him the key. "The point of your escorting me home has not escaped me, Charley."

He frowned.

"I know you were meant to soften me up before I talked to my board, so let me give you a message to take back."

He waited.

"If your employers think we cannot see behind the subterfuge of brotherly love to their real reason for wanting to shut us down, then they are mistaken."

"And that reason is what, Meg?"

"Oh, come now, Charley. It doesn't take a genius to understand that the senator and Mr. Winters will profit if the market is depressed."

"I don't see that at all," he said, inserting the key, turning it in the lock, starting to open the door. "It's one for all and all for—"

He glanced down. "Here now. Looks like someone sent you a telegram." He stooped, picked up an envelope, handed it to her.

"Wait a minute. I'll light the lamp," he said.

"Thank you." She wondered if it was a message from Bill.

She waited in the doorway until a soft glow of light filled the small room. She wished she hadn't been so short with Charley. He was just doing what he was told; a loyal employee, like her father. With the envelope in hand, she moved to the lamp, still wondering who would send a telegram on Christmas Eve.

She worked her thumb under the flap, pulled out the yellow sheet, and opened it.

MISS MEGGEN KENDALL
GENERAL DELIVERY
GOLDFIELD, NEVADA

HILARY KENDALL SUFFERED STROKE STOP HOLDING
HER OWN STOP
WILL BE IN TOUCH STOP GWENDOLYN PHILPOTT

Meg's heart stopped. She reread the telegram, placed it on the table. "My aunt's had a stroke."

Charley frowned. "Is there anything I can do?"

She stared at him, seeing her aunt, her weathered leather flat-brimmed cowboy hat over her white hair, hiking up mountain trails ahead of her, seldom even pausing to catch her breath, pointing out the scarlet paintbrush or delicate wild asters with the walking stick she'd carved years before. This was a woman Meg had always looked up to, depended on all her life. This was not a woman who had a stroke.

"Is there anything I can do?" he repeated.

"Oh, no. Thank you. Mrs. Philpott says she's holding her own."

"Then I'll be leaving. If you change your mind, let me know."

As she closed the door behind him, it occurred to her Charley had been at her side when she'd buried her father. Now her aunt might be about to die. Meg pulled in a deep breath and tried to push away the possibility.

She'd intended to write to Aunt Hilary tonight. It had been weeks since she'd sent a letter, almost as long since she'd received one. Her aunt continued to make it plain she didn't approve of Meg's decision to stay in Goldfield. As an English teacher, Aunt Hilary had a way with words that, if she chose, could cut right to the heart.

Meg remembered when she'd first come to live in Boulder, she'd disobeyed her aunt and torn her one good dress, playing mumblety-peg with the boy up the street. When Aunt Hilary discovered what had happened, she'd sat Meg down on the back step and given her the scolding of her life. That night, Meg had crawled into bed and cried herself to sleep, praying her mother would miraculously come down from heaven and save her. Her aunt could be a stern taskmaster, yet—

For some crazy reason, Meg wondered if Mrs. Philpott would still give her traditional Christmas day reception. It was always the same. Cold, rare roast beef, sliced wafer thin, on tiny rounds of rye bread, Brie cheese and crackers, sherry. Aunt Hilary was always invited. In a university town, the genteel poor like Meg and Aunt Hilary were generally accepted as equals to the lawyers, bank presidents, and doctors. Everyone would politely pretend not to notice Aunt Hilary wore the same hunter green silk she'd worn for years. Everyone but Aunt Hilary.

Meg had planned that as soon as she sold her stock, she would write to Mr. Meckley at Boulder's First National about setting up a sizable trust for her aunt. And she wanted to buy the house she'd lived in for twenty years but her aunt couldn't afford to buy. A woman owning a house was important. No matter what, Aunt Hilary would have a place of her own.

Based on today's bid price, Meg's ten thousand shares of Fourth of July would bring nearly a hundred thousand dollars. Half of that would be for Aunt Hilary's benefit. Yet it might be too late.

She had been too late for her father. Yet in a strange way, by coming to Goldfield after his death, she probably had grown to know him more fully than she ever had when he was alive, felt his love and energy within herself as she learned about herself. How ironic that the closeness she felt with her father, the new choices she'd made, had separated her further from her aunt, her only living family.

Absently, Meg removed her borrowed cloak, put it on the end of the cot. Only old people had strokes. Her aunt was sixty-three. A stroke could be incapacitating, and Aunt Hilary was a woman of such independence. Meg couldn't imagine her unable to teach and hike and do for herself.

Meg sat down heavily, her elbows on the table, her forehead in her hands. The telegram said Aunt Hilary was holding her own. Yet if her condition wasn't grave, why would Mrs. Philpott have sent word? Should she catch the morning train and go back to Boulder? But if she did, what good could she be? Bring her trays, read to her? It wouldn't be a day before Aunt Hilary would send her packing.

And there were also three other women counting on her. As a team, they had a chance at dreams that until they'd started the exchange had seemed unattainable. The scheme the senator wanted them to go along with could destroy everything. He'd already tried to divide the group by appealing only to her instead of to the entire board. If she left, he'd try to do it again.

John Burlingame was the president of the bank the senator controlled, so Emma would be the most vulnerable. It was hard to say who the senator would approach next, maybe Verna. Divide and conquer. That was the senator's ploy. Somehow, she had to prevent that from happening. Perhaps the thing to do was to wait until the telegraph office opened at dawn, contact Mrs. Philpott first for the latest news about Aunt Hilary, then decide.

Heavyhearted, Meg unhooked the bodice of Tess's gown, carefully pulled it over her head and, with shaking hands, spread it over the back of the chair. She had a duty to Aunt Hilary. Her friends depended on her. God in heaven, how could she possibly be in two places at once?

CHAPTER 23

*S*orry, boys," Vic said, pointing to the clock over the bar, both hands pointing straight up. "We're closing down. It's Christmas."

"So what?" a man grumbled as he shuffled past Tess, who was holding open the door.

Tess had asked the same question when Vic had suggested they shut down Christmas day in honor of the Christ Child's birthday. Religion had never been part of her life. She'd seen a few pictures in books of Baby Jesus with his mother and father and a few animals in a stable, fellahs in turbans and capes kneeling before him. She liked the picture all right, but Christmas and the birth of Jesus, brotherly love, all that kind of thing, had no meaning for her.

After the last customer had stepped out the door, most to return to a frigid tent, she locked the door, turned off the lights over the gaming tables, and began to lift the chairs up on the tabletops to make way for the floors to get a good scrubbing in the morning. It seemed quieter than usual outside, maybe because the stamp mills were silent.

As she put up the last chair and Vic returned to the bar to gather the glasses, she realized she wasn't ready to call it a night.

"How about if I make us some coffee and put out some of the fruit cake Mrs. Archibald sent over?" she asked Vic.

"Sounds good to me. I'll be with you in a few minutes."

In the kitchen, she was just tying on her apron when she heard Teddy's sharp bark. Someone, probably a drunk, was at the front door. Vic would take care of it. She scooped out lumps of coal, dropped them into the stove's firebox, slammed the door shut.

Vic called to her. He sounded alarmed, which wasn't like him, and she hurried back into the saloon.

In the dim light of the high-ceilinged room, she saw Vic by the door, talking to someone, then realized it was Bill Brown. From here, it looked like he was holding a child in his arms. At the sound of her footsteps, Vic came toward her, took her arm.

"It's Jenny Lynn, Tess. But she's okay. Bill found her in the waiting room at the Tonopah depot."

Tess stared at him wide-eyed for an instant, trying to understand what he'd told her, then rushed to Bill and the child in his arms.

"She's fast asleep," Bill said in a near-whisper. "I was picking up freight at the Tonopah depot, and the stationmaster told me a little girl had come in on the last train but nobody had met her. If it hadn't been for the tag with your name on it, pinned on her coat—"

"There was a tag on Jenny Lynn?" Tess asked, feeling tears running down her cheeks as she reached for her daughter, pale, cheeks smudged, hair disheveled.

"That she made it here from Colorado Springs with no address and just your name is nothing short of a miracle, if you ask me," Bill said, stepping back toward the door.

"How can I ever thank you?" Tess said.

"I'm just glad I was the one who found her."

Tess glanced at Vic. "See if Bill needs a drink of anythin', will you? I'm takin' Jenny Lynn up to bed."

By the time Vic came upstairs, Tess had removed Jenny Lynn's worn, high-topped shoes, their soles with holes as big as fifty-cent pieces, and covered her with a quilt.

Standing next to Vic at the end of the bed, Tess gazed down at her daughter and started to cry. "Look at her, Vic. There's no meat on her. She's like a little bundle of sticks."

Vic put an arm around Tess's shoulders. "Maybe we ought to go downstairs, let her sleep."

Tess sniffed, rubbed away the tears with the back of her hands. "I can't leave her."

"There's nothing to worry about. She's safe now."

"But if she wakes up, she won't know where she is. She'll be frightened."

"Okay. Stay."

Tess glanced at him. "What if she caught somethin', Vic? I couldn't stand it if anythin' happened to her."

He gave Tess's shoulders a squeeze. "She'll be fine. She's with you now."

Tess shifted her gaze to her sleeping daughter. It had been almost a year since Tess had told her she had taken a job in a traveling vaudeville show to make them enough money for the ranch. When Jenny Lynn woke up and saw she was above a saloon, she'd know her mother had lied to her. "Vic, what am I goin' to do? Jenny Lynn thinks I'm an actress."

"She doesn't care what you are, Tess. You're her mother." Vic took her arm, started to lead her to the high-backed rocker in the corner. "Sit. You can see Jenny Lynn fine from here. Sleep a little, if you can. I'll be downstairs if you need me."

Tess glanced at him uncertainly. "Maybe if I bring it up closer."

Finally, the rocker next to the bed, she sat down, her hands gripping the armrests, and Vic tiptoed out of the room.

After a few minutes, she let herself sit back. The Briggles must have turned her out. The thought made Tess's blood boil. By some miracle, like Bill had said, Jenny Lynn had made it here, safe. Tess thought of her stock. There wasn't quite enough, but if the Red Top went up to six next week, she'd sell it and have enough to leave.

Tess took in a long breath, relaxed a little, and began to rock.

The steady motion was soothing, and she felt herself growing sleepy. Outside, some drunks were singing Christmas carols, and she thought of the pictures of Baby Jesus in the manger again, remembered tales his birth had been a miracle. With half-closed eyes, Tess studied the sleeping little girl. Jenny Lynn was skinnier and bigger, but there was no doubt in the world she had the same sweet expression as the Christ child in those pictures. A mother could see the resemblance.

This was the child of her heart. What kind of a mother was she to leave Jenny Lynn alone, defenseless in a world that didn't give a damn about her? Tess had made a promise to herself the day Jenny Lynn was born that she would do anything, go anywhere, to make certain her daughter had the kind of life she'd never had. And look what she'd done. Good intentions didn't count. She'd abandoned her daughter, left her in a place where she wasn't loved and, as it turned out, in terrible danger. Of all the people in the world, Tess knew what it was like to be young and alone.

God or somebody had been looking after Jenny Lynn, had given Tess another chance to do the right thing. Tess wiped away her tears with the back of her hands, closed her eyes. A moment later she was asleep.

CHAPTER 24

Verna put a shovelful of coal in the feed box of the heater, lit a match to the tinder, and closed the door. Straightening, she hugged herself against the cold. It would take a while before the room heated up. Maybe she'd go back to bed, then she remembered it was Christmas.

She padded in her bedroom slippers over to the front window, pushed her glasses up her nose, and peered up into the gray sky of early morning. It even looked cold today. She glanced up and down the street, saw only one rider and a freight wagon. The boardwalks were nearly empty. Not much doing. Probably because of the strike or because it was Christmas, but she doubted it.

Verna went back to the heater, adjusted the draft. It was beginning to heat nicely. She decided to tidy the place up and get dressed, then fix herself a little breakfast. After that she'd go calling to deliver her presents, such as they were.

She ducked back through the curtain and, to her astonishment, saw Meg peering through the window at her. Instinctively, Verna adjusted her robe around her, tightened its chord, wishing now she hadn't put off dressing.

"Merry Christmas," she said as she pulled the door open and Meg stepped inside.

"I'm on my way to the telegraph office," Meg said, grimly.

"What's wrong?"

Meg told her about her aunt. "I don't really know how bad the stroke is. I'd go to Boulder in a minute, but with Nolan wanting us to close down—"

"Shut down the exchange?"

Meg nodded. "He cornered me at the party last night and wanted me to make a decision then and there. Of course, I said there'd have to be a meeting of our board to make a decision like that."

"Why didn't you just say no?"

"I guess I could have, but he said the Mining Stock Exchange had already agreed to close. If that's true, I'm not sure we could hold our own. He's going to send a messenger for our answer at noon."

Verna regarded Meg with amazement. How anyone at her young age could be so collected, in spite of everything, was a wonder.

"He may just have to wait," Verna said, pulling herself together. "I'll go tell Emma and Tess. They'll probably want to meet as soon as possible. Where will I look for you?"

"The telegraph office, I guess," Meg said. "No, wait—"

For the first time Verna picked up the sound of a Meg in distress. "I'll send Jimmy to get you at your house."

*   *   *

Panting to catch her breath, Verna gave the Burlingames' front bell a firm twist. She could see lights through the frosted glass of the front door, a good sign they were up. She stamped her feet impatiently in the early morning cold. She was about to ring the bell again when the door opened.

Still in her bathrobe, Emma peered out at her, an anxious look on her face. "Oh, Verna. I'm glad you came. Come in."

"I apologize for the early hour."

Emma stepped back and motioned for her to come inside. "I take it you heard about the senator's proposal?"

"That's why I'm here. Meg stopped on the way to the telegraph office. She asked me to talk to you and Tess."

"Is something wrong with Meg?"

Verna explained as much as she knew about Meg's aunt. "Whether she goes to Colorado or not depends on what she learns when she hears back from her aunt's friend."

Emma shook her head, her forehead wrinkled into a deep frown. "Duty never fails to call at the most inconvenient times."

"Isn't that the truth?" Verna glanced about to make sure John Burlingame was out of earshot. "What does Mr. Burlingame think of all this business about shutting down?"

"The man's under a terrible strain. Doesn't know whether he's afoot or on horseback."

"I can imagine."

"The senator and Mr. Winters have a right, of course, to set policy for the bank. And, as the president, he must carry it out."

Verna folded her arms over her bosom, nodded. "Good old duty again."

Emma sighed deeply. Verna had never seen her so dejected.

"But isn't there a chance the Mining Stock Exchange board might figure it was worth risking their wrath to stay open?"

Emma eyed her. "That's what Mr. Burlingame is hoping for."

"When will the matter be decided?"

"Ten o'clock. At the Montezuma Club," Emma said.

"Not exactly what the gents had planned on doing Christmas morning, I'd guess. But then, in Goldfield, nothing runs according to the usual schedule."

Emma looked at Verna speculatively. "If the men decide to suspend operations, we can't really stay open. Can we?"

"There's no law against it if we did. Least not as far as I know. Whether it's a good idea is another question."

"What do you think Tess will say when she hears?"

Verna gave a little laugh. "It won't be fit for ladies' ears, I can tell you that much."

Emma chuckled. "Let's meet at the exchange at noon."

Verna shrugged. "Anytime is fine, as long as we decide, up or down."

* * *

Squinting in the midwinter sun, Verna hurried across town to the Ajax Saloon to let Tess know about the meeting. The events of the morning so far depressed her. On the surface, a person might think shutting down the exchange would make little difference to her. Her needs were simple. Yet the thousand dollars she'd hidden beneath the coal bucket next to her heater wasn't enough to keep her out of the poorhouse for long. Tess and Meg had even bigger dreams they wanted to make good on. For Emma, the exchange had to do with her independence.

Winters and Nolan knew all too well the San Francisco exchange, the New York Curb, Chicago—all looked to the Goldfield exchanges as the harbingers of the general health of the camp's mining operations.

Her own problem was Amos, as it always was. She had no idea how much Amos had borrowed on the little stock he owned. But if the market crashed, he'd beg her to lend him enough to cover his debts. Before she could even blink, her thousand dollars would disappear like smoke. And the senator and Winters would step in and buy his stock and everyone else's stock that had to be sold at a loss for a song. They'd have virtual control of the Goldfield market.

This afternoon when it came time to decide whether to shut down, she was going to vote "no."

* * *

The Ajax was closed when Verna stopped by, and she went to the back door, thinking she might find Cookie, only to be greeted by Vic. His gray hair disheveled, it was plain she'd wakened him. He explained about Jenny Lynn's dramatic appearance. Both she and Tess were still asleep upstairs. Verna left the message about the meeting at noon.

On her way back to the *Star*, Verna noted that, like every other mining camp where she'd lived, the saloons and dance halls she passed were going great guns. Men seemed to drink earlier and heavier on Christmas. Fights invariably broke out. Over the years, she'd made it a practice to stay off the streets that day, which made her wonder about the wisdom of wandering around town now.

To her, Christmas was not what the storybooks would have a person believe. Growing up in the back of the sutler's place in Fort Kearney, it had been like any other day. If there really was a jolly old Saint Nick, he'd always missed paying a call on her and Amos.

She wondered what Amos was doing today. She'd expected a letter. No, she hadn't expected a letter. She'd hoped for a letter. Amos hadn't even sent one of his frantic telegrams for a month or more. He could be sick. He could've moved on, though she doubted it. Her brother wasn't much but he was pretty good at letting her know his whereabouts.

Her thoughts returned to the possibility of his being sick. He could have the croup. Ever since that terrible winter in 1873 in Denver when they'd had to live in that shack by the Platte, he'd had a weakness in the chest. Mustard plasters helped. Trouble was he wouldn't fix them himself.

By the time she unlocked her door, her spirits were lower than they had been in months. She was ashamed she'd let herself get so down in the dumps. She unpinned her hat. Maybe if she fixed something to eat, made a fresh pot of coffee . . . Her gaze fell on the string bag, holding the few presents she'd bought for the Earnest children. She'd deliberately set it out on the table last night as a reminder to take it to them first thing. And here it was nearly noon. Seeing their happy faces was bound to improve her disposition. She repinned her hat, picked up the string bag, and set off again.

But when she reached the Earnests' tar paper–covered tent, no one answered her knock. No smoke came from the stovepipe.

There were no sounds of children's high voices. As she placed the string bag by the door, she wondered if it was worth the risk to leave it. She'd picked out a red knit cap for baby Mikey, a little doll with a real china head for Mary Lou, and two of those new naval-blue hill box kites for Jimmy. She didn't want them stolen.

Originally, she'd had her eyes on the Eclipse tricycle wagon she'd seen advertised in the Sears catalog for Jimmy. It was supposed to be the latest thing, its body made of sheet steel and painted bright red with gold trim. The lock corner handle could be used to pull or steer the wagon. Jimmy could give his sister and brother a ride at the same time. The four-dollar price, however, was a little steep.

Cross with herself that she hadn't come sooner, Verna started back down the hill, the string bag and its contents still under one arm, when she heard a woman's voice calling her. "Heh, lady!"

Verna glanced around and saw a tired-looking woman wiping her hands on a filthy apron, in the doorway of a neighboring tent.

"If you're lookin' for Miz Earnest and the kids, they're at the union hall."

Verna nodded, smiled her thanks. The only reason a miner's wife and children would be at the union hall was for a free bowl of soup. Strike pay didn't go far in Goldfield. Verna thought of Mrs. Earnest and her fierce pride and knew the woman had to be desperate to take a union handout. She probably told herself her husband had earned it with his union dues, which would be true. Yet a bowl of watery soup was not what any mother wanted for a Christmas dinner for her family. A woman's spirit could be crushed by such things.

Verna glanced down at the packages in the bag, walked over to the woman. "I came to bring some presents for the children. I don't want to leave them in the doorway. I was wondering if you'd see they got them."

The woman tucked stray locks of mousy-brown hair behind her ears. "Will they know who brought 'em?"

"Do you think they'd believe the Christmas elves?"

She and the woman exchanged smiles.

"If they don't, they should," the woman said.

"Then the Christmas elves it is," Verna said, and she handed the bag to her.

As she trudged back down the hill, Verna grew disgruntled and out of sorts again. Swallowing disappointments with a cheery face had become a way of life. You learn to make do, some old lady had told her once when she'd been a little girl, and Verna had. Yet why should the Earnest family have to go to the union hall and take handouts, instead being at home with a full larder?

Though mining camps had never been kind to women and children, it seemed to her Goldfield was the worst. After the giant merger, when the Goldfield Consolidated Mines Company had been created, the senator and Winters had all but eliminated the practice of high-grading. The other owners had followed suit. Once the working stiffs were closed off from the chance to make more than wages, the union had decided to retaliate and deliberately called a strike two weeks before the leasing deadline. Never mind that Christmas occurred at the same time. The strike, the merger, all of it was about money, about power. Not about families. If a man wanted to bring his wife and kids with him to Goldfield, that was his lookout. It was a matter of business, the way the world worked.

The Bible said something about "suffer the little children." And they certainly did. She, for one, was sick of it. It was high time those responsible be held accountable. Neither the companies nor the union had paid any attention to her earlier editorials, so there was no reason to believe they would now. Still, there was something to be said for the squeaky wheel principle. Right after the meeting this afternoon, she was going to sit down and give Goldfield a piece of her mind.

CHAPTER 25

$\mathcal{M}$eg gave Emma and Verna each a hug as they left the exchange. Fearful of leaving her daughter after the harrowing journey from Colorado Springs, Tess had sent over her proxy. The senator hadn't even bothered to put any further pressure on them. Apparently, he'd thought they were just a bunch of stupid women who couldn't figure out his scheme, but he was wrong. After only a few minutes of discussion, they'd taken the vote. The final tally: four to nothing in favor of staying open.

Earlier, the Mining Stock Exchange had sent word that they, too, had decided not to close. Meg was pleasantly surprised. Tomorrow both exchanges would be ready for business as usual.

The last order of business before she left was to write the senator and Mr. Winters an official letter informing them of the decision. She walked back to the table and sat down. Reaching for pen and ink, she felt the warmth of the early afternoon sun streaming through the nearby window soak through the thin wool of her traveling suit. In her skirt pocket was the latest telegram Mrs. Philpott had sent this morning. Her aunt's condition hadn't changed. Meg planned to take the afternoon train to Tonopah, then on to Salt Lake City and Denver, finally catching the Interurban to Boulder. If she made all her connections, she should make the trip in two days.

She dipped the pen in the ink, tapped off the excess, and wrote a short note, stating the proposal to suspend operations of the ladies' exchange had been duly considered and rejected. As she pressed a piece of blotter paper over her signature, she heard the front door slam, a man's voice she recognized as Bill's calling out a hearty merry Christmas to someone at the restaurant, the sound of boots hitting the worn wood steps, taking them two at a time. In the back of her head she'd been expecting him for hours, but now that he was here she still wasn't ready to say good-bye before he set off for San Francisco.

Day before yesterday, he'd walked her home from the exchange and told her of his decision.

"The strike's to blame. Even the freight business is down," he'd said. "A guy by the name of George Cleats offered me cash for the whole caboodle. I couldn't turn it down."

She'd glanced up at him, already missing him. "I suppose not."

"With a break in the weather, I figure I better get going."

But she didn't want him to leave, not now. When she returned to Goldfield from Boulder, she wanted to feel the comfort of his arms around her, to laugh at his jokes again. She knew it was selfish. He had his own dreams. She'd known his plans for two months. Occasionally, they'd joked about her part in those plans, how once he returned from the cross-country race and had time to look into likely locations for a garage large enough to display automobiles, she'd be ready to sell her seat on the exchange here and join him. She'd rent a room until she found a house, then order the automobiles Bill recommended, hire mechanics, and open for business. It was all said lightly, in fun. To take the matter seriously, they might have to face the consequences of how they felt about each other.

Meg returned the pen to the holder, drew in a deep breath. An instant later, Bill appeared through the doorway.

Hatless, wearing a hip-length leather jacket over his jodhpurs, a red plaid scarf around his neck, he smiled when he saw her. "Merry Christmas."

"Merry Christmas to you."

As he stepped into the room, he nearly fell over her valise, and it tipped over. He picked it up, propped it against the wall by the door. "What's this?"

She told him about Aunt Hilary.

"I'm sorry. I imagine it'll mean a lot to her to have you there." She smiled up at him.

"I ran into Verna on the way over here. She told me about your decision." He chuckled. "Very soon, Winters and Nolan will be two very unhappy men."

"I hope so."

An expectant silence hung in the air.

"Say, I almost forgot." He pulled a slim package wrapped in brown paper and string out of a jacket pocket, and handed it to her. "For you."

"Oh, no."

He grinned. "Oh, no? You haven't even seen what it is."

"It's just that I realized your present is still on top of my chiffonnier."

"You can send it to me."

"It's gloves. I thought you could use them on your trip."

"They'll be even better for the cross-country tour."

They looked at each other for a moment without speaking. "So you're really going?"

"With any luck, I'll make the twenty miles to Beatty by dark."

"It shouldn't be a bad trip as long as you stay on the road."

They smiled, sharing the memories of punctured tires, forays along dry creek beds.

He pulled up a nearby chair, swung it around to sit on it backward. Resting his folded arms across the top of the ladder-back, he looked at the package in her hands. "Aren't you going to open it?"

"I wish I hadn't forgotten yours." She could feel him watching her as she worked the string off the package. Folding back the paper, she saw a red leather-bound book. Across the front, embossed in gold, was the title, KIM, and the author's name, Rudyard Kipling.

"Have you read it?"

She shook her head. Fighting back tears, not daring to look at him, she concentrated on the book cover. "I've wanted to."

"First, I thought of some of his poetry, but then I saw this and—"

She raised her eyes and saw the gold flecks in his dark eyes.

"Remember me when you read it."

She pulled in a breath, heard its ragged edge. If she wasn't careful she might cry and she didn't want to do that. If she let her feelings take over, even in tears, she was afraid they would sweep her away, pull her off course, that she would forget who she was, how essential her freedom was.

He stood up, leaned over, and took the book from her. Pulling her to her feet, he guided her around the table into his arms, holding her against him, then kissing her deeply, and something stirred inside her. She kissed him back with a kind of savageness, biting at his lips, thrusting her tongue into his mouth, feeling his in hers until, suddenly, as frantically and quickly as it began, it was over, and they stepped away from each other.

"Did anyone ever tell you how well you kiss?" she asked, her heart still pounding.

He smiled down at her, refusing to play her game, fished into his pocket, drew out a scrap of paper, and handed it to her. "It's my cousin's address."

The paper clutched in her hand, she stared up at him, her heart too full to think of anything else to say. Finally, she glanced at the clock to the right of the board still filled with prices now two days out-of-date. It was nearly two. "Would you mind giving me a lift to the depot?"

"Just say the word."

"I still need to get our letter to the senator to his office at the John Cook Bank."

"I'll drop it off on my way out of town."

"Well." She gathered her notebook, the few papers Verna and Emma had left behind, the pen and inkwell, and put them in the large bottom drawer of the cashier's desk reserved for executive committee documents. Bill picked up her valise. "Ready?"

She folded the letter to the senator and inserted it in the envelope. "Ready."

* * *

The engine of the afternoon train to Tonopah belched steam. The door to the mail car yawned, waiting for baggage. Aside from the single passenger car, the others were freight cars loaded with ore. Men with rifles cradled in their arms stood guard.

"I've meant to ask you what kind of automobile you plan to buy," she said, desperate for conversation as Bill pulled up to the depot.

He shrugged. "What color do you think it should be?"

She studied his profile. Until this instant, she'd never noticed the bump, perhaps the result of a fight, just below the bridge of his nose. "I didn't know there was a choice."

"There is if you paint the machine yourself."

She gave a little laugh. "Red, I think. I had a bright red sled called the Red Flyer when I was little." She could see it, see her friend, Johnny Phillips, his orange stocking cap pulled down so low it nearly covered his eyes. She remembered sitting behind him, arms around his waist as they flew down the snow-covered hill high over Boulder, confident nothing bad could possibly happen to her with Johnny at the helm. When Johnny had moved away, it had nearly broken her heart. Now, sitting beside Bill, the same feelings filled her heart.

"Red it is then."

He shifted the gears to neutral, pulled back on the brake.

"Drive carefully," she said.

"Always."

"No side roads."

He laughed. "Only when absolutely necessary."

They climbed out of his cutdown automobile. Every time she saw a machine like it she would remember the first day they'd met, how hot it had been, how he'd driven her to the Mohawk Mines Company. Bill lifted her valise out of the backseat and followed Meg to the ticket window, where she purchased a ticket straight through to Denver, though she would have at least three changes in between.

The engine's whistle screeched; steam whooshed from between the wheels of the cars; the conductor in a dust-caked black jacket and flat brimmed cap beckoned for her to get on. Still carrying her valise, Bill helped her up the steep steps, saw her inside.

Glancing about the empty car, she chose a window seat. Bill shoved her valise into the overhead rack.

"All aboard!" shouted the conductor outside.

Bill bent down and kissed her lightly. She smiled, looked away to hide her tears. A moment later, he was gone.

CHAPTER 26

*T*ess poured a shot of bourbon and slid the stubby glass down the bar. The mood of the customers at the Ajax was dour, not good for business on a New Year's eve. Tess went to the window and watched her daughter skip rope, relieved that the long, cold trip from Colorado Springs hadn't seemed to have done her any harm.

It warmed Tess's heart to see her every day, to be able to tuck her into bed each night. Yet the fact remained that Goldfield wasn't a fit place for a child, particularly a little girl. Plainly, her daughter's unexpected arrival had changed Tess's timetable about leaving.

The child's pale-brown braids, tied with large pink ribbons, flopped rhythmically against her back. Her high sweet voice chanted a rhyme: "One a-button, two a-button, three a-button, four . . ."

Three men with thick beards, in miner's coats, came up and said something to Jenny Lynn, and she stopped, smiling up at them in that eager way she had with everyone. Instantly, Tess was out the door.

"Jenny Lynn, come inside, baby."

"I'm jumpin' rope, Mama."

"I can see that, baby, but it's gettin' cold out."

"Oh, Mama—"

"Do as I say, Jenny Lynn. Right now."

Her daughter's large blue eyes gazed at her, pleading and sad as Teddy's when he was scolded. It broke Tess's heart to speak harshly to her, but she couldn't be too careful with all the bad types passing the Ajax.

Jenny Lynn came slowly through the door, not looking at Tess, the skip rope dragging on the floor behind her.

"They were nice men, Mama. They said they liked my song."

Tess hugged her daughter to her, kissed the top of her hair, feeling its softness, smelling the rose scent Tess had rinsed it in. "I'm sure they did. It's just that after your big trip, I don't want you over-doin' it."

Tess felt Vic's level look, and she glanced over at the bar. "Don't you have nothin' better to do than listen in on my conversations?"

Without replying, he unscrewed the top of a beer bottle, slid it to the only customer at the bar, who took it with him to one of the faro tables. Tess squatted down in front of her daughter. "I'll bet if you go back to the kitchen Cookie has somethin' good for you."

"Hot chocolate?"

"Could be. You better go see." Tess gave Jenny Lynn a gentle swat on her behind, and the little girl skipped through the maze of tables, smiling at the few customers, and disappeared down the narrow hallway.

Tess stepped behind the bar. "Jenny Lynn is my kid and she does what I tell her."

Vic arched an eyebrow.

"Seein' those bums out there tells me I've gotta go."

"Now?"

"I know it's sudden, and I'm sorry to leave you in the lurch. But I can't have Jenny Lynn stayin' here—not in the saloon, not in Goldfield."

"What are you going to use for money to live on?" Vic pulled a stool up close to her and sat down.

"I've got my stocks. At yesterday's prices I figure I can cash in at about three thousand. Add that to my half of this place, which should be about a thousand—"

"A saloon doesn't sell like a share of mining stock."

"Sure, I know."

In the past any talk about breaking up their partnership had been in fun. But today she caught a pleading tone beneath Vic's words, and his eyes held such a soulful look it made her feel bad.

"Listen, once the strike's over, business will be up strong as ever," she said. "You'll have another partner inside a month."

"What if I don't want another partner."

"Well, hell, you wouldn't have to have one. That's up to you. If you went solo, you'd be the only boss, without me to give you fits every time you wanted to do somethin'."

"I don't want you to go, Tess." His voice was husky, barely above a whisper.

She met his gaze, saw the desire. She'd grown up with men who lusted after her, like Jake. What she saw in Vic's eyes was different, loving. She smiled at him affectionately, anxious not to hurt his feelings.

"I mean you should use your head. Winter's no time to start up a ranch."

"You're right there."

"So stay."

She tried to explain. "Jenny Lynn and me are goin' to rent a room in Steamboat till spring. She can go to school like regular kids."

"There's a school here in town."

"I know, but I have to go," Tess said as gently as she could. "I'll sign the place over to you and you can send me the money when you can."

*   *   *

Later that night as she gave a final tuck to Jenny Lynn's bedcovers, Tess thought about Vic's reaction to her decision to leave. She wasn't really surprised. They'd worked together every day for nearly nine months. But she'd never thought of Vic as anything but just dependable Vic, always there when she needed him. She had never imagined the feel of his weight on her, of him thrust inside her. He was a good and wonderful friend, whom she'd miss very much, but nothing more.

The laughter and tinny piano from below were signs business was picking up again. Vic would need her help downstairs. She went over to the mirror above the chiffonnier to check her appearance, and started at the reflection of Jake, standing behind her in the doorway. She spun around, held a finger to her lips.

"Touching little scene with the kid just now."

"Shush," she whispered, pushing him out of the room and closing the door. "You got your nerve, comin' up here to my rooms, uninvited."

His smile spread, revealing his sparkling white teeth. "How much cash do you have?"

A flash of anger erupted inside her. "I haven't seen you in weeks, and you ask me for money again." She shoved past him toward the head of the stairs, but he caught her wrist and stopped her.

"Whatever you've got will do."

"The answer was no before. It's still no."

"Sign over your stock then."

"Jenny Lynn and I are leavin' by the end of the week. That stock is our seed money."

Their eyes met. He seemed to be studying her as he slowly rubbed the back of his neck. "Okay."

She eyed him, suspicious. It was not like him to give in.

"But don't go think I'm not throwing in the towel."

"Where'll you get the money?" she couldn't help asking.

He chucked her under the chin, ignoring her question. "If anyone asks, say I'm just going to stay out of circulation for a while."

"You're a fool if you come back to Goldfield."

He shrugged, flashing that grin that had melted her heart so many times. "I've had a good run here."

For an instant, she almost felt sorry for him. She reached up and put her arms around his neck, pulled him toward her so she could kiss him. The man was a charming sonofabitch. She almost hated to see him go.

CHAPTER 27

Verna frowned as she watched Jimmy hoist a bundle of papers up on one shoulder and stagger out the door into the biting cold. He'd come to work every day. Yet not till today had she noticed how thin he was, all bones. Pale as a ghost except for the flush of his cheeks. She suspected he might be sick. Though his father was back at work, which meant more money for food and coal, the weeks of doing without had already taken their toll.

She sighed, closed the door. The room suddenly seemed cold. A fresh, hot cup of coffee would taste good. She walked back to the stove and saw she needed to refill the supply tank with coal oil. The advertisement for the stove had assured customers the process was so simple a child could do it, which was true. What they had forgotten to mention was the weight of a can of coal oil. At the moment, she didn't want to struggle with it. She went over to the table by the window where she had put the one letter that had been waiting for her at the post office this morning.

The waning day outside held the transparent brightness of January. The wind caught bits of garbage and trash, tossing them through the air. She glanced down at the envelope before her. Even with her poor eyesight, she recognized Amos's handwriting. She'd been expecting it for months.

Working her thumb under the flap, she pried the envelope open and removed the single sheet of white, lined paper, like a schoolboy's. She unfolded it, reached in her skirt pocket for her glasses, and put them on.

> *Dear Sister,*
> *Hope you are well. I am the same.*

She raised her eyes from the paper, envisioning her brother hunched over the sheet, trying not to blot the paper. Schoolwork had never been one of his interests. Thinking of it, she wasn't sure what his interests were except being part of the newest adventure. Stable and dependable he was not. But, shoot, the enticement of whatever lay beyond the next hill filled the world's storybooks. Who was she to criticize? She adjusted her glasses, read on.

> *Bullfrog goes poorly lately. Water is scarce. The mines find*
> *operation hard. I am told of new action outside Tucson. I*
> *believe that is where I will go within the week.*
> *Your brother, Amos Bates.*

Verna reread the words and gave a rueful smile. What did she know about Tucson? She closed her eyes, picturing the nation's map, recalling the location, south of Nevada, close to the border with Mexico. From what she'd read, it was desert, like Goldfield. The prospect of moving there held no appeal.

The dry air, the relatively mild temperatures were fine. But, dear Lord, the gray expanses of nothing, the harshness, the unrelenting wind and sand, with not a green tree or grass, was more than her aging soul could take. She did not think she'd go to Tucson, or anyplace near it. She stood, amazed at what she'd decided.

Amos Bates would have to do for himself without her. She frowned. Could he? He'd always maintained he could, but then came the frantic telegrams for funds. He'd never actually asked her to follow him, she realized. That was her doing, and now it was time to cease. If a man at fifty-eight couldn't conduct his life responsibly, there was no hope for him. Nothing she could do would change it.

She sighed, took a sip of the cold coffee. Slowly, it began to occur to her that for the first time in her life she could do what she wanted, when she wanted. She was free of Amos.

She rose, stared around the room, astonished at the realization. She could go to Zamboanga, and who would care? She chuckled, picturing herself on a Pacific island amid half-clothed natives. Or she might go to England instead. Bates was a good English name. She might trace where the family came from. The four thousand dollars in the John Cook Bank would pay the fare and then some. Before she went blind, she'd be able to see all the places she'd read about.

Just then, out of the window, she caught sight of a large man whom she recognized as one of the deputy sheriffs. Like the others, he was an aging, has-been gunfighter, trading on his meager reputation. Slung over one shoulder was a small man, no larger than a boy. The deputy strode across the street. To her surprise, she realized he was heading her way.

Amos immediately flashed into her mind, but Amos was twice the size of the man the deputy was carrying. Curious and apprehensive all at once, she went to the door. The instant she opened it, the deputy stepped inside. Verna glanced at the limp form over his shoulder. Without even looking at the face, she knew it was Jimmy Earnest. She was sure he was dead.

CHAPTER 28

$\mathcal{M}$eg stepped off the 12:02 train from Salt Lake City, flagged a redcap, pointed out her valise, and followed him along the crowded platform toward the nearest entrance to Denver's Union Station.

The January day was clear and cold, the air crisp. She ached from the hours of sitting and looked forward to the short walk to the Interurban Station where she'd catch a train to Boulder. She had sent a telegram from Salt Lake to Mrs. Philpott, telling of her approximate arrival time.

Meg made her way along the marble floors, past the rows of high-backed benches of gleaming, dark wood filled with waiting passengers, out through the huge entrance doors. The redcap offered to call her a cab, but she refused, tipped him, and took her valise.

Directly in front of her, she saw the familiar wrought iron gateway with its huge WELCOME sign, arched over the bottom of Seventeenth Street. A web of telephone wires crisscrossed the air above the street clogged with freight wagons and automobiles, a few carriages. She felt a little like the country mouse who had come to visit her city cousin. Only instead of a city cousin, she had come to visit an aunt who might or might not still be alive.

* * *

Meg was panting by the time she reached Mrs. Philpott's house on the crest of Mapleton Hill. Mounting the stairs to the broad porch, Meg put down her valise and tried to catch her breath. The porch wrapped around one side of the pale brick house. The far end had a magnificent view of the side gardens of the house and the sandstone flatirons looming beyond. Furnished with white rattan chairs and lounges in the summer, the small space had been screened against the mosquitos all Boulder claimed didn't exist. It was there on August afternoons before she'd entered high school where she had sat listening to Aunt Hilary and Mrs. Philpott plan her career in medicine.

Meg approached the massive front door with its etched glass oval framed by gleaming mahogany, pushed the bell, and waited. A moment later the door opened and Rosie, who had worked for Mrs. Philpott for years, greeted her with only a cold stare.

"Hello, Rosie," Meg said brightly.

"Mrs. Philpott thought it was you ringin'." The maid reached for Meg's valise. "You're to go into the library."

Meg was puzzled at Rosie's abrupt reception. "How's Aunt Hilary?" she asked as she stepped into the large front hall.

Rosie shrugged, put down her valise by the door. "I'm sure you'll be needin' to ask Mrs. Philpott about that. I'm to bring tea." With a wave of her hand toward the library, she turned her back and walked toward the pantry and the kitchen beyond.

Meg glanced about the familiar hallway, up the stairs. She wondered if it was only her imagination, but she felt a decided chill in the air. Rosie, who'd always been so friendly, seemed angry. Meg suspected she was merely reflecting the tension of the last few days over Aunt Hilary's stroke.

With a sense of trepidation, Meg went into the library, where she'd spent so many wonderful hours in her growing-up years. Unlike most libraries she'd been in where only matched sets of unread books were on display, this one was lined floor to ceiling with Mrs. Philpott's personal choices, each one carefully chosen and treasured. A large couch in the center of the room faced a fireplace and a crackling fire. Just behind the couch was a long table covered with a silk scarf, a Tiffany lamp, and more books. In front of it was a low table on which a tray with cups and saucers, and a plate of little cakes had been placed. An Oriental rug, its patterns in shades of blue and burgundy, covered the oak floor. Normally so inviting, the room now held a sense of foreboding.

Meg heard firm footsteps descending the stairs, heels striking the polished floor of the hallway. A moment later Mrs. Philpott entered the room, bringing with her the scent of the lilac toilet water she always wore.

"My dear," she said, giving Meg a perfunctory peck on the cheek. The tone was cool.

"I can't thank you enough for telegraphing," Meg said. "I came as soon as I could."

The large-boned, older woman, dressed in a fashionable afternoon silk suit the color of claret wine, didn't reply. Tucking an errant strand of gray hair up into the knot on the top of her head, she took a seat on the far end of the couch, laid her hand on the cushion next to her. "Sit here where I can see you." It was a command, not a request.

Just then Rosie reappeared, bearing a silver teapot that she set down next to the cups. After she was gone, Mrs. Philpott leaned toward the low table in front of her, picked up the teapot, and turned to Meg. "Lemon?"

"Please."

"Take one of those cakes with the sesame seeds. They're one of Cook's specialties." Mrs. Philpott poured herself a cup of tea, sat back, and surveyed Meg.

"Hilary's been asking for you."

"How is she doing?"

"The stroke paralyzed her left side. Speech is a problem. It's hard to make out what she says."

"Will it be—permanent? The paralysis, I mean."

"Your aunt is a determined woman. And a brave one. Two qualities I have always admired."

Meg nodded, suddenly shaken by the intensity of Mrs. Philpott's love for her aunt. These two women had defied society by making their own way in the world. Both had been beauties in their youth. Meg knew Aunt Hilary had once been engaged to a distant cousin from Boston, that Mrs. Philpott had been briefly married to a charming gambler before she bullied him into a divorce. Aunt Hilary had decided against denying her western heritage by living with a man who wouldn't leave the house he'd been born in and had come home. Mrs. Philpott had resurrected her late father's nearly moribund canning factories north of Denver.

Each had refused to surrender except to what she believed in. They had been her examples. Yet watching the pain in Mrs. Philpott's eyes as she talked about how Aunt Hilary had collapsed on the ice while skating on Varsity Lake, Meg saw not an icon of perfection but a human being who hurt, who feared her dearest friend might die.

Together they had built their visions of Meg going to medical school. Though she'd known that staying in Goldfield would disappoint them, until now she hadn't realized how much. All Boulder knew how proud they were of her. Yet she had walked away, almost arrogantly taking them for granted, as if she had an inborn right to do what she chose. She could only imagine the embarrassment they'd felt as they'd tried to explain away her decision. She didn't regret that decision. She did regret that she couldn't have made it without hurting two people who loved her.

Meg took another sip of tea, dimly aware of its exotic scent. "Will Aunt Hilary be able to teach again?"

"*She* thinks so."

Meg shook her head and chuckled at the picture of her aunt's look of disdain at the merest suggestion she might be unable to do something. Mrs. Philpott studied her for an instant, then smiled, as if reading Meg's mind.

"Can I see her?"

"Of course." Mrs. Philpott rose, held out a hand to Meg. "She's in the rose room with a view of the mountains."

* * *

Aunt Hilary was propped against three or four pillows, her long, white hair fanned out around her. When Meg thought of her aunt, she thought of Athena with helmet and sword. Now, as Meg approached the bed and Aunt Hilary turned her head, Meg was stunned to see the ashen face, one side immobile as if frozen, the other straining to smile.

Meg widened her eyes against her tears, leaned over the bed, and kissed her aunt on the cheek. "Merry Christmas" was all Meg could think to say.

Her aunt mumbled something Meg couldn't understand.

"Wait a minute," Meg said, determined to keep smiling. She carried the stool that had been placed in front of the dressing table, placed it next to the bed, and sat down. "Mrs. Philpott said you're doing fine."

Aunt Hilary jerked her head away, as if in protest.

Meg took one of her aunt's hands, feeling its blue-veined ridges beneath the baby-soft skin. Never before had she thought of her aunt as fragile or vulnerable. Now she was both.

"I came as soon as I could."

Her aunt fixed her with an unblinking gaze for a moment, as if assessing the truth of what she'd said.

Meg pulled in a deep breath, smiled. "You must do everything Dr. Mauer says. None of your tricks."

Her aunt mumbled something. Meg thought it sounded like "poppycock."

"I'll let you rest, but I'll be here when you wake up."

Her aunt closed her eyes, and Meg tiptoed out of the room.

* * *

Dr. Mauer came by that evening. He seemed glad to see Meg. As he examined her aunt, she stood at the back of the room, then followed him into the hall. He told her the cause of Aunt Hilary's stroke was probably her high blood pressure. Meg felt she knew him well enough to ask if her absence might have contributed to her aunt's stroke. He patted her arm, confessed that though no one knew the exact causes of a stroke, emotional upset might be a contributing factor.

Later that night, Meg sat on the window seat of the room adjoining her aunt's, the throw from the loveseat over her shoulders, her arms around her knees drawn up to her chest, nightdress pulled down over her toes, and gazed down the hill at the lights of Boulder's downtown and to those of the college campus on the hill beyond, recalling her childhood years. Doors were never locked. A runaway team made the *Camera* headlines. A child was protected, secure, growing up in Boulder. Her father had been right to bring her here to live with his sister. Instinct, blind hope, had told him his sister's strength would never fail.

Meg thought about Aunt Hilary. All these years, Meg had seen only the strong woman with high expectations, who knew exactly what path to take and when to take it. Yet the woman who lay in the next room was totally vulnerable. For the first time, Meg realized the burden her aunt had assumed when she'd taken Meg to raise.

She tried to imagine what it would be like, suddenly having a slightly wild, six-year-old little girl entrusted to her care, the responsibility of bringing up someone else's child. Even someone as strong as her aunt must have had moments when she'd wondered: Am I doing the right thing? Am I making the right decisions?

Meg suddenly realized that behind the sharp words of disapproval over her staying in Goldfield was her aunt's agony that she had somehow failed in her job of raising her. What she owed Aunt Hilary now was not filial devotion but proof that she had brought up a responsible, intelligent woman who had the ability to make her way in the world, to become.

Beyond the exchange, Meg had little concrete to show for her five months in Goldfield. She had yet to solve the mystery of her father's death. She still held the Fourth of July stock. She'd talked a good deal about starting her own business, even toyed with the idea of selling automobiles. More and more women were driving every day. It would be a moneymaker, she was sure. It was just a matter of gathering the loose ends together and getting started.

* * *

As she had done every morning in the four days since her arrival, Meg dressed in her dark-blue wool skirt and a starched shirtwaist, tied on her shoes, and went downstairs. Because Mrs. Philpott had a tray brought up to her room and the nurse ate in the kitchen, Meg had breakfast alone.

The dining room was off to the right of the front hallway. The mahogany table was large enough to easily accommodate twenty people. A chandelier, its crystals twinkling in the sunlight, hung above it. On the Queen Anne sideboard was a magnificent silver tea set, said to have belonged to Mrs. Philpott's grandmother. Meg took her customary place at the far end of the table by the window.

As she unfolded her napkin and placed it in her lap, the grandfather clock in the library struck eight. Dr. Mauer would be by for his morning visit in half an hour.

The swinging door between the pantry and the dining room opened and Rosie appeared, carrying a silver coffeepot in one hand and a plate heaped with eggs and bacon and toast in the other.

"You got a telegram, miss. The boy delivered it not more than fifteen minutes ago." Rosie plunked the plate down in front of Meg, poured the coffee. She drew a buff-colored envelope out of her apron pocket and handed it to Meg.

"Sure and somebody's died," Rosie said, her eyes on the telegram.

Meg glanced up at her, smiled. "My, but aren't you the cheery one this morning."

"And why else does a person send a telegram?"

"It could be good news, you know." Meg slid her table knife beneath the flap, slit open the envelope, removed the message.

"What's it say?"

Meg unfolded the sheet. What she read made her heart stop.

"Well?"

Meg continued to stare at the words. "It's from a friend of mine."

"And?"

"Mrs. Burlingame's her name. She tells me they might have to close the stock exchange because of the pneumonia."

"In Goldfield, you're talkin' about?"

Meg nodded, trying to understand what could have happened. There'd been no cases of pneumonia when she'd left a week ago. Or, at least, she hadn't heard of any. But with the strike, miners and their families were eating poorly, living without heat in their tents. An outbreak of pneumonia should come as no surprise.

During the years of working in Dr. Mauer's office on weekends all through her high school and college years, Meg had only observed the disease from a distance, but she knew it was particularly virulent in the cold and among those with an insufficient diet. She thought of Verna's beloved Jimmy Earnest and all the other children like him. If there was a classic example of the worst possible conditions for the spread of pneumonia, it would be Goldfield. No one would want to venture out unless they had to. It only made sense to shut down the exchange. Yet, it still seemed a drastic step to take.

She'd heard that such doctors as there were in Goldfield were all drunks. She didn't pretend to be a trained nurse, but she could help. She pushed back from the table, folded her napkin.

"And where do ya' think you're off to without your breakfast?"

"I have to leave, Rosie."

"Right this minute?"

"Not quite. I want to talk to Mrs. Philpott first."

An hour later, Meg was packed, had explained the situation as best she could to Aunt Hilary and promised she'd write. Valise in hand, a cold north wind snatching at her skirts, Meg strode down the hill to the Interurban Station. With luck, she'd make the next train leaving Denver for Goldfield and be there day after tomorrow.

CHAPTER 29

$\mathcal{D}$ust motes danced in the bands of winter sunlight streaming through the front windows. Teddy had already taken his station by the door. The strong smell of lye soap, used to scrub down the floor each day, mixed with stale cigar smoke hung in the air. As Tess entered the silent saloon to start working on last night's books, instinct, a sixth sense, turned on inside her. Something was wrong.

Sucking in her breath, she threaded her way around the tables, chairs still stacked on their tops, went around the far end of the bar where the safe was, and found it open. For an instant, she was afraid to go closer, to learn the truth. Then, knowing there was nothing else to do, she went over, squatted, peered inside. Her three large account books were there. So far so good. She sat on the floor, her skirts spread around her, put the ledgers on her lap. Holding her breath, she opened the first, hoping against hope her stock certificates were still between the pages where she'd put them.

Carefully, she lifted the hard-backed cover of the ledger on top. Staring back at her was the first of the dozens of lined, yellow sheets filled with small, neat figures entered in her hand. She turned

each page, one at a time, until she came to the blank pages at the
back. Even those she went through. Nothing. The stock certificates
were gone. Despair gripped her as she glanced into the empty safe.
Even the envelope with last night's receipts was missing.

"Mama, Cookie says I gotta eat my oatmeal," wailed Jenny Lynn
from the doorway to the kitchen.

Tess let out a long breath, realized she was trembling. Getting
to her feet, she smoothed her skirt, put the account books on the
bar. Small feet ran down the hallway from the kitchen. Jenny Lynn
burst into the room.

"Mama—"

"Go back and do as Cookie says, baby."

"But Mama, I don't feel good."

"You heard me. Do it now." Tess heard the snap behind her
words, saw the dismay in her daughter's face. More kindly, struggling for calm, Tess said, "If you're goin' to take care of your own
pony on the ranch, you have to be big and strong."

Jenny Lynn looked up at her with tear-filled eyes, turned and
went back to the kitchen.

In the silence of the saloon, Tess wondered where Vic was, then
remembered it was the day he picked up supplies from the depot.
She and Vic had the only keys to the safe. It wasn't much of a safe,
as safes went. Normally, they never kept cash around for more than
six hours before they took it to the bank. There wasn't much profit
for someone to rob them. Until early this morning.

Yesterday she'd brought some of her stock certificates from the
exchange with the intention of signing them over to the Steamboat Springs bank and sending them off today. Vic hadn't been
happy about having them around and reminded her to sign them
over before she put them in the safe. She'd forgotten.

Heartsick, she leaned on the bar, absently running her hands
along its satiny surface, and gazed out the window at the passing
twenty-mule team. The value of the stolen stocks equaled the cost
of a wagon, a four-horse team, and enough hay to get them through
till summer. Except for her share of the Ajax when Vic managed

to sell it and a little cash upstairs in her pocketbook, she'd been wiped out. She was back where she'd started last summer.

She felt her anger, deep down inside, churning, building until she was a hair away from exploding. She clenched her teeth, narrowed her eyes, and glared at the ceiling, reviewing names and faces. Suddenly, she slapped the bar so hard her palms stung, knowing as certainly as she knew her own name who had stolen her dream. "Goddamn you, Jake. Goddamn you to hell."

* * *

When Vic came back from the depot, Tess was waiting for him by the door.

"We were robbed." She nodded her head toward the bar. "Somebody managed to open the safe."

He frowned, went past her to have a look.

"I knew better. I shoulda signed 'em over."

Vic examined the empty safe, shook his head. "At least, there wasn't much cash."

"It was Jake."

He glanced at her, didn't say anything.

"You warned me."

He shrugged.

The anger at her foolishness, at Jake, rushed through her again, and she spun around to glare out the window. "It's what I was goin' to use for the equipment, for us movin'. Goddamn him."

Vic came over and stood beside her. "I've saved some money back you can have."

She reached out and patted his arm. "Thanks."

"If you bought some Mohawk with it, you could double it in no time."

She eyed him and felt a lurch of affection. "You're a generous man, Vic Ajax."

"You'd do the same."

"You give me too much credit." She looked over her shoulder at the bar. "Right now, all I want is to—"

"Tess, even if you could find Jake, shooting him won't get your stock back."

"Shootin', hell. I'd like to string the bastard up by his balls."

"Let the postal inspectors take care of him."

"Hah! He'll worm his way out of it like he does everythin' else. You wait and see."

"He won't come back here. Not after this."

"You wanna bet?"

She suddenly felt Jenny Lynn beside her. Automatically, Tess put a hand on her head. The child felt hot. Tess squatted, inspected her face. "Sweetheart, you're burnin' up."

"My tummy feels all bad."

Tess frowned, took her daughter's hands. Jimmy Earnest had been lying close to death for days with the pneumonia that had been sweeping the camp. Hundreds of miners were too sick to go down to the mines. An epidemic was in the making. She had to take Jenny Lynn and get out.

"Vic, you got to manage without me." She stood, scooped Jenny Lynn up in her arms. "I think Jenny Lynn might have the pneumonia they're talkin' about."

"You want to leave now? Why?" Vic placed a hand on her daughter's forehead. "For God's sake, Tess. The kid's sick."

"She'll be okay till we get to Salt Lake."

"Did Jake steal your brains, too? She needs a doctor."

Tess looked down with terror at the feverish child in her arms. "Then get one."

* * *

Tess had taken Jenny Lynn up to bed. Not knowing what else to do, she'd started bathing her with cool cloths, but no sooner had she arranged one on her daughter's chest or back, then the cloth grew warm, and Tess had to replace it. Hours had gone by since Vic had left and still no sign of him or the doctor.

Finally, she heard a door close. She straightened, went to the head of the stairs, saw only Vic, and she panicked.

"Where's the doctor?"

"He's over in Montezuma," Vic said as he slowly climbed the stairs.

"But I need him now."

"So does half the county."

Vic followed her into the bedroom, stood beside her at the foot of the little bed Clem Little had made for Jenny Lynn.

"She started wheezin' a few minutes ago." She glanced at Vic. "God, if only I knew what to do. If only there was a hospital. At least there'd be nurses."

Vic put an arm around her shoulders. "I'll go back to the doc's and wait for him."

Tess felt tears trickle down her cheeks. "Vic, nothin' in this world matters but Jenny Lynn. I just can't lose her. I just can't."

CHAPTER 30

A stethoscope dangling around her neck, Meg straightened and pushed back a wisp of hair that had fallen over her eyes. Two weeks ago when she'd returned from Boulder and had seen the seriousness of the situation, she had asked Tess and Vic if they'd be willing to convert the Ajax into a makeshift hospital. They had instantly agreed.

The gaming tables and the chairs had been replaced by cots, the large room dimly lit by two kerosene lamps instead of the electric lights Meg thought too harsh for the patients' eyes. Wearily, she eyed the rows of seriously ill women and children lying on cots. She had hoped that by now she would have received word about Aunt Hilary's progress. So far, none had come.

When Meg had suggested the hospital to the five doctors in town, only Dr. Hudson had seen the sense of it or cared. Another hospital for men had been set up in a gambling hall a few blocks away. This one was exclusively for women and children. At first, Meg thought the hospital would solve the problem. Then she realized Dr. Hudson still had to make housecalls from dawn to midnight. He couldn't be everyplace at once.

When she'd returned to Goldfield, she'd gone to Dr. Hudson,

briefly explained her experience in a doctor's office, and offered her help. Before she had left his office, he had come up with a plan: he would see the patient, prescribe treatment; she would make the return visits. At first, some men had objected to her demands that they expose their chests so she could listen to their lungs. But, soon, too sick to cause much fuss, they relented.

Meg had returned from today's rounds of house visits an hour ago. The last call she'd made was to check on Emma, whose fever continued to hover around 102 degrees. An adult couldn't sustain a fever that high for very long and live. Before Meg left, she'd explained to John Burlingame again the importance of continually applying cold compresses. He had seized her arm, pleaded with her to stay. As gently as she could, she'd escaped his hold and promised to come the next day.

She hadn't slept for eighteen hours. Her back ached. Her head ached. It seemed impossible that three weeks ago her chief concern had been the price of stocks.

The door to the kitchen opened, and Tess appeared, carrying pitchers of water. Between nursing Jenny Lynn, who lay upstairs in bed, and doing her bit to care for the others, Tess's normally high color had disappeared. Meg worried that she, too, would become ill.

"How's Jenny Lynn?" Meg asked as she took a pitcher from Tess.

"She's still coughin' up yellowish stuff."

"How are the aches?"

"Terrible." Tears glistened in Tess's eyes.

"Keep giving her plenty of water, and give her a teaspoon of brandy. It'll help her sleep."

Tess nodded, put the other two pitchers of water on the bar, returned to the back of the room and the stairs.

Meg rubbed the small of her back, made her way slowly down the row, listening and looking. She paused at the side of a heavy-set woman with the telltale bluish color that meant she was starving for oxygen. Meg would have thought from the sturdiness of her appearance, the woman would have escaped the disease. For the past few hours she'd been mumbling, delirious.

The woman reached up and grasped Meg's arm. "Janie girl, you haven't forgotten the lads' supper, have ya'?"

Meg knelt beside her, placed the head of the stethoscope on the woman's chest, heard the bubbling sound of lungs nearly filled with bacteria. "I haven't forgotten," Meg said gently as the woman began to cough up thick, red phlegm. Unless a miracle occurred, she would be dead by midnight.

Meg got to her feet, went to the corner where Jimmy Earnest slept. His fever had broken earlier today, and Meg had managed to persuade Verna, who had been spending nearly every waking hour with him, to go home for some sleep herself. Meg took his wrist, felt his pulse, counted. It had slowed. He hadn't vomited for several days. If all continued to go well, he could go back to Verna's soon. She lifted up the sheet, saw that he had soiled himself again. Obviously, the diarrhea was still a problem.

A young woman—a sister of one of the patients, Meg seemed to recall—dozed in a chair nearby. Meg went over to her, tapped her arm, and the girl opened her eyes. "The boy in the bed in the corner needs his sheets changed."

The girl nodded, pushed to her feet, went to obey.

Meg heard the door open, felt a blast of cold wind. She glanced over her shoulder, saw Dr. Hudson, carrying his black medical bag, struggle to shut the door. He shrugged off his sheepskin coat, re-moved his broad-brimmed hat. Clean-shaven, with a thick head of light-brown hair, Dr. Hudson was a man of average height. He had the wiry build of someone never content to be still. He looked more like some of the middle-age prospectors he treated than the doctors she'd known. There was something about his quiet man-ner that made a person immediately trust him.

She went over to him. "Let me get you some stew."

He gave her a tired smile. "Sounds good."

She led the way to the kitchen, dished out a bowl of stew from the pot Cookie kept full on the back of the stove, placed it on the table before him.

"Coffee?"

"Please."

She poured them both a cup, sat down opposite him. As he ate, she reported the condition of the patients she'd been caring for.

"I'll need you to come with me tonight. I got word about several men over at the Montezuma Queen too sick to come in. I don't think I should wait till daylight."

She nodded. "Tess can take care of things for a while."

The doctor sipped at his coffee for a moment, sat back. "I understand you ladies closed down the exchange."

"Having people jammed together unnecessarily didn't seem very smart to us. Anyway, the sick and dying seemed a little more important than trading stock."

He nodded, yawned. "Isn't the other one still in operation?"

She was too tired to summon the anger she'd felt when she first learned the Mining Stock Exchange hadn't closed. Refusing to submit to Nolan and Winters' proposal to suspend operations was one thing; ignoring a community crisis was something else. "I suppose someone has to keep the wheels of commerce going."

He raised an eyebrow. "I guess."

She rose. "More stew?"

"No thanks." He studied her curiously. "Miss Bates tells me you were admitted to Johns Hopkins Medical School. Quite an accomplishment for a young woman."

She picked up his bowl and cup, carried them to the sink.

"You should have gone. You're as good as a lot of doctors I've seen who've practiced quite a while. You have a feel for it."

"Thank you." Meg appreciated the compliment. What he'd said about her skill was true. She did have a feel for it. The look of near-adoration in the eyes of some of the patients, as if she were capable of miracles, was a humbling experience. Yet with that adoration came a certain debt that could trap you.

"I'm serious. You shouldn't throw away a chance like that."
She leaned against the sink.

"Doctors, decent ones, are as scarce as hens' teeth out here," he
said. "If you hadn't believed it before, the last days should have convinced you."

"Some say a woman doctor has difficulty . . . establishing a practice."

He raised a skeptical eyebrow, got to his feet. Everything about
his manner toward the standard excuse she'd let roll off her tongue
was one of disbelief. If there'd been time, she might have told him
that medicine had been the dream other women held for her, that
her dream, to be ever realized, had to be of her own making.

Wearily, he asked for his coat, putting an end to the discussion.
"It's time we be on our way."

*   *   *

Meg sat beside the doctor, an ancient quilt wrapped around them
to guard against the cold as he drove the rig through the dark streets
to the outskirts of town and into the desert. Back in the kitchen,
he had essentially told her she'd tossed aside her abilities and the
opportunity to serve others as if she took them for granted. She
thought of all the girls she'd grown up with whom she'd regarded
as frivolous. Plainly, Dr. Hudson considered her in the same light.

She pulled the quilt up to her chin and tried to put the nagging
thought behind her. The Montezuma Queen mine with its sick
miners was north of Goldfield. As she glanced about, she realized
Dr. Hudson was taking the same road as she and Bill when he'd
first driven her to see the mine.

She gazed up at the black velvet sky, studded with brilliant stars,
and recognized the outline of the Big Dipper, the Little Dipper
below. The memory of that November night, sitting on the lap robe
with Bill, gazing at the same stars, flooded over her. She remembered every word of their conversation, how she'd still felt a little
giddy from the champagne. She wondered if he'd reached San
Francisco yet.

In the moon's half-light, Dr. Hudson guided the horse through the eerie desert landscape with the sureness of someone who knew where he was going, and she felt herself relax. If she wasn't careful, she would fall asleep. A coyote yipped, other coyotes joined in until their voices became a chorus. Otherwise, there was only silence. She and the doctor didn't speak. It took too much energy.

*   *   *

John Hudson removed the stethoscope from his ears. Letting the instrument dangle around his neck, he looked up at Meg, who was standing on the other side of the cot where Slim Pattison lay.

"Microbes in the lungs lodge in air sacs where the blood normally exchanges carbon dioxide for oxygen. There they multiply rapidly and the air sacs soon fill with fluid, overcoming the white blood cells produced by the body to fight infection." His voice had that removed quality of a teacher lecturing students.

Meg wondered if his reciting the definition of pneumonia was for her benefit, the patient's, or a desperate effort to keep his mind on track.

"Doc, I'll be okay. The men in the bunkhouse across the way are the ones who need you," Slim Pattison said.

"I'm going to leave you some morphine. Try to drink lots of water. Other than that, there's nothing to do but rest and pray a little." The doctor straightened, returned his stethoscope to his black medical bag.

Glancing about the room, he said, "It's damn cold in here, Slim. Have one of the men keep the stove up."

Slim Pattison gave a shallow cough, nodded.

"Miss Kendall and I will try to get back in a few days."

Slim Pattison glanced at Meg. "I didn't realize you were a nurse, too."

She smiled. "You get well. I don't want our Montezuma stock to take a dive."

He attempted to match her smile, but the result was more of a grimace. "Your dad would be right proud of you."

"I hope so." She glanced at Dr. Hudson, who was shrugging into his coat, but his face was a mask. Apparently, he hadn't heard Slim Pattison's comment.

She put on her coat, and they walked across the hard-packed sand to the bunkhouse, built since Meg's last visit.

Inside, they discovered three dead men beneath a piece of gray tarp on the plank floor, pockmarked by bloody spittle. A dozen other miners, alive, lay on their bunks. A few stirred, glanced at Meg and John Hudson as they entered. The others didn't move. She smelled dried vomit and urine. Death seemed to hang in the air. She should be used to it by now, but she wasn't.

She felt a flood of sadness, knowing each death meant to someone what her father's death had meant to her. She'd managed to fight off hopelessness in the face of so much of it, but she'd have to be dead herself to get used to it.

* * *

The eastern horizon was edged with a thin, rosy line. Another day was about to begin. In half an hour the sky would be filled with daylight. As John Hudson guided the rig back through the nearly empty streets toward the Ajax, Meg was amazed her eyes were still open.

"Shall I drop you by your house?" Dr. Hudson suggested.

"Thanks, but the Ajax's fine. I promised Tess I'd look in on her daughter."

The rig turned onto Myers. The doctor maneuvered his horse around a twenty-mule team pulling a string of ore wagons. Just ahead was the Ajax. A lone touring car, black, caked with dust, was parked in front. Meg's heart skipped a beat.

She climbed down from the rig. Dr. Hudson said he'd meet her at the gambling hall–hospital at noon, and he drove off.

Meg stood on the boardwalk, gazed at the touring car, felt a surge of hope that it might be Bill's. Missing him as she always did, she'd been only half what she could be with him by her side. She glanced up and down the street. This early, the other saloons along the street were closed. Unlike the Ajax, they hadn't yet turned themselves into hospitals, though as the epidemic grew, which it was bound to do, they might. The tents between the board buildings looked drab, starkly exposed in the half-light of day.

From the eastern edge of town, the distinctive blast of the whistle at the Fourth of July mine signaling the next shift echoed across the desert. Once the pneumonia faded, she'd be able to think of mines and the gold they produced again, but not now.

She walked over to the touring car, studied it. Unlike Bill's automobile, the fenders, the top, the seats were all in place. She turned away, opened the door to the Ajax. Inside, patients stirred on their cots, coughed, moaned. Little had changed in the twelve hours she'd been absent. She felt light-headed and remembered she hadn't eaten since yesterday. She decided to get some breakfast before she checked on Jenny Lynn.

As she entered the kitchen, Meg saw the broad back of tall man, a man with dark brown hair, seated at the table. He wore a leather jacket. She caught in her breath. "Bill?"

He glanced over his shoulder, saw her, and stood. An instant later, he was folding her into his arms. "I came as soon as I heard."

CHAPTER 31

Verna unlocked the door of the *Star* and went inside. Nearly drunk with exhaustion, she lifted the curtain dividing the room and walked to the stove, then forgot what she was going to do. Emma Burlingame was dead. This morning Verna had stood with Tess and Meg at the grave site, watching John Burlingame's bewildered expression, and knew how he felt. Of the three women who ran the ladies' exchange, Emma had been closest to Verna's own age. She'd always had a special feeling for Emma, admired her. Not two days ago when Verna had gone by to see her, she thought she looked some better. It seemed impossible she was dead.

In other circumstances, there probably would have been a reception for friends after the funeral, but the epidemic made folks leery of gathering in groups. So Meg and Bill had taken John back to the empty house, with its painted china and silver tea set Emma had been so proud of, where they had gathered only three months earlier with such high hopes.

As Verna undressed and put on her nightdress, she wondered what would happen to the ladies' exchange once the epidemic subsided. With Emma gone, nothing would be the same. Automatically, Verna folded her skirt and petticoat, shirtwaist, her corset and underthings, her stockings, arranged them neatly over the back of the chair by the cot. Next to it, she placed her shoes, side by side. She lay down on the cot, drew the blankets up under her chin.

Her heart felt like a lump of lead in her chest. She closed her eyes. It was only by some miracle that she wasn't the one in that pine coffin, probably should be. With no husband, no real ties, it would have been fairer, but then whoever said anything in life, or death, was fair?

*   *   *

When Verna finally awoke, she lay without moving for several moments, clinging to a dream she'd had about Jimmy in which he was riding a new bicycle as he delivered papers. She smiled. At least the Lord had spared her darling Jimmy.

She sat up, glanced past the curtain to the window, saw the gray light of dawn. She'd slept straight through the night. Emma's funeral must have worn her out more than she'd realized. She got up, squatted on the chamber pot. As she relieved herself, she set out her plan for the day. She'd heat some water, bathe, put on a change of clothes. It would lift her spirits.

She filled the soup kettle, the biggest pot she had, with water, and put it on one of the burners. As she waited for it to heat, she went to the type stand, opened the drawer, and let her gaze travel fondly over the rows of type. It had been three weeks since she'd put out the last edition with the editorial about the union and the Goldfield Consolidated Mines Company. At the time, she'd secretly hoped for an official visit from the union and, if not Winters and Nolan in person, at least a representative of the company. But she hadn't received so much as a letter of objection. Probably with the epidemic raging, no one had even taken the time to read it.

Verna stood at the window, arms folded, watching the passersby, the snarl of traffic. Outwardly, Goldfield seemed about the same as before the consolidation and the strike, and the epidemic that followed. Yet there was something missing. Gone was the old devil-may-care, live-and-let-live spirit.

The crackdown on high-grading since the major consolidation had squashed the miners' hopes of making quick money. The prospectors' nose for gold wasn't enough. Success in Goldfield required shafts hundreds of feet deep using pumps and electric engines. It took big money and big machines to make fortunes now. Even at Emma's funeral yesterday, the conversation around her had a discouraged, dark feel to it.

* * *

A week passed. Verna pushed her worries to the back of her mind. Jimmy was stronger, but his mother was worn out caring for his sister and baby brother, who'd also come down with pneumonia. When Verna approached Mrs. Earnest with the idea that she could watch out for Jimmy for a while, the poor woman was too tired to object.

The day Bill finally carried Jimmy, wrapped in a blanket, from the automobile into the *Star* and settled him on the cot, Verna felt as if she'd died and gone to heaven.

"How's that?" she asked, plumping up the pillow she'd bought yesterday at Vogler's and sticking it under his head.

"Aw, Miz Bates, you'd think I was like one of them china dolls."

"One of *those* china dolls."

Jimmy grinned up at her.

"I rounded up some of those dime westerns you like. Even found a new one by somebody named Zane Grey."

"Wow!"

"Chicken soup's on the bill of fare for now. When your stomach's better, I'll make some stew. We've got to fatten you up."

"You shouldn't be fussing with me this way."

She gave his shoulder a brisk little pat. "You let me be the judge of that, young man. Now get some rest."

That night Meg came to listen to Jimmy's chest. Tucked under her arm was a copy of Kipling's *The Jungle Book*, a present from Bill

Brown. Verna fixed a fresh pot of coffee, cut two generous slices of bread from the loaf she'd bought from Swenson's bakery. It seemed like old times, the two of them seated across the table from each other, just talking. Finally, Verna sat by the darkened window and watched Meg, the kerosene lamp moved close for good light, her chair pulled up to Jimmy's cot, as she read of the adventures of Mowgli in the faroff jungles of India. If it hadn't been for the nagging, ill-defined uneasiness in the back of Verna's thoughts, her world would have been perfect.

*   *   *

The following Monday, the early darkness of the winter evening had already settled over the camp when Verna hurried back from visiting the other Earnest children. Two of the remaining fresh apples she'd bought for the Earnest family as special treats bulged in her pocketbook. She could hardly wait to see Jimmy's face when he saw them. He was sitting up now, getting stronger every day.

Verna stood on the corner and took a deep breath as she waited impatiently for the traffic to thin so she could cross the street. She crinkled her nose at the acrid smell, sniffed. Smoke, she was sure of it.

She glanced at the man next to her. "Do you smell smoke?"

He stared at her for an instant, maybe not understanding. "Smoke?" Then his eyes widened. He tipped back his head, took in a deep breath. "Jesus, you're right."

A fire bell suddenly sounded. A moment later the entire camp seemed to explode with terrified cries of "Fire!" A kerosene stove could catch, a cigarette could be carelessly tossed, anything. Constant wind and inadequate water supply increased the danger. The possibility of fire was always in the back of everyone's mind.

As the people streamed by her, Verna craned her head this way and that, wondering where the fire was. Suddenly, she saw the column of smoke, billowing up into the night sky, close, in the next block where the *Star* was. Fear clutched her heart. She ran into the street, dodged rearing horses until she reached the other side. Elbowing and pushing through the frantic crowd, she could think of nothing but Jimmy trapped in a raging inferno.

She turned the corner, her heart pounding. She stopped to catch her breath and watched in horror as the canvas of the tent next to the *Star* became blazing shreds, flapping in the wind, tinder to set the *Star* on fire. The orange light of the blaze illuminated the dark. The heat was ferocious, but she kept moving closer, and as she did, she knew, absolutely, the fire had been deliberately set. Whoever was responsible, the union or the companies, she didn't know nor did she care. Her editorials had finally hit a nerve, and now Jimmy was paying the price.

A team of men pulling a fire wagon raced past her, stopped in front of the tent. Two men pumped water from the tank on the wagon. Others held the hose and trained a weak stream on what remained of the tent. Verna ducked past them, headed toward the door to the *Star*.

A hand pulled her back. "You can't go in there."

"I've got to," she screamed as she tried to wrench free.

Out of the corner of her eye, she saw a line of men rolling beer barrels from a nearby saloon down the center of the street. They were coming this way. With so little water to fight the fire, beer was the only alternative. The man holding her turned to watch them, and his grasp loosened just enough for her to escape.

"Miz Bates," someone called as she ran forward. "Stay back."

The windowpanes exploded, sending shards of glass flying. Smoke poured out into the cold, night air. For an instant, she stood transfixed in terror, unable to move. Everything she owned was being consumed by the flames, but none of it was important compared to Jimmy.

Pictures of him flashed through her mind, how he had come to work even when he was sick because he knew how much she depended on him, how his whole face had filled with a smile as he'd watched the circus movie. The little she'd done for him, he'd given back a hundredfold. The sky was orange with flames, the heat from the fire nearly unbearable. She might not be able to save him this time, but she wouldn't risk anything less than he had for her. She pulled off her coat, held it over her head, and ran, unnoticed, past men wetting down the firefighters with the beer.

* * *

Excruciating pain consumed her. Time passed. The pain numbed, then resurfaced. Verna opened her eyes to blackness. It occurred to her she might be dying.

A man's voice, a man she knew but couldn't place, reached through her fog. "Miss Bates, it's Dr. Hudson. You're at Miss Wallace's. You've been badly burned. What you feel are the compresses soaked with tannic acid I'm having Miss Kendall apply to your arms and face. I've given you some morphine for the pain. Miss Kendall will stay with you and give you more as you need it."

"Is Jimmy—"

"I'm here, Miz Bates," said the dearest voice in the world.

Verna attempted to reach out to him, but the pain stopped her short. She asked about her eyes.

"They were probably scorched by the smoke and the heat," the doctor said. "It's best to keep the bandages on for a while."

"But my sight will come back, won't it?" In the split-second pause it took for the doctor to give her a reassuring answer, Verna knew he had some doubt.

After he had left and the room was quiet, she thought about the prospect of her blindness. If it had to be, she wished she could have continued to go blind in stages as she'd been doing, giving her a chance to adjust.

Verna was grateful Tess had made room for her. Meg was nursing her as tenderly as if she were kin. Jimmy was nearby. Yet that night, as she heard the familiar sounds of the camp beyond the windows, she felt more alone, more hopeless, than she had in all her life.

She knew it was her own fear that made her feel alone, but she couldn't help it. She'd always taken care of herself, of others, too. Now she was dependent on the kindness of others. At best, she felt uncomfortable. At the worst, it was terrifying.

* * *

Verna sank back against the pillows, listening to Tess's quick footsteps as she went back downstairs to the kitchen with Verna's supper tray. Yesterday Dr. Hudson had removed the bandage from her eyes. Her world was gradually beginning to turn gray. She couldn't distinguish forms or faces, but the blackness had lost its grip. Meg had assured her the burns on her hands and arms were healing nicely.

Vic told her the fire had been kept to a single block, nothing short of a miracle, given the board shacks and tents that made up most of the camp. She had to press Jimmy before he'd admit that nothing remained of the *Star*. Everything she owned was gone, including her savings she'd kept under the floorboards.

If John Burlingame was still in the banking business by the time she was back on her feet, she was reasonably sure he'd loan her enough to buy new equipment and replace her few belongings. But a loan wouldn't cover her lost savings. Depression settled over her like a dark cloud so thick it wouldn't let so much as a ray of sunshine through.

If she had the cash and the ladies' stock exchange reopened, she supposed she should try investing again, but at the moment, she didn't have the heart to take another risk.

CHAPTER 32

*A*s Tess carried Verna's breakfast tray down the Ajax's steep stairs, she decided the first chance she had today she'd talk to Vic about signing over her share of the saloon. Whatever it amounted to plus the money from the sale of her seat on the exchange, once it reopened, were now her only assets. She'd have to be careful Vic didn't give her too much. With business down since the epidemic, he needed the money, too.

The bitterness she felt about Jake stealing her stocks, leaving her pretty much where she'd started, was strangling the life out of her. She'd reported the theft to the sheriff, knowing he wouldn't or couldn't do anything about it. Jake hadn't left a trace. Vic kept telling her the postal inspectors would catch up with him, but she doubted it. So now that Jenny Lynn was on her feet again, Tess wanted to get out of here, make a new start. Whatever appeal Goldfield once had was long gone.

She'd have enough cash to get to Steamboat Springs. Once there she'd earn enough waiting tables or such to make the mortgage payments and taxes for a year or so. She'd only have enough now to buy a few calves. Maybe she'd hunt up an old widower on a neighboring ranch who needed a housekeeper and wouldn't mind a kid in the bargain.

With Verna's breakfast tray on one hip, Tess glanced about the large, familiar room, its chairs neatly arranged on the tabletops. She was proud of the Ajax. She'd be leaving a little part of herself in this place, and in the exchange. She'd miss them both, but she'd miss Vic more, though Meg and Verna weren't far behind. Still, it was always a mistake to come to depend on people too much. She hadn't meant to stay this long.

Out of the corner of her eye, she noticed two men, their hands clutching their hats, heads bent against the sand-filled wind, passing in front of the plate glass window. She smiled. If the mines closed down tomorrow and the camp turned into a ghost town, the wind would still be around.

Tess walked down the short hall and into the kitchen, put the tray on the drainboard. Cookie was already preparing the lunch spread. Jenny Lynn sat at the table, spooning oatmeal into her mouth, her eyes on a copy of McGuffey's reader propped in front of her.

"It's not polite to read at the table," Tess said, kissing the top of her daughter's head.

Jenny Lynn glanced up at her. To see her cheeks rosy again was nothing short of a miracle.

"All the kids have to recite at the program."

"What program?"

Jenny Lynn smiled an angelic smile. "It's Friday night. I told you."

"Sure, I remember now." But Tess didn't remember. Her daughter was the center of her life and all Tess could think of was Jake and the money she'd lost. The sooner she left this place, the better.

"So I gotta memorize this poem."

Tess tried to look stern. "Then memorize, but eat all your oatmeal."

She looked over at Cookie. "Don't go overboard on the sandwiches. With business down the way it is, I don't want to be throwin' out food."

Without so much as a glance her way, Cookie merely picked up another thick slab of bread, slathered it with butter. If he wasn't such a good cook, she'd fire him.

Tess walked over to the stove, removed the blue enameled cup from the warming shelf where Cookie always kept it waiting for her, and poured herself some coffee. Holding the cup gingerly by the handle, she sipped the steaming black liquid, watching her daughter lost in her book, and thought about last night's receipts.

She'd taken it for granted that the day she converted the Ajax from a hospital back to a saloon, their old customers would come flocking back, but they hadn't. She'd picked up rumors that some in camp said Jenny Lynn was to blame for the epidemic, that she'd brought the pneumonia with her from Colorado Springs. The mere idea that people believed a little kid was responsible for such a thing, when everyone knew it was the cold and not enough to eat that had done it, was another reason for moving out.

The back door opened, and Vic staggered in, a box of supplies on one shoulder. He grinned at her, said good morning to Jenny Lynn. It was almost like the three of them were family. That part would be hard to leave.

Vic lowered the box onto the floor, glanced at Jenny Lynn. "Aren't you supposed to be in school?"

Jenny Lynn looked up from her book. "Ma! What time is it?"

"Near to nine."

Jenny Lynn shot out of her chair. "Oh, Ma, I'm gonna be late."

"No, you're not. Just run fast. But not too fast or you'll get a stitch in your side."

An instant later Jenny Lynn was out the back door and gone.

Vic leaned down, began to remove cans from the box he'd brought in. "The way that kid buries her nose in a book, she's bound to amount to something."

Tess smiled, put her cup in the sink, took her apron off the hook on the back of the door, and tied it around her waist. She should have started the bread an hour ago. "Not around here, she's not."

Vic raised an eyebrow, as if he knew what was coming next.

"As a matter of fact, I've been needin' to talk to you again about sellin' out my half."

Vic didn't say anything.

She cleared the table, went to get the mixing bowl she always used. "With business down, I don't know how much it would be worth, but—"

"I thought Cookie made the bread."

"He doesn't knead it enough."

"Tess—"

"Save it, Vic. I've made up my mind."

"You can plug your ears if you want, Tess. But I'm going to say it anyway."

"It won't do any good. Besides, I've got bread to bake."

Vic pulled one of the straight-backed chairs away from the table, sat down. "You don't know the front end from the rear of a cow."

"Thanks to Jake wipin' me out, I'll have plenty of time to learn."

"What you do know, Tess Wallace, is about feeding people."

Tess ignored him and walked around the chair Vic was holding for her to the back porch where the flour was kept.

"Damn it, Tess, hear me out on this."

She lifted the lid off the flour barrel, saw Cookie had already taken some out and left the scoop behind. She could feel Vic behind her.

"You came to Goldfield with the idea of a restaurant, remember?"

She cracked a smile in spite of herself as she went past him to get the mixing bowl she'd forgotten. "So?"

"So, you being the cook you are and me pretty handy at most anything . . ."

She stopped, looked over her shoulder at him. "Last I looked you were the owner of the Ajax."

"I plan to sell out."

"Since when?"

"Since you got this cockeyed idea," he said defiantly.

She stared at him.

"We'll say I'm your uncle."

"What in the hell are you talkin' about?"

"Outside of a mining camp, a man who starts a business with an unmarried lady, a lady with a kid, has to be explained."

She regarded his dark eyes, liquid with feeling. "Are you sayin' we should run a restaurant together?"

"You got to admit it only makes sense."

She gave a deep sigh. The ranch was her dream. She couldn't let it go. Yet her head told her she could do a lot worse than to have a kind, decent man like Vic to look after her and Jenny Lynn. She suspected he was trying to work up his nerve to ask her to marry him, but appreciating a man's kindness wasn't the same as loving him. Or was it? The truth was she wasn't sure she knew what loving a man was all about.

She placed her hands on his chest, gazed at his necktie, afraid to look into his eyes.

"I'd take care of you. And Jenny Lynn."

"Vic, it just wouldn't work."

"You're the most beautiful, the finest lady I've ever known."

They looked at each other, old friends whose relationship would never be the same again. Then, almost fearfully, with an unfamiliar tenderness inside her, she put her arms around his neck and smiled into his luminous, soulful eyes.

"And with you that goes double."

"See, so why not—" Vic began.

"Shush," she said, gently touching a finger to his lips. "You gotta stop worryin', Vic. Everything'll be fine. But I've got to do it my way."

CHAPTER 33

$\mathcal{M}$eg walked around the Oldsmobile again, inspecting it more carefully this time. Though she'd talked about buying a car for months, she'd always had Bill's to use in a pinch. Now he was about to leave, again; and with the exchange reopening, she'd still need transportation to visit any potential new listings. Even with the consolidation and not as many mines opening up as there once had, there were bound to be some.

Her Fourth of July stock remained in the John Cook Bank, where she'd put it during the epidemic. It seemed odd she hadn't heard so much as a rumor about the suit in weeks. But then she'd been out of circulation so long, she had a great deal to catch up on.

She'd have to sit down and really study the situation, review the July's latest statement on its assets before making any decisions about how to proceed. Tess had talked to her about selling her seat. Since Verna had lost everything in the fire, she had nothing left to invest. And Emma was gone. They would have to elect another president. Nothing would be the same. Of the four friends who had started the venture, she would be the only one left.

"What do you think?" Bill asked from beyond her thoughts.

She refocused her attention on the car. "It looks fine. The finish on the bottom of the fenders is pretty badly nicked but—"

"The Olds is reliable," he said.

"True." This model had no doors and no top. She didn't care whether she had doors, but she'd need a top to shield against the Goldfield summer heat. Maybe Bill could fashion something for her before he left.

Before he left . . . Though the words had slid through her mind a thousand times, she had steadfastly refused to confront the reality of them. Soon she'd have to.

"Well?" Bill ran a hand along the gearshift.

"Oh, it's splendid. A real find."

"The guy who owned it said he'd hardly driven it, but he lies through his teeth," he said.

"The engine's sound, isn't it?"

"Come take a look." He lifted the hood and they ducked their heads, peered at the engine. "I checked the hoses and tightened the fan belt. I also put in some more oil. You better keep an eye on that."

She nodded.

"If you have any trouble, George Cleats can give you a hand."

"I don't see why he had to change the name from Brown to Cleats Transportation Company."

Bill chuckled, stepped backward, one hand still on the hood. "Heh, it's his now. I'm just glad I could get rid of it as fast as I did."

She ducked her head, straightened. Bill lowered the hood in place, shoved it firmly closed, pulled a rag out of his back pocket, and wiped his hands.

Meg regarded him. "Business is bound to bounce back though."

"If you mean Goldfield's economy, it might. But if history's any measure, mining camps usually don't last long."

"What about places like Leadville and Cripple Creek? The mines there are still open—"

"Open, maybe. More important is what are their production levels?"

Her father would have known the answer. A day didn't go by that she didn't think of him.

Bill studied the nearest tire, gave it a haphazard kick with the toe of his left boot. "Either way, I'm anxious to get started for San Francisco. If I hold off much longer, they'll start the race without me."

She smiled. "They wouldn't dare."

"I'm not going to chance it. That's for sure." He walked around the Olds again. "Two hundred, used. Not cheap, but what is in Goldfield?"

She felt disconnected, almost like an eavesdropper as she heard the words, the talk about her automobile, when she knew they were actually saying good-bye, and she blurted out, "Maybe we better give it a test drive before I decide."

"Right now?"

She looked sideways at him. "Why not?"

"I thought you were going to open up the exchange today."

She gazed up at the clear sky. Her concern about the status of the exchange and the Fourth of July suit didn't seem that important at the moment. "It's too nice a morning to be cooped up inside. I'll tackle all that when we get back."

* * *

Her duster around her, a veil over her hat and tied securely under her chin, her goggles in place, Meg shifted the gears into first. A little nervous, she pressed her foot down gently on the gas pedal, eased the car forward and away from the boardwalk into the middle of the street, right in back of a plodding twenty-mule team pulling a string of ore wagons.

"Where do you want to go?" She pulled out from around the wagons, saw the street was nearly empty of other traffic, and drove past them.

"This is your party."

She thought of the possibilities, someplace where she could drive as fast as the car would go. "What about the salt flats?"

* * *

About seven miles north of town, Meg slowed and turned left off the road through a break in the jumble of the gray, frowsy-looking saltbush and cactus. Immediately, she felt the wheels of the car sink, and for an instant her heart clutched at the thought of getting stuck.

"It's okay," Bill said, reading her mind. "Just keep it steady. Follow the tracks if you can. The closer we get to the flats, the harder it'll get."

She gripped the steering wheel tighter. Thankfully, the sun was at her back, out of her eyes. It was hot, and she could feel the sweat beneath the duster and her shirtwaist trickling down her sides. For about a mile, she dodged around Joshua trees and clumps of sage until finally she drew up to the edge of the hard-packed ellipse of sand. She braked to a stop, and they both climbed out.

Swatting the dust and sand off her duster, she surveyed the desolate expanse of packed sand. "It does look like a racetrack, doesn't it?"

He walked onto the edge, stamped his feet on it. "Solid as cement."

Meg turned a complete circle, surveying the landscape. "Your cross-country race ought to stop here and try it."

"I think the route's farther north, going east across Utah and Wyoming."

"You could take a detour."

"I suppose."

She shielded her eyes, gazed across the flats. "Think how much fun it would be, all those cars racing around out there."

"It really isn't a race, you know."

She glanced at him.

"They call it a tour. A reliability tour. Charles Glidden, a Boston millionaire, thought the idea up. He and the American Automobile Association sponsor them. This will be the first one in the West. Anyway, the cars are allowed to go only at fixed speeds. The thinking is that if the public sees some stalwart, upstanding citizens driving across country in regular automobiles, it'll build public confidence and sell more machines."

Looking at Bill with his cap turned backward as usual, she nearly laughed at the picture of his driving in the company of proper businessmen probably wearing high silk hats, their machines driven by chauffeurs. "I didn't realize you were in such important company," she teased.

He grinned. "They let some of us young bucks go along to patch tires."

"Your Boston connections probably don't hurt either."

He shrugged, put an arm around her shoulders. "Not to change the subject, but I thought we came out here to run a little race ourselves."

She glanced up at him. "Well, let's go then."

* * *

Tearing along, her eyes squinting through the goggles, she leaned over the steering wheel as she'd seen pictures of racers doing, and started into the third swing around the huge oval. Her foot on the gas pedal was pushed to the floor.

"What was the time on that stretch?" she shouted.

"Fifty."

"I can't seem to go any faster."

"Fifty will do. Pull up when you go around the next bend. You've proved the point."

She gave a little nod, let up on the gas. The car slowed, and her heart slowed with it. The exhilaration she'd felt roaring across the hard-packed sand was as intoxicating as French champagne. The car rolled to a stop, and she pulled back on the handbrake.

"Wow! You don't spare the horses." He lifted the goggles off his eyes, grinned at her. "It's good the children weren't in the back. We might have lost them on the turns."

She glanced at him, cocked her head. In the six months they'd known each other, it had always been the same—kidding, saying absurd things. Life was to be enjoyed, Bill said. "How many children are we talking about here?"

"Oh, four seems like a good round number."

"Boys or girls?"

"Both, I think." He reached over and placed a hand around the back of her neck, began to knead it. "The problem is the boys might decide to go to Harvard."

She grinned. "And the girls might want to go to medical school. Either way, it wouldn't be good."

He slowly pulled her toward him, kissed her. Putting her arms around his neck, she kissed him back. The kisses went on. His hands moved over her back, her arms, over her breasts.

"What's happening here?" he mumbled huskily as he began to nibble at her lips.

"I think you're kissing me." She could hardly breathe. She ached with wanting him. The smell of him, the feel of him caressing her consumed her. If she allowed it to happen, they would be making love in another moment in the broad daylight, stretched out on the sand.

Summoning all her strength, she pulled away from him, saw the familiar gold flecks in his dark eyes.

"Marry me, Meg."

"You're leaving for San Francisco."

"They have ministers in San Francisco."

"Then you're going cross-country, for months."

"You could come along."

She smiled, traced a finger along his chin line. "I don't think that would be a good idea."

"Then marry me when I get back. Your Aunt Hilary can come."

"How about your mother and father?"

"What about them?"

"I can't imagine they'd approve of your having a wife who intends to open a garage and sell cars."

"Probably not much more than they do my driving them. Anyway, we'll be in San Francisco."

"I'm not much of a cook."

He took her hands in his, held them tight. "I love you. I don't care if you're the worst cook in the world. We'll hire a girl to do that. Will you or won't you marry me?"

She gazed lovingly into his brown eyes, knowing that this was a very special man. She'd never known any other like him. If she married him, he wouldn't be her lord and master, but her partner. He shared her passions. She shared his.

"I don't approve of hiring a nanny to take care of the children."

He grinned at her. "I don't either." He dug inside his shirt, pulled out a gold chain with a small, enameled medallion hanging from it, slipped it over his neck, and put it in her hands. "For now, this will have to take the place of a ring. Gram gave it to me."

She gazed at the intricately carved medal, no bigger than a dime.

"He's hard to really see clearly, but that's Saint Christopher on there. He's supposed to guard you from harm."

She clasped the gold-backed circle to her breasts. "I love you, Bill Brown, and will for the rest of my life."

* * *

Agreeing they would meet for dinner, Meg dropped Bill off at what was now Cleats Garage, blew him a kiss, and drove off. She felt lightheaded. For no earthly reason, tears filled her eyes. She was going to get married.

Up to now, she'd turned up her nose at lovesick girls who mooned over their fiancés. Suddenly, she was one of them. The only difference was that instead of mooning over Bill, her feelings were ones of unadulterated lust. She wondered how many other women ached to make love with a man as much as she ached to make love with Bill. As she drew up to the Imperial and braked to a stop, she decided if Aunt Hilary knew how she felt, she'd be shocked. Or maybe she wouldn't.

Meg climbed out, swatted the dust off herself, straightened her skirts and hat. As she pulled open the door to the restaurant and didn't see the usual line of lunch customers waiting, she wondered what time it was. Perhaps all of Goldfield's economy was hurting.

Standing at the bottom of the stairs, Meg looked up, half-expecting to hear Mr. Linton's baritone, calling out the bids and asks, the din of investors anxious to get in before the price went up or to sell before it went down. Now there was only silence.

Soon that would change. The place would have to be swept. Mr. Linton had left town, but they'd find someone else. She reached in her pocketbook for the key and climbed the stairs, only to find the door ajar. The key still in one hand, she peeked inside, not knowing what or whom she would find.

The familiar room was empty, the air warm, stuffy, like the inside of an old trunk that had been locked up for years. There was no sign of anyone. Only mice tracks etched the skim of sand that had blown through the window cracks and accumulated on the floor.

She walked past the orderly row of chairs to the cashier's cage, peered inside. The slots large enough to file the ledger books were empty. The inkwells looked dried up. She moved to the podium, idly ran a finger over its dust-thick edge.

From the floor below, she heard the front door open and close, heavy footsteps climbing the stairs. She turned and saw John Burlingame come through the door.

"I came by earlier, but you weren't here," he said. Meg thought he looked tired, older since Emma's death. "I used Mrs. Burlingame's key."

Somehow, Meg had forgotten each board member had her own key.

"I've been wanting to talk to you. You and Miss Bates. And Miss Wallace, of course."

Meg glanced about. "Shall we sit down?"

He ran a hand over the seat of the nearest chair, shook his head in a sad kind of way, and pulled out a handkerchief from a pocket in his trousers. "Mrs. Burlingame was always complaining about the dust and sand."

"It certainly is a problem."

John Burlingame dusted off two chairs, and they sat down. He crossed his legs, pulled at the bottom of his vest. "After considerable thought, I decided there was nothing else to be done but close."

She wasn't certain she'd heard him right. "Close what?"

"The ladies' exchange."

"But I'm here to reopen it."

He gave a tired smile. "That's what Miss Bates told me. So before you went to any trouble—"

Meg sat up straighter. "Mr. Burlingame, how is it that you came to the conclusion that we should close?"

"As your president. Of course, you know how much it saddens me. Mrs. Burlingame put so much store in the ladies' exchange, but having inherited her seat—"

"Mr. Burlingame, we loved Emma almost as much as you did. Nevertheless, I must emphasize you are not the president. The ladies' exchange duly adopted a constitution which sets out an orderly process for replacing officers. Nowhere does it mention that an office can be inherited. That would be quite irregular. I'm sure Tess and Verna will be more than happy to meet as a board for the purpose of holding an election."

"I—"

"I'm afraid I must insist."

"Very well. If that's what you want, I'll go along."

"Those are our rules, Mr. Burlingame. You helped us establish them, remember?"

John Burlingame waved her comment away, as if it was a pesky fly, and rose. "The fact remains, Miss Kendall, that the ladies' exchange no longer has sufficient listings to warrant being in business."

"I beg your pardon," Meg said, indignant.

"It's true. With the exception of your own stock, the Fourth of July, every other listing that was offered by the ladies' exchange is no longer in existence."

"How's that?"

"When the leases ran out, those mines reverted to Goldfield Consolidated. The senator and Mr. Winters bought up most of the surrounding mines for insurance. In other words, almost all the independent mines are now under Goldfield Consolidated Mines."

"But what about the brokerage houses that traded with us? We were counting on them to list their new issues with us."

"Miss Kendall, don't you see? There aren't any new listings. Not of any size. Certainly not enough to fuel two stock exchanges."

She gazed, unseeing, out the filthy window, trying to comprehend what John Burlingame was saying.

"I'm sorry."

She glanced at him. "Verna and Tess had counted on the money from the sale of their seats."

"I guessed as much."

She rose, walked to the board, stared at the empty squares, returned to where Mr. Burlingame stood. "Apparently, while Goldfield was trying to survive the epidemic, the senator and Mr. Winters were busily buying up mines."

John Burlingame gave her a level look. "You can't blame them."

She sighed. "I suppose not. It's business, isn't it?"

"It is indeed." Mr. Burlingame picked up his bowler from a nearby chair. "Of course, you are welcome to trade your Fourth of July with us. I'm sure I can arrange the waving of the commission charge."

Meg smiled. "Thank you."

"I mean it."

"I want to talk to Verna and Tess. We need to hold a formal board meeting."

Mr. Burlingame put on his hat, adjusted its angle.

"I suppose there are steps one takes to dissolve a business," Meg said, walking him to the door.

"Just close the doors. It's that simple."

Chapter 34

$\mathcal{T}$ess opened the nearest window of the exchange. "Lord a'mighty, you'd think it was summer instead of March with this heat." She came back to sit down at the table. Meg sat across from her. Verna was to her right. The account books were piled in the center. Beside it was the magnificent cake Mrs. Archibald had baked for the occasion. The butterscotch frosting was decorated with little sugar roses. Tess had never been much of a fancy baker herself, but she admired the artistry. Once she got the ranch going, she'd teach herself how.

Meg had come by the Ajax last night during the evening rush, such as it was these days, told her about John Burlingame's visit, and said they had to have an emergency board meeting. She'd been all-business, but Tess had caught the anxiety in her voice. Closing the exchange would be tough on Meg. It was like her baby. She'd brought it into the world, breathed life into it with her father's stock, fed it. For Tess, the exchange was only a means to an end. Now she no longer had any stock to trade or money to buy more. If the exchange folded, so be it, except . . .

A sadness hung over the room.

"It don't seem the same without Emma," Tess said.

Meg and Verna merely nodded. There was nothing to say. They had known Emma for a brief three months. Yet she'd become an important part of their lives. As their official leader, she'd been their link to the other exchange. More than that, she had been their friend. Tess would never forget the morning after the Petticord party, sitting next to Emma in this very room, the way she'd quietly overlooked Tess's insults and told her how she admired her. Emma had been one in a million.

"Well." Meg moved a pad of paper in front of her, picked up a pencil. "We better get started."

There'd never been a formal vote taken on who would take Emma's place as president, but Meg seemed a natural successor. They voted to donate the furniture to Mrs. Archibald as a token of thanks for letting them use the room, rent free. Meg withdrew her Fourth of July stock from the assets. Verna made the motion, with a second from Tess, that the Ladies' Goldfield Stock Exchange go out of business. Everyone drew in a long breath. Meg called for the vote. The ayes had it unanimously. The entire meeting, start to finish, took five minutes.

For an instant, they glanced at each other as if at a loss to know what to do next. They eyed the cake, and Verna picked up the cake knife.

"I feel like I'm at a wake," she said, expertly cutting a piece and sliding it onto one of the three plates Mrs. Archibald had provided.

"Too quiet for a wake." Tess took the plate, completely filled by the slice of cake. "There's no booze."

Meg accepted the second piece of cake. "I just wish . . ."

Tess caught the wistful tone of her friend's voice. "Sweetie, if wishes were horses, beggars would ride."

"That ought to be on my brother's headstone," Verna said wryly.

Tess chuckled as she picked up her piece of cake, took a bite, and swallowed. Beneath Verna's motherly exterior was a toughness Tess admired. Tess licked her fingers. The cake's texture was light as air. She could taste the vanilla and maybe a drop of something else. Brandy? Cognac? Just a hint. In the frosting.

"Whatever happened to Amos anyway?" Tess asked, brushing a scattering of crumbs off her skirt.

"Last I heard he was in New Mexico. Las Cruces or someplace like that."

Out of the corner of her eye, Tess saw Meg staring down at her cake, not eating it. The usual starch was gone. "Eh, cheer up, Meg. This isn't your fault. The consolidation, the times, whatever— that's what did it. We had a good run. We all made money."

Meg glanced at her, morosely. "But you've lost a thousand dollars you could have had with the sale of your seat." She turned to Verna. "So have you. In fact, you weren't even going to invest at all until I talked you into it, and now look."

"Poppycock! It was me, not you, who bet on that fight. I'd stayed clear of gambling all my life till I won that four dollars on Gans. After that, the stock market was a natural."

Meg looked away, not replying. Beyond the room was the day's noise—bullwhackers' shouts, horses neighing, the honk of automobiles, the ever-present rhythm of the stamp mills. After a moment or two, she said, "Funny. I'd almost forgotten about the fight."

"I sure haven't," Tess said, feeling the familiar bite of regret over her stolen shares. "Good old Jake robbed me even then."

"That fight made the organizers a lot of money," Meg said thoughtfully, as she stood and began to pace the room.

Tess watched her circle the table. She could almost hear the wheels whirring inside Meg's head. Something was up.

Finally, too impatient to wait any longer, Tess said, "Okay. You've got somethin' on your mind. Spit it out."

Meg eyed Tess and Verna. "We'll have a race. Charge for seats. Just like they did at the fight. And, in the process, we'll get more than any two thousand dollars." Meg grinned from ear to ear as she surveyed her two friends for their reaction.

"I don't know," Tess said. "Who in his right mind would pay to watch a collection of nags in this town?"

"Not horses, silly. It's going to be an automobile race. Shiny as patent leather. Brand-new touring cars. Cadillacs, Renos, Thomas

Flyers, Pierces." Meg shot a glance at Verna. "You'll take care of the publicity. People will come from everywhere. Los Angeles. San Francisco. Just to see these gorgeous cars. It will be like before."

Tess eyed her skeptically. "You sound like you've been smokin' that sweet stuff in Hop Fiends' Gulch."

"Is that all you can say, Tess Wallace? I come up with a solution that's perfect and—"

Tess held up both hands in a gesture of surrender. "Okay. You're goin' to have an auto race, with tourin' cars."

"*We* are goin' to have an auto race," said Meg firmly.

"You and Verna, maybe. I'm leavin' for Steamboat Springs."

"Well, you're just going to have to wait until after the race because you'll be in charge of the refreshments and contacting all the saloons to contribute beer and such."

"Meg, dear, do you really think anyone is going to come and bet on an auto race in Goldfield, Nevada?" Verna ventured, gently.

"They came to see a prizefight."

"Sure, they did," Tess said. "But a national championship was at stake. I don't see the draw on this one."

"We're going to have the very men who are taking part in the first-ever cross-country race detour to Goldfield."

"You mean, the cars would just tear into town and out again?" Tess asked.

Meg didn't answer at first. Finally, she said, "No. It's going to be on the salt flats. We'll set up bleachers."

"I suppose Bill is goin' to be in on this?" Tess said.

"Well, of course. He's a member of the cross-country group. He can arrange everything."

Tess wasn't so sure.

"Of course, it really isn't a race. They call it a reliability tour."

Tess cocked an eyebrow.

"Though if we persuaded them, they might agree to call it a race," Meg said.

"Who's 'they'?" asked Verna.

"The American Automobile Association and the men who own the automobiles."

Tess leaned back in her chair. "Rich men."

"Mostly."

"And they bet on these reliability tours, do they?" Tess asked.

"Well, not generally, but—"

"You're somethin' else, Meg Kendall." Tess regarded her friend with affection. "How many people in the world would cook up something like this just to help two friends on their uppers?"

Meg came up behind Tess, hugged her. "You'd do the same, if it were me. You know you would. Besides, I'll make money, too."

Tess glanced around at her. "You really think this thing can work?"

"If we started a stock exchange, we can certainly organize an auto race."

Tess met Meg's flashing eyes. If Tess didn't miss her bet, the American Automobile Association or whatever the hell it was called was about to learn what it was like to deal with a woman like Meg Kendall. It might almost be worthwhile sticking around to see what happened.

CHAPTER 35

$\mathcal{M}$eg left the Imperial, torn between regrets over the closing of the exchange and excitement over the prospects of the race. She suspected her father wouldn't have been surprised over the death of the ladies' exchange. Nothing was permanent in a mining camp. Still, she'd not only accomplished what she'd set out to do but had also come to know three, now two, wonderful women who had became her friends.

What better way to take the sting off and go out in grand fashion than with an auto race? Even with consolidation and a downturn in business, nothing could squash people's insatiable urge to experience something new and make quick money in the process.

Yet before she and Verna and Tess tackled the details of the race, she had unfinished business of her own to take care of. The nagging, unanswered questions over her father's death hung over her like a dark cloud. Then there was her Fourth of July stock. She knew it was time to dispose of it. John Burlingame had offered to act as her broker with no charge.

Meg walked to the corner, turned onto Fifth, and headed in the direction of the John Cook Bank. Bits of trash, caught up in the warm wind, swirled around her ankles. She squinted in the bright sunlight as she paused at the end of the block to let the traffic go by. To her amazement, she saw Charley Thompson waiting on the opposite corner. It had been weeks since she'd even seen him. An older, gray-haired man who looked familiar stood next to him. Looking more closely, she realized it was Charley's father, Sumner Thompson.

Seeing him again, tall and dignified, she was impressed, as she had been that night at dinner last fall, by his reassuring manner. Why hadn't she thought of Mr. Thompson before? As the senator's and Mr. Winter's attorney, he had to be informed about the workings of their mine operations. She sensed he was the one person she could trust who was able to give her real answers about her father's death.

She hurried across the street, hailed them. Sumner Thompson looked her way, smiled, tipped his soft-brimmed fedora.

"Miss Kendall, what a delightful surprise."

She caught her breath, returned his smile. "I'm so glad I caught you."

Charley cleared his throat, and she colored, embarrassed that she'd completely ignored him. "Charley, how are you?" she asked now.

"Is that an Olds you're driving around town?"

"It is indeed," she said, mildly surprised he would have noticed. She returned her gaze to his father.

"Mr. Thompson, if it isn't an imposition, I would appreciate the opportunity to speak to you on a matter of business."

"It would be my pleasure. It just so happens I expect to be in town for the remainder of the week."

"Would there be a chance we could meet this afternoon?"

He and Charley exchanged glances.

"Of course, if that interrupts your plans . . ."

Sumner Thompson smiled at her. "Not at all. In fact, right now would be fine. I have a small office on the second floor of the Nolan Building." He offered her his arm. "Shall we go?"

* * *

Meg gave an inadvertent shiver as she glanced up and down the hall as she waited for Mr. Thompson to unlock the door. It was the first time she'd been in the Nolan Building. Its stone exterior gave it an aura of permanence unique in a camp constructed largely of raw lumber and canvas. The offices downstairs housed the headquarters of the Goldfield Consolidated Mines Company. Behind two of those doors sat the owners, the men probably responsible for her father's death. She was about to enter their attorney's office. Quite literally, she was in the midst of enemy territory. Yet for a reason she couldn't explain, she believed Sumner Thompson was an honorable man who would try to help her.

Once his key found its notch, Sumner Thompson opened the door, stood aside, and motioned for her to enter. The office was about as she had expected—just big enough to hold the usual roll-top pine desk, a swivel chair, two glass-front bookcases filled with large volumes, probably law books. To her right, against the wall, were two straight-backed chairs for visitors. A coatrack stood in the corner. The single window offered a view to the street below.

Sumner Thompson removed his hat, placed it on the top hook of the coatrack.

"It seems stuffy in here. Would you mind if I open the window?"

"Not at all."

He opened the window an inch and asked if he could take her cloak. She unfastened it, handed it to him, and he hung it on the coatrack below his hat.

They sat down, he in the swivel chair, she in one of the wood chairs. She settled her skirts, impatient to begin.

"As you may remember, Mr. Thompson, my father worked as a mining engineer for the Mohawk Mines Company. Last August he was killed in an accident. Or, at least, that's what I was told."

The lenses of his pince-nez gave his blue eyes a gentle appearance.

"I take it you are not entirely convinced that the tragedy *was* an accident."

She glanced down at her hands clasped in her lap. "I'm not sure what to think." She told him about her father's warning. For the moment, she decided not to mention the stock. "I realize you represent the senator and Mr. Winters, but at this point I don't know who else to ask who might know the facts."

He gave her a sympathetic smile. "Surely you know accidents are a daily occurrence in mines."

"I've also been told there's no possible way to prove my father's death was anything but accidental."

"I fear that's probably the case."

She sighed deeply.

"Your father, as I recall, was a friend of Mr. Eckles," he said.

She eyed him, a little surprised he had remembered. "Yes, he was."

"Have you discussed the matter with Mr. Eckles?"

"Briefly."

"But Mr. Eckles didn't put your mind at rest."

"Not really, though it was plain he had no use for the senator or Mr. Winters."

"I'm not surprised." Mr. Thompson leaned his elbows on the arms of the swivel chair, made a tent of his fingers. "Charley tells me you were one of the founders of the ladies' stock exchange."

She nodded, a little puzzled at the turn in the conversation.

"As such, I presume you've been following the suit against my clients still pending in district court."

"I'm afraid all I know is rumor. Frankly, I'm amazed the court never shut down the three mines in question. Amazed and pleased, I might add."

He gave a wry kind of smile. "It sounds as if you have a personal interest."

"I do," she admitted. With a slip of the tongue, she'd revealed more than she had intended. Now there was nothing to do but tell him the entire story. "My father left me ten thousand shares of Fourth of July."

His left eyebrow shot up. "Ah, that explains it."

"I beg your pardon?"

"Where the remaining stock was."

"I don't understand."

Tapping his fingertips together, Mr. Thompson swung the swivel chair around and gazed out the window for a moment. As she stared at the back of his head with its well-trimmed gray hair, his square shoulders in the good tweed jacket, she recalled how carefully she'd always tried to keep track of the number of Fourth of July shares traded at the exchange.

In those mad weeks before Christmas, it had seemed all but her ten thousand shares had exchanged hands every day and all handled through one broker, Phil Steiner. Had he been commissioned by Nolan and Winters to buy up the Fourth of July and thereby drive up the price? Had he suspected she might know who had the outstanding stock? Was that why he had invited her to the Christmas Eve party?

Mr. Thompson turned back to face her. "You are a wealthy young woman, Miss Kendall."

"Not as rich as I would have been two months ago."

"True."

She leaned forward, impatient to return to the reason for the meeting. "Mr. Thompson, I must know about my father's death."

She studied his carefully composed face with its sympathetic eyes, searching for the answer, but found none.

"Is there nothing you can tell me?"

He removed his pince-nez, rubbed the bridge of his nose. Without looking at her, he said, "Mr. Eckles is in town. Perhaps you should pay him another visit."

CHAPTER 36

*V*erna could see well enough to fend for herself now, high time she was out of Tess's hair. The day after they'd voted to close the exchange, Verna had moved into the Rochester Hotel with her sole possessions—a change of underthings and a new shirtwaist from the Bon Ton—in a battered straw valise.

Her room was on the second floor, its window overlooking the street. It was so tiny she had to turn sideways to get between the dresser and the single bed. It reeked of ancient vomit and sweat. It wasn't the Ritz, but it would do. Once she gave the floor another good scrub, it would be fine. And, given her lack of resources, the weekly room and board of five dollars was within her price range.

Meg had insisted on lending her fifty dollars. When Verna had started to object, Meg had cut her off, said it was just to tide her over until the auto race. Without much choice, Verna had swallowed her pride and taken the money, but just until. . .

Until what? The auto race might net her the fifty dollars she would owe Meg. Might. After that, what? She could ask Frank Tribble at the *Tattler* for a job as a copy editor. Out of sympathy for her situation, he might agree to take her on, though probably not for long, certainly not after she overlooked obvious errors a pair of good eyes would have caught in a minute.

Truth be known, she didn't want to stay in Goldfield anymore. Its only appeal were the friends she'd made and Jimmy. Emma was dead. Tess and Meg would be gone soon. It was only natural Jimmy would move on to wherever his father got work.

The treeless, never-ending gray cast that hung over the surrounding desert shriveled her soul. Her feet and legs swelled into giants stumps in the heat. She longed for the scent of pine trees, the sound of their needles stirring in the light breeze. She wanted to go back to Colorado. But, at the moment, she had more immediate matters to tackle.

She sat down on the lumpy mattress, felt her stays jab into her sagging breasts as she stared at the peeling, dingy gray wallpaper, and thought about the auto race again. In spite of her skepticism, she had to admit it had possibilities. Automobiles, particularly when driven by rich men, had a magic about them that could draw a good crowd. If her job was publicity, she better get to it.

She pushed to her feet, tugged her corset back down into place. She better scout up Jimmy. News releases didn't get written and sent out by themselves.

* * *

Verna was halfway up High-grade Hill when she had to stop to catch her breath again. More and more these days her body failed to cooperate with what she intended to do. As she felt her heartbeat slow, she gazed toward the familiar tar paper–covered tent that was the Earnest family's home. She hoped Jimmy was home. If he wasn't, maybe she'd send little Mary Lou to run fetch him.

She set out again, careful to stay on the high side of the wagon ruts. As Verna came closer, the woman who lived next door stepped out of her tent, waved a greeting. Verna waved back.

"If you're lookin' for the Earnests, you just missed 'em."

"Jimmy, too?"

The thin woman tucked loose strands of mousy hair behind her ears. "The whole family. Seems the mister's got him a job in Creede."

Verna tried to digest the news. She'd expected such a thing would happen, but not so soon. The timing couldn't be worse. "When did they leave?"

"Half hour, maybe. They were bound for the afternoon train."

"Did they leave a message, a note maybe?"

The woman shook her head. " 'Fraid not."

Verna gazed at the door of the Earnests' deserted tent, her heart gripped with disappointment and with anger. Why hadn't Jimmy come by to tell her he was leaving? It was the least he could have done. She wondered what time it was. She wished she had a watch. She glanced up at the sky. Judging by the position of the sun in the western sky, it was close to train time.

Without another word to the woman, Verna hurried back down the hill. She turned her ankle once on the rutted road, caught herself before she fell, hobbled on. Close to the bottom, a blast of the train whistle ricocheted through the dry air. Her heart pounded. Tears of frustration clouded her eyes. She blinked them away. She was so close. She had to get to the depot before the train pulled out. She dodged a mule train, a freight wagon whose team nearly ran her down. The depot, the train with its three cars was just ahead.

She saw the steam whooshing out from between the wheels, heard the impatient pant of the engine. She tried to run. A line of people stood waiting to board the lone passenger car. Her chest felt as if it might explode at any minute. She waved, called Jimmy's name, but no sound came out of her mouth.

The conductor climbed down from the passenger car and moved among the small crowd of passengers. There were several children among them. A woman picked one of them up, held the child in her arms. In that instant, Verna caught a glimpse of a thin boy, a battered cap turned backward on his head, wearing clothes too small for him. Jimmy. Gathering all her strength, she waved with both hands, praying he'd glance her way.

CHAPTER 37

The daylight was nearly gone when Meg rounded the corner and came in sight of the bottle house. A tall, rangy man with salt-and-pepper hair leaned against the door. He seemed to be waiting for her. Even at this distance, instinct told her it was Pete Eckles. It was almost as if he'd known she was looking for him.

"Meg Kendall!" he called when he saw her.

She summoned a smile as she approached.

"I'd hoped we'd get together."

"I, too." She dug the door key out of her pocketbook, opened the door, invited him to come in. She went to the stove and reached for the box on the shelf above it for a match. Turning to the table, she lifted the glass chimney of the lamp, held the match to the wick, and adjusted the flame so it wouldn't smoke.

As she blew out the match, she was aware of the size of Pete Eckles as he continued to stand by the door, how he seemed to fill the small room. It made her uneasy.

"Please. Sit down, won't you? May I get you some coffee?"

"No thanks on the coffee, but I'll sit for a spell." He pulled out the nearest wood chair, settled himself, and smiled. "I 'spose you've been wonderin' why I haven't gotten in touch with you."

"I had. Yes."

"In this business, it's all a matter of timin'." He nodded, as if re-flecting on the truth of his words as he looked around him. "This was your dad's place. You've got it fixed up right nice."

She smiled, took the chair across the table from him.

"The man was a genius."

Her uneasiness ebbed slightly. After all, she was sitting in her father's house with a man who had been his friend, a man who was praising him.

"I've been told he was a fine mining engineer," she said quietly.

"The best."

Their gazes held for a long moment until he said, "Well, now. Best get on to business."

She straightened.

"Fact is, I came to tell you it was time."

"Time?"

"To sign over your Fourth of July shares."

"How do you know I haven't sold them already?"

He cocked an eyebrow, laughed. "Damnation if you aren't as smart as your dad. He'd be proud of you."

For a reason she couldn't explain, the compliment put her off.

"Here's the deal." He hunched forward, his neck jutting forward, and leaned his elbows on the table. "I'll buy the whole shootin' match from you for an eighth above the market."

When she didn't respond, he asked, "Is anybody offerin' you more?"

She shook her head.

"Whatever the offer," he said. "I'll match it and add an eighth."

"That's most generous."

"I'm talkin' good business here, Meg. And old times. Your dad and me. Who better to sell his shares to than me?"

She tried to smile.

"I hope you're not thinkin' to push up the price on me. My offer is fair." He stood. "As usual, I'll be at the Casey when you want to get in touch with me."

As he stepped over the threshold, he stopped, looked back at her. "Meg, I'm a generous man, so I'll make that a quarter of a point over any price you can get. That's a lot of money, Meg."

She watched him stride down the boardwalk, round the corner out of sight. She'd forgotten to ask him about her father's death.

* * *

Her head too full of contradictions, Meg didn't sleep well that night. In the morning, she went to Mr. Thompson's office and found him in. She told him about her brief meeting with Mr. Eckles. He listened, nodded.

"I'd like to get back to your concern about your father's death," he said.

"Please."

"It's important you understand that the senator and Mr. Winters view mines as an investment to be made the most of as rapidly as possible. The fine points of digging out a new drift correctly was, and is, of absolutely no interest to them."

"But it was to my father."

Mr. Thompson nodded. "I understand the three of them had some rather heated arguments on the subject. My guess is that the senator and Mr. Winters would have fired any other mining engineer for insubordination, but your father was too skilled. In fact, the last such argument between them took place over the very issue involved in the suit."

"Which was trespass."

"Exactly." He stood, went to the window, gazed down at the street for a moment, then turned back. "Apparently, your father's map of the area in question gave absolutely no indications of trespass. An independent survey of the area we commissioned since then substantiates that fact. As I say, your father was the best."

She smiled, warmed by the words.

"As a result, we felt confident that should the case come to trial, there would be no question of the outcome."

"I see."

"We had heard, though it is only rumor, that your father also showed that map to Mr. Eckles, who was a friend. In fact, as I understand it, your father once did some early mapping of the Fourth for Eckles."

"I believe so."

He sat down again. "So there we are. Two men—the senator and Mr. Winters—bent on profit, another man—your father—who cared only for finding the next seam of rich ore. Disagreement was inevitable. As to murder, absolutely not." He smiled sympathetically.

She gazed toward the window, going over Mr. Thompson's explanation in her mind again. The logic of it was clear. She took in a deep breath, let it out slowly, and felt a great weight lift from her heart. She wondered why she hadn't thought of it herself. She looked at Mr. Thompson, at his steady blue eyes, and smiled. "Thank you."

He nodded. For a moment, they sat without speaking. Finally, he said, "If I may, I'd like to return to the matter of the stock."

"Of course."

"Your shares of stock are vital to Mr. Eckles. With them, he remains the majority stockholder of the Fourth of July mine. He holds the winning hand. Without them, he is just another stockholder."

"I don't understand."

"Let me explain it this way." He rocked absently back and forth in his chair a few times. "You've lived in Goldfield long enough to know that when a mine shuts down, the digging ceases, the pumps stop. As a result, the deepest levels often fill with water. Most importantly, production comes to a halt. Without ore coming out, no one makes money. It is a situation to be avoided at all costs. Agreed?"

"Agreed."

"So when Mr. Eckles filed suit for trespass against my clients and the court decided the suit was not a frivolous one and decided to proceed, there was always the possibility the court would decide to shut both parties down until the matter came to trial.

"You may remember when I first met you, Miss Kendall, I was here on business. The business was about the suit. Mr. Eckles came to me with a proposition. He would arrange to hold off any court action regarding a shutdown if we came up with the money to settle. We protested, of course. Said the suit had no basis in fact. Said we had the proof. Eckles only laughed and said the next move was up to us."

"But if you had the maps to prove—"

"I'm afraid experts can be bought to prove anything, including trespass. In other words, Eckles said that if we could come up with enough money to buy him out at his price, he would settle out of court and production would continue, uninterrupted."

She remembered the talk before Christmas of Sumner Thompson visiting bankers in New York.

"You mentioned that you thought someone was attempting to acquire all the stock. The someone was Mr. Winters and the senator. Of course, no one but the transfer clerk for a company knows who the stock owner is. Nevertheless, we knew how much stock was originally issued. As you do. Even before you and I met yesterday, it was clear ten thousand shares were outstanding. Your shares, as it happens, are the determining factor of who is the majority stockholder of the Fourth of July."

"What, exactly, are you saying?"

"In plain English, I believe you should sell your shares to the senator and Mr. Winters."

She stared at him. To sell her father's shares to the very men for whom he'd had no use was immoral, absurd. "Mr. Eckles said he'd best any offer I received."

He gave her a wry smile. "But did he tell you what his price to us was to settle the suit?"

She shook her head.

"I didn't think so. Perhaps you better go back and ask him."

* * *

Charged with a strange kind of energy, Meg left Mr. Thompson's office and strode to the Fourth of July office, refusing to be put off by either clerks or the superintendent until she came face-to-face with Pete Eckles.

He looked up from his desk, smiled when he saw who it was. "Good girl, Meg. So what's the price I have to match?"

"I need to know what price you told the Goldfield Consolidated you'd settle for."

He didn't move a muscle.

"It's only fair that I know."

A smile curled one corner of his mouth. "Sorry, darlin'. But that's none of your business."

"With all due respect, I think it is. From what I understand, my ten thousand shares—my father's ten thousand shares—are going to help make you a fortune."

His smile held, but she noticed a twitch had developed in his left eye. "Are you playin' some kind of game here, missy?"

"It's my inheritance I'm trying to protect, Mr. Eckles."

"Heh, you're lookin' at the man who gave those shares to Jim Kendall." He squinted the left eye shut, as if to control the twitch. "I repeat. Gave them to him."

"You gave those shares to my father as payment for work well done. You said so yourself."

"So I did." He puckered his lips and nodded thoughtfully, stared at the floor, then glanced up at her and said, "You see, when you get right down to it, darlin', it's all about loyalty."

"I don't—"

"Your dad and me were like brothers. When he showed me that map of his and said I was wrong about trespass, I said he had to prove it. So he took me down, showed me the drift."

Meg stared at him. "You went down in the Haywood-Mohawk?"

He laughed. "Jim fixed it so nobody saw us."

"You actually were in the area Dad had mapped?"

"You betcha."

In that instant, Meg was certain Pete Eckles had killed her father. He hadn't done it himself. He was too smart for that. But he'd killed him, nonetheless.

Pete Eckles tipped back in his chair, relaxed, a look of confidence on his wrinkled face, as if certain he had fooled her. "Now about your shares—"

"I'll be in touch," she said, backing toward the door.

"You do that, darlin'. Don't forget. I'll match whatever you get and add an eighth."

"I thought you said a quarter." She heard the edge in her voice.

Pete Eckles cocked an eyebrow. "Did I? Well, sure, if that's what I said, you know you can count on it."

* * *

The cold fury, the hatred Meg felt toward Pete Eckles propelled her blindly out the door of the Fourth of July office, past miners on their way home from their shift, past ore wagons until she stood at the entrance of the Nolan Building.

Eckles had deliberately used her father's skill, used his friendship, to make himself rich. He had never felt anything for her father. Yet Eckles knew if her father had ever testified at the trial, he would tell the truth: The Fourth of July was guilty of trespass, not the other way around. Eckles would have lost everything. Now he intended to cheat her and use the shares her father had given her to gain ultimate control of the company, thus forcing the Goldfield Consolidated Mines to pay his price if they wanted to settle out of court.

Meg climbed the stairs to Mr. Thompson's second-floor office, tapped on the door, opened it, and looked in.

Seeing her, he rose to his feet. "Miss Kendall. Good morning. Come in."

"I came to tell you I've decided to sell my shares to Goldfield Consolidated."

He motioned for her to come in, invited her to sit down.

"Thank you. I'll stand."

"Very well."

"I want to check today's prices first. Then I'll be back."

"The senator and Mr. Winters will be grateful."

"I must be frank, Mr. Thompson. I don't care whether your clients are grateful or not. I've met them only once. What I do know of them, I don't like."

Sumner Thompson gave her a level look.

"Mr. Eckles guaranteed me a quarter point above whatever price I was offered. I will expect the same from your clients."

Mr. Thompson nodded.

She went to the door, then paused and turned back to him. "I want you to know how grateful I am for your help, Mr. Thompson."

"Quite the contrary. It is I who am grateful."

"I know I can't prove Pete Eckles killed my father. Even if I could, it wouldn't bring him back."

Mr. Thompson nodded sympathetically.

"My father didn't care a hoot about money. It was the mines he loved. He thought Pete Eckles shared that love, but he didn't."

"Apparently not."

"I should be pleased that the matter is settled, but somehow it makes me a little sad. It's the part of mining that was my father's blind spot. The greed, I mean. When I first came to Goldfield, I didn't see it either."

"Money, I fear, is what it's all about," Mr. Thompson said gently, opening the door for her.

"I know." She extended her hand to him. "Well, then. I guess this is good-bye."

He held her hand between his for a moment, studied her. "What will you do now?"

"Oh, I thought I'd mentioned it. The ladies' exchange is sponsoring an auto race."

"An auto race?"

"Like the prizefight. Remember?"

"Indeed I do."

"We intend to advertise widely to attract a good crowd. There'll be a charge for seats. And, I suspect, some bets will be made," she said with a laugh.

Mr. Thompson's eyes danced behind the lenses of his pince-nez. "In Goldfield, that goes without saying."

"I hope you'll come. Charley, too, of course."

"When will this grand affair take place?" he asked.

"In about three weeks. The exact date hasn't been set yet. It'll be announced in the paper. You won't be able to miss it." She glanced down the empty hall. She felt a great weight lift from her heart. It was time to get on with her life.

"I hope the auto race and whatever comes after it will go well for you," said Mr. Thompson.

Standing on tiptoe, Meg gave him a quick kiss on the cheek, and they parted.

CHAPTER 38

A buzz of voices swarmed overhead. Everything was black. For a terrifying second, Verna thought she'd gone blind, then realized her eyelids were closed. Something hard stabbed into the back of her left shoulder, and it dawned on her that she was lying on the ground. She opened her eyes to see Jimmy Earnest peering down at her, an anxious expression on his face.

"Miz Bates, are you okay?"

Summoning all her energy, she raised onto one elbow. "What happened?"

"You tripped and fell. You must have hit your head."

Verna blinked, remembering her desperate effort to catch Jimmy before the train left. "You're still here. You haven't left."

He took her arm, half-lifted her to her feet. "I'm goin' to get you over to the shade where you can sit."

Verna looked over at the train. "You never told me you were leaving."

"I should've, I know, but Dad decided suddenlike to take this new job—"

They had reached the bench outside the depot entrance, and she sat down heavily.

"Sit down," she said to Jimmy, who did as he was told.

"Can I get you some water or something, Miz Bates?" he asked.

"Not a thing, but thank you. I'm fine."

For a moment, they gazed at the train. Crates were being unloaded from a freight wagon into one end of the mail car.

"There's going to be an auto race in a few weeks right here in Goldfield. Did you know that?" She eyed Jimmy for his reaction.

"An auto race?"

"We ladies are putting it on. I'm in charge of the promotion. That's why I was looking for you. I just naturally thought you could give me a hand with it."

"Gosh," he said in a tone of amazement. Then he sighed. "I sure wish I could help you, Miz Bates. I'd like that more than anything."

Verna scanned the milling collection of passengers. "Where's your father?"

He gave a nod of his head toward the locomotive. "Talking to Mr. Phelps, the engineer."

"Do you suppose your father would consider allowing you to stay here for a while? Just until the race is over?"

"I . . ." He glanced at the ground. "I'm plenty old enough to go down into the mines. Dad thinks I could be a car man's helper."

She pretended not to hear what she'd known all along would probably be the boy's fate. "Would you like to stay?" she asked.

His face instantly broke into a broad smile. "You bet I would."

Verna swatted the dust off her skirt. "All right then. You run over to your dad and ask him to come over. We'll see what he says."

* * *

Standing in front of her, his arms folded resolutely across his chest, Mr. Earnest listened to Verna explain her idea, then shook his head. "You're a good woman, Miss Bates, but Jimmy's wages are needed."

"But he'd be part of bringing Goldfield back to life. Think of it. He'd be promoting the auto race and—"

"I ain't heard of no auto race."

"I realize that," she said, knowing the entire scheme was still in the heads of three women and Bill Brown. But Verna had spent years making up her life as it went along. "The news isn't out yet, but I can assure you it'll be a national event."

"I still don't see what the boy here's got to do with an auto race."

"Jimmy's become my right-hand man, Mr. Earnest. He's learning to be a first-rate writer. We're depending on his help to put out the articles about the race. I can't do it without him."

"There's others in town."

"Not of ability, however." Verna smiled affectionately at Jimmy, then looked back at his glowering, obviously unmoved father. "If you don't mind me getting a little personal, Mr. Earnest."

He shrugged.

"You and I are part of the older generation. Times are changing and these young folks like Jimmy need a chance to better themselves . . ."

"Miss Bates, what Jimmy does is my business."

"I realize that, but just think of the opportunity. He'll meet famous auto racers. What he writes will be read by thousands of people all over the country. Besides, he'd only have to stay here another month at the most." Verna looked for some sign that Mr. Earnest was weakening, but none appeared.

"There's a mucker's job open now. It might be gone in a month."

Verna gazed down at her hands clenched in her lap, unable to imagine how long her dear Jimmy would last mucking out a drift. The job was hard for a grown man. She was desperate to find something that would move this stubborn man. Finally, she looked up and said, "Mr. Earnest, if you are willing to let Jimmy remain in Goldfield with me until after the race, I will pay for his room and board and add five dollars a week beside."

Mr. Earnest gazed at her thoughtfully, pursed his lips. Verna saw hope.

"Well?" she asked, brightly.

He continued to study her.

"On further thought, given Jimmy might be earning six dollars a week in the mine, I'll raise his pay to six."

Mr. Earnest glanced at his son. "For a month?"

"A month," Verna agreed. There'd be nothing left of the fifty dollars Meg had loaned her, but who cared?

*   *   *

Verna felt like a new woman. Jimmy would be with her, at least for a while. The weather was warm but not hot. She had a purpose in life again.

The very next day, Verna met Tess, Meg, and Bill in the kitchen of the Ajax, and they began to map out their plans. Bill was to leave for San Francisco the next day. He'd already wired his cousin, who was rich and somebody important in northern California, and asked him to speak to the powers-that-be in the American Automobile Association about sanctioning the detour from the already established route. Verna was optimistic, sure the automobile association wouldn't turn down one of its own.

Bill left a few days later. The race committee, including Jimmy, got down to serious business. Meg would talk to the town board, get its support. Verna and Jimmy would take care of publicity. They'd have to have a reviewing stand. The charge for seats would be a dollar in the front row, a dollar more for the next two rows, five dollars at the top, where the view of the track would be the best. It was a foregone conclusion that Tess would take care of the refreshments.

Following the meeting, Verna was ready to start promoting. She'd need a desk, space to work. She paid a call on Frank Tribble at the *Tattler*. Apparently relieved she hadn't come to ask him for a job, he immediately agreed to let her use his back room and his press whenever she wanted.

By the end of the week, she and Jimmy were spending twelve hours a day, writing up articles about the race and sending them to every western newspaper. The angle was the zany idea that rich men in fancy new automobiles were to race across a dried lake bed, next door to the country's richest gold field. The improbability of the site and the kind of men doing the racing made for great copy.

Verna's head burst with plans. There were times she forgot where she was, what time it was. Twice she left her hotel room and was almost in the lobby when she realized she still had on her bathrobe and bedroom slippers. She hadn't been this energized in months. If only half the number of people came to the race who'd been to the fight, it would still be a success.

The Masons agreed to build the reviewing stand. The town board said it would arrange for extra cars to be put on both the morning and afternoon trains of the Goldfield and Tonopah the day before, the day of, and the day after the race. Tess and Vic would be in charge of the concessions stand. Meg said she'd arrange for flags to be made. The entire camp, Verna along with it, had come alive again.

Then came the telegram.

Verna was sitting at her makeshift desk in the rear of the *Tattler*, oblivious of the voices and the thump of the press a few yards away as she worked on the next story, when she felt someone's hand on her shoulder. She started, looked up, and saw Meg. Her expression was grim. She handed Verna a telegram.

"They aren't coming," Meg said.

"Who isn't, dear?"

"It's all there."

Verna took the telegram and read.

PURPOSE ADMIRABLE STOP SORRY GLIDDEN
RELIABILITY TOURS CANNOT ENDORSE STOP HAVE
SO ADVISED LA AND SF AAA STOP CHARLES
GLIDDEN ESQUIRE

"What'll we do?" wailed Meg.

Verna glanced up at her. "This Charles Glidden. Who is he anyway?"

"Bill says he's in charge of the reliability tour. He finances it, I guess, and he's very important. A millionaire, I think." Meg's eyes misted. "How could he do such a thing?"

Verna stood. "Tell you what. Let's go over to the Ajax and have Tess fix a fresh pot of coffee. Then—"

"Coffee?" She glared at Verna. "We don't have time for coffee. We have to do something. Now."

"Come on. We can't talk here." Verna put an arm around Meg's shoulders. "This calls for a meeting of the board."

CHAPTER 39

*S*weating, yearning for some shade, Tess watched Vic and Clem Little, shirtless, the tops of their union suits plastered against their chests, pound nails into the frame of the refreshment stand. Tomorrow's race was going to be a scorcher.

For the hundredth time, she offered a silent thanks to Bill Brown. When old man Glidden had put thumbs-down on the touring cars detouring to Goldfield, Bill had stepped in and saved the day. Several of his friends who owned race cars agreed to come instead. Bill had even persuaded none other than the famous Barney Oldfield to enter. The race was turning out to be as big an event as the fight.

In the bed of Clem's freight wagon were the remaining boards needed for the stand. Finally, she was going to have the chance to sell beer on the spot and make the money she should have made at the prizefight. If Jake were still around, it could well be another story. One way or another he'd manage to take the concession out of her hands as he had before. The damn part of it was she'd probably let him.

She didn't like to think about Jake or about how she'd let him yank her around like a pet dog. The man was a revolting sonofa-bitch and she'd been a fool not to see it. For someone who'd made her way in the world since she was thirteen, she should've known better than to leave stock certificates in that safe.

As she gazed across the desert, past the refreshment stand-in-the-making toward the racetrack, she could almost see the throng of spectators, smell their money. She was sure to recoup the thousand dollars she might have made from the sale of her exchange seat, maybe more. She envisioned the sportsmen in their checked suits moving among the crowd, taking bets—hers among them, and she smiled. Bill Brown would be the winner by a length. It would be the easiest money she'd ever made.

Then, from out of nowhere, a notion edged into the back of her mind, grew to a hunch, a sixth sense that Jake would be at the race. Not in a checked suit, but he'd be there. Smooth as always, working the suckers, making his pile. The possibility made her blood boil.

Tess heard Clem call her.

"Heh, Tess. What d'ya think?"

"Looks great!"

Vic grinned at her, mopped his forehead and neck with a huge, red handkerchief. "We gotta have American flags on top."

She tilted her head, studying the small board structure.

"If I can't find any, at least red, white, and blue bunting."

"For sure," Tess said, impressed by Vic's patriotism when he wasn't even a citizen. Yet that was Vic. When she'd first known him, he'd confused her. The men she knew were callous, cruel. A few—like Jake—were sexy. Vic was real, genuine, decent. She wished she had room in her life for his love.

It wasn't long before the men finished. They stowed their tools in the wagon. Standing back aways with Tess, they surveyed their work, decided the refreshment stand looked sturdy, ready for business. Tomorrow she and Vic would bring out sandwiches, sarsa-parilla, and beer to sell. She glanced at the sun high overhead.

Noon. She still had to boil the beef brisket for the sandwiches, and she was anxious to get back to town before Jenny Lynn came home from school.

*   *   *

Clem Little at the reins, Tess sat between him and Vic as they sat up on the box of the Studebaker and bounced along the rutted road back to Goldfield. The brilliant light shimmered like quicksilver above the desert road stretching out ahead of them, playing tricks on her eyes. Tess felt herself growing sleepy. She leaned her head on Vic's shoulder, let her eyes close. Next thing she knew they were on the edge of Goldfield.

Tess gazed around her. The camp was bigger, the shacks and tents more spread out than when she'd first arrived. But the ugliness, the bleakness was the same. She remembered that day, staring out the stage window, not surprised at what she saw. She hadn't been able to pick out the saloons or the pleasure houses—the whorehouses and the cribs, the hophouses—but she'd known they were there. Mining camps were all the same. Soon that would all be behind her.

Unwillingly, she thought of Jake again. She'd known she was smarter than most women, savvier about the world. When she'd met Jake she'd seen right away he was the same. In a strange kind of way their friendship had opened her heart. Maybe without Jake, the good and the bad of him, she wouldn't have been able finally to see what was now between her and Vic.

Clem guided the team through the maze of mule trains and riders. Up ahead, a drunk stumbled into the traffic. A warning shout went up. Horses reared. Immediately, a crowd of curiosity seekers gathered, but blood and guts were not her cup of tea.

As she looked in the opposite direction, she saw a tall, broadshouldered man, with dark hair beneath his smart fedora, coming out of the corner saloon. He was clean-shaven and handsome, well dressed. Her heart stopped. Jake Stratton.

She turned away, stunned. The drunk was carried to the boardwalk. The snarl of traffic loosened. Clem flicked the reins over the rumps of his team. The buckboard moved on, past the saloon Jake had stepped out of. Out of the corner of her eye, she searched for some sign of him. He had disappeared, but tomorrow he'd be at the race.

Once he'd told her that Goldfield had been good to him. Not anymore. She'd make sure of it.

She touched Clem on the arm. "Do me a favor, will you? Drop me off at the sheriff's office. I've got some business to take care of."

CHAPTER 40

$\mathcal{M}$eg pulled open the door of the Imperial and climbed the stairs to the familiar room that had once housed the ladies' exchange and was now the race headquarters. Beyond the windows the warm air was so thick with anticipation she could almost taste it. She smiled, rolled up the sleeves of her shirtwaist. So far their plans had gone like clockwork.

An hour earlier, the entire length of Main Street had been lined with people eager for a good look at the racing machines and their drivers. Though the mayor had led the parade in his Reno touring car, Barney Oldfield had been the star attraction. Broad-faced, a cigar stuck in one corner of his mouth, younger-looking than she'd imagined, he'd sat beside his mechanic in the trim Winton, waved at the cheering crowd that lined the street.

The rest of the drivers and their mechanics had followed in a variety of racers—Fiats, a Renault, two DeDietrichs, a Benz, a Panhard—like mammoth tin cans turned on their sides, balanced on a frame with four wheels. Bringing up the rear, looking for all the world like a cheeky, little boy trailing, full-grown men, had been Bill, alone, in his Packard Gray Wolf. Small, the car was half the size of all but Barney Oldfield's machine.

Bill had written her about the Gray Wolf, about its leaf spring suspension, about the aluminum body, which made it so lightweight, about how excited he was to have a chance to drive it. The car had come in second in the Vanderbilt Cup race he and his friend had been in two years ago, and he'd had to pull out all the stops to be allowed to enter it in the Goldfield race.

Meg unpinned her hat, put it on the chair next to the door, and walked over to the table piled with papers containing the details of tomorrow's events. She and Tess and Verna had gone over them last night, but because Meg was the chairman of the event, they had told her it was up to her to give everything a final look.

The mayor and the sheriff, as well as the town board, were to assemble at the racetrack tomorrow morning by nine o'clock. The Wobblies' brass band would begin entertaining at ten. Then the mayor was to bring greetings from the citizens of Goldfield and turn the podium over to the sheriff, who would hold up the winner's trophy, ordered all the way from Los Angeles and donated by the Goldfield Consolidated Mines Company. Finally, acting on behalf of the planning committee, Meg was to introduce the racers, who would then proceed to their machines.

There'd been considerable debate over the rules for the race until Bill stepped in and took charge. The fifty-lap course was a rectangle, a half mile wide by a mile and a half long, designated by four poles painted red, white, and blue. A judge, wearing a red armband on his left sleeve, would be stationed by each pole. Though there'd be no restrictions on engine size or design of the machine, only the driver and his mechanic could work on the car. All spare parts must be carried. Fuel would be stored in a specific area to the north of the stands. Any repairs or tire changes would be done inside the borders of the course.

Meg straightened the pile of papers, glanced out the window. It was growing dark. By now, the machines were parked in the open space by the depot so those who wanted could get a closer look.

A gala dinner was scheduled for eight o'clock at the Palm Grill in honor of the race participants and the dignitaries, who by now constituted half the camp. The private dining room had been reserved. If just the invited guests showed up, it would hold everyone. Gate-crashers being close to a tradition in Goldfield, she prayed the quantities of elk steak, tiny boiled potatoes, fresh salad, pecan pie, and, of course, champagne that had been ordered would be enough.

Meg gave the pages of details a final check. Satisfied, she pinned on her hat. She had to get home and change before Bill came by to pick her up. Maybe then she'd finally have a chance to tell him about the sale of her Fourth of July stock and about her encounter with Pete Eckles.

*   *   *

Meg wore an off-the-shoulder French blue chiffon evening dress, belted at the waist in a wide band of deeper blue taffeta with seed pearl trim. Her silk slippers were the same blue. Her elbow-length white gloves were the softest kid. She had pinned a white, silk rose, etched in seed pearls, in her hair. Bill's medallion hung between her breasts. Every bit of clothing—including her corset cover, her drawers, her petticoat—had been specially ordered from the haute couture department of Denver's Daniels and Fishers. She was a little embarrassed by how much she'd paid for it. Generally, clothes didn't mean that much to her, but tonight was special. And as she passed the mirror in the entrance of the Palm Grill and saw her reflection, she decided every penny had been worth it.

Bill stood behind her, his hands surreptitiously encircling her waist as she greeted people. The feel of them distracted her. She couldn't seem to remember anyone's name. Finally, she turned around, made a little face. "Go away, Bill Brown. I can't concentrate with you around."

He grinned down at her. "That's the idea."

"I mean it. Go talk to your friends. I have to count noses and see whether there'll be enough to eat."

He squeezed her hand, kissed her with his eyes, and melted into the crowd.

She spotted Verna and Tess across the crowded room. They were standing with Vic and Clem Little, who were dressed for the occasion, stiff as two toy soldiers in linen collars and cuffs, silk ties, and coats. John Burlingame and Charley Thompson were nearby with Senator Nolan and George Winters, all in proper evening dress.

Guests continued to push into the room until it was nearly impossible to move. She thanked heaven none of the men were smoking or it would have been impossible to breathe. Lou Clancy, who ran the Palm Grill, shouted to her that dinner would have to be delayed until they had time to set up more tables. She nodded. Maybe it was just as well. People were laughing, shouting out bets to one another, passing gold pieces and bills to John Burlingame, who seemed to be holding the bets, calling for more champagne. If the meal was delayed long enough, no one would care or know what they'd eaten.

An hour went by. Meg was listening to Bill's racing friends, arguing about the latest odds. Trickles of perspiration ran down the sides of her cheeks. She pushed past knots of guests toward the window to get some air. As she stood, fanning herself with her hands, she felt a hand on her elbow, turned, and saw Pete Eckles, a full glass of champagne in either hand.

Her heart skipped a beat.

"Champagne?" he said, handing her a glass.

She stared at him. "What are you doing here?" She had presumed he'd left town. Never had she imagined he would come to the celebration.

"Come one, come all. That's what we say in Goldfield."

"Is it?" she asked, coldly.

"Heh, no hard feelings. Business is business. You got the better of me. It doesn't happen that often, but it happens. Let bygones be bygones. That's what I say."

She was so close to him, she smelled the tobacco on his breath and something else, faint but disagreeably distinct.

"I hear the race was your idea."

"Not really." She stepped back from him as far as she could, took in a deep breath to steady herself. Castor oil. That was what she smelled. Her aunt had threatened her with the nasty stuff often enough that she'd never forget it.

"So who are you puttin' your money on?" Pete Eckles asked.

"All the drivers are equally well qualified."

"With Barney Oldfield in the race? Who are you kiddin'?"

"I'm an official of the race."

"Oh, come on. You have to be bettin' on someone."

She gave him an icy look. "If I was, I wouldn't tell you."

He shrugged. "Suit yourself. But I think I've got a bet you won't be able to resist."

In spite of herself, she was curious. "Which is?"

"I'll bet one of the cars don't finish the race. I'll give you ten to one odds."

"That's no bet. Lots of cars don't finish races. Bill told me seven of the eighteen cars in the Vanderbilt Cup didn't finish."

"I heard about that race. I also heard it was the crowd that broke it up."

"Mr. Eckles, I'm really not interested."

He held up a hand, as if in surrender. "Okay. I'll bet you *two* cars don't finish."

She narrowed her eyes, suspicious. "Which ones?"

"If I named them I'd have to *get* odds, not give them."

Meg crossed her arms. "Nevertheless, it's Bill's and Barney Old-field's cars you have in mind."

"It would sure make sense." He grinned, revealing his mouth-ful of yellow teeth. "The whole world knows Brown's little tin can and that ridiculous Winton of Oldfield's aren't strong enough to last the course."

Meg raised an eyebrow. She'd heard similar comments through the day. Like all the other scoffers, Eckles thought a machine with twenty-five horsepower like Bill's, or even Mr. Oldfield's compar-atively larger car, couldn't compete against such cars as a Benz with five times the power. Yet Bill had a feel for engines, for racing. He was convinced the smaller machines were the wave of the future, and she believed him.

"I'm not interested."

He gave a twisted kind of grin. "Afraid you'll lose this time?"

She wanted no part of Pete Eckles. Yet to back off from his bet was to say she didn't believe in Bill. "How much money do you have in mind?"

"A thousand."

She fought to hide her gasp. Wagering a thousand dollars on a single auto race? Still, wasn't that what she hoped everyone else would do?

"All right," she said. "It's a deal."

* * *

Meg stood at the south end of the dried lake, its bottom of sun-dried sand hard enough to hold the weight of one-ton race cars, and touched the red ribbon strung between two poles as the ceremonial starting gate for the race. Her heart full to overflowing, she closed her eyes, listened to the sounds that seemed to magnify and reverberate in the dry, desert air. The excited babble of hundreds of voices, the high laughter of children, flags snapping in the wind, an occasional distant backfire from an arriving automobile, filled the air.

The racers weren't expected to assemble for another hour, yet people had been arriving since daybreak. The union had erected an officials' platform in the center of the racetrack, even draping it with red, white, and blue bunting. The bleachers, with an awning big enough to hold five hundred people, were at the west side of the track so the sun wouldn't be in anyone's eyes. Off to the left aways was Vic and Tess's refreshment stand, also with an awning so customers could be out of the sun when they ate.

The Tonopah-Goldfield railroad had offered a special rate for those coming in from Reno and Los Angeles. The *Tattler* had outdone itself with a constant barrage of articles detailing the lives of the race contestants, particularly the famous Barney Oldfield. Men, women, and children from miles around, as far away as Los Angeles and Salt Lake City, had flocked to Goldfield.

Hitch rails for horses, traps, and buckboards, set up five hundred yards away from the track, were full. Verna had arranged for the water wagon to bring in a trough for the animals, though there'd be a charge. Autos had a separate spot to park.

Last night as Bill had walked her back to the bottle house, she finally had had the chance to tell him about her conversation with Pete Eckles, about their bet.

He'd only laughed, drew her into his arms. "Don't you worry about a thing."

She'd pushed him away. "He frightens me, Bill."

"He's a has-been."

"I don't trust him. There he was in full evening clothes, smelling of castor oil, and—"

"Castor oil?"

"I'd know that smell anywhere."

"So would I. I use it in my crankcase."

Instantly, a flick of fear had run through her. "You don't suppose he's done something to your car?"

"Look." He'd pulled her close again. "I'll take care of the car. You take care of your end. Just don't worry. It'll all work out fine."

Now as she watched the members of the town board make their way through the crowd toward the officials' platform, Meg prayed Bill was right. Off to the south, in the direction of town, just like clockwork, she heard the roar of engines. Cheers broke out. Her heart did flip-flops as she cupped her hands around her eyes to shield them from the brilliant sun and saw a giant plume of dust arching into the cloudless, blue sky. In what seemed only a moment or two, the ten cars came into view. One after another, the driver's silk scarves flying out behind them, the racing cars roared up to the starting line and came to a dramatic stop.

Then, all at once, everything she planned just happened. It was like seeing herself on the screen in a moving picture show. There she was, smiling, bringing greetings on behalf of the race committee, thanking everyone: the union, the senator and Mr. Winters. The list went on.

Mayor Gaines introduced the race contestants. Once again, the crowd roared its approval. The major offered her his arm. It was time for the race to begin.

As they walked across the platform toward the steps, Meg paused, looked past the faces of the people below her, and the reel stopped.

To her left, Meg saw the refreshment stand. In front of it, Jenny Lynn was perched on Vic's shoulders for a better view. Tess was beside them, talking earnestly to the sheriff. Meg shifted her gaze, searching for Verna. The mayor cleared his throat, obviously impatient to move along. Meg pretended not to notice as she continued to look for the familiar, stocky figure. She finally spotted Jimmy Earnest. Verna had to be nearby. And she was. Pencil in one hand, notepad in the other, she was interviewing the senator, probably for the post-race issue of the *Tattler*. Meg chuckled inwardly as she imagined the edge the article would have.

In a matter of days, no more than a week or two at most, she and Verna and Tess would go their separate ways. Tess with her daughter to Steamboat Springs, Verna to some other Colorado mountain town to work on a newspaper as long as her eyesight held. Which town Meg didn't know, but it would be in thin, cool air among the pines. And, Meg, if everything went according to plan, would go to San Francisco.

A person would be hard put to find a trio with less in common. Yet they'd become friends who'd put up with each other's foibles, trusted each other, had grown to love each other, like family. The part about love had never been spoken of in so many words. Tess, particularly, would have been embarrassed and probably made a joke of it. Still, Meg knew they felt it, knew it was true. They'd never forget each other, but the thousand miles or more that would be between them was too great a distance for anything but occasional visits at the most, unless they guarded against it, so that, gradually, because of age or maybe babies to care for, the visits would become less frequent until they stopped altogether.

The mayor cleared his throat, again. Meg glanced at him, smiled. Her arm through his, they walked down the steps toward the starting line and the waiting racing cars.

*   *   *

The early April day was pleasantly cool, in spite of the unrelenting sun overhead. The spectators had barely settled down for an afternoon of cheering for their favorites and serious beer drinking when a DeDietrich tried to take too sharp a turn and tipped over. Gasps mingled with groans. With one car out of the race, the field had suddenly narrowed to nine.

Standing in the midst of the other officials, Meg tried to stay as close to the edge of the track as possible. She narrowed her eyes against the blowing sand and inspected the latest figures chalked on the lap board. Bill was the leader.

Just then, his trim, little Gray Wolf tore by, with Barney Oldfield, hunched over the steering wheel of his Winton, close behind. Out of the corner of her eye, she saw a Fiat with a flat pull into the designated center of the course. The weight of the cars, coupled with the speed, was rough on tires, but some, like the Fiat as well as Bill's and Barney Oldfield's cars, carried the allowable limit of three new tires and tubes already mounted on rims that the Frenchman Michelin had developed. Instead of the relatively lengthy process the driver and mechanic faced having to take the flat tire off the rim, replace it with another, then pump it up, the men in the cars carrying the rimmed spares could unbolt the flat, remove it, replace it with one of the spare sets in two to three minutes. Even Bill, who drove alone, could do it, saving precious minutes.

As she watched the Fiat roll back onto the track, she felt a hand on her arm. She turned her head and realized Pete Eckles was beside her, shouting something.

"What?" She cupped one ear. The roar of the engines had nearly deafened her.

"For a while there I thought you might win the ten thousand." She stared at him. In the excitement, she'd managed to forget their bet. "The bet was about two cars. Only one's dropped out."

"Till now." He pointed toward the south end of the course. "Your friend seems to be havin' trouble."

She swung her gaze to where he pointed and saw that a car had fallen so far back it was as if the brake had been applied or the car had run out of fuel or, worse, the oil had been drained. Even from this distance, she knew it was the Gray Wolf. Groans came from the stands.

She stood on tiptoe for a better view. Bill couldn't lose. He just couldn't. She gathered her skirts, ran along the course, shouting encouragement, urging him on. The small car started to move faster, but not by much. Three cars passed him. Bill was loosing lap money at a great rate. Half the camp was betting on him, including Verna and Tess, and herself.

"It's Brown's tin can all right," said Eckles. "He's out of it for sure."

"Not a chance," she said, stubbornly.

He snorted in disbelief. "I'll bet you."

She knew he was egging her on, but she couldn't control her anger.

"Well? What about it? If you're so set on him, how 'bout another bet?" Eckles asked, his mouth close to her ear, his breath stinking of bourbon.

She eyed him, repulsed.

"I've got another hundred thousand that says he won't win, and I'll still give you ten-to-one odds!"

She glared at him, knowing he'd set her up, played to her loyalty to Bill, with the full intention of recouping the hundred thousand dollars she'd made on the sale of her stock. She wasn't about to back down now. She spun around, called to the mayor to come over.

"You don't trust me?" Eckles asked.

"Just call it insurance." She turned to the mayor. "I want you to serve as a witness, Mr. Gaines."

The mayor glanced from Meg to Eckles, an amused look on his face. "A little wager, is it?"

"You could say that." Meg heard her voice, cold and hard.

"I'm putting up a hundred thousand and givin' the little lady ten-to-one odds Bill Brown won't win."

Meg met Eckles's icy, blue eyes. "Mr. Eckles has just made me a million dollars richer."

* * *

By the lap board, Bill had five laps to go. Though still near the back of the pack, he slowly overtook and passed one car after another, until, with a burst of speed, the Gray Wolf was streaking around the track. Yet, unless it regained the lost time, Bill would be lucky to place fourth.

Meg's legs ached from the hours of standing, but the race was nearing its end. In the next few minutes, the fate of her bet with Eckles and the bets of two friends, money they depended on desperately, would be settled.

Fans had abandoned their seats and were strung out along the track, shouting encouragement to their favorites. Excitement reverberated across the flats. When Meg had warned the sheriff last week that the crowd might break up the race, arrangements had been made to hire men who'd keep people back, but she didn't see a sign of anyone doing that. If people surged out onto the track, it could be a disaster.

Suddenly, with no warning, the Gray Wolf left the pack and limped into the center of the course with a flat. Meg held her hands to her mouth, hardly able to breathe as she watched Bill vault out of the cockpit, immediately unbolt the offending tire, replace it with the last of his three spares, throw his tools in the cockpit, climb in himself, and tear off again.

Eckles sidled up to her. "He does that well. It's too bad. A touch of the brakes now at the speed he's going—" He snapped his left thumb and forefinger together for emphasis—"that tire could go, just like that."

Meg turned her back to him. Bill only had three more laps to go. Surely, his tires would hold that long. He sped past. This was his forty-ninth lap. Meg ran to the other side of the track, saw him shoot past one car after the other. He was gaining on the leaders of the pack. If only he could keep the torrid pace, he had a chance to come in first. Then, suddenly, he disappeared from view. Her heart sank. She elbowed past people lining the track, straining for some sign of him.

"If Brown's out to pick up fuel now, he's dead in the water," a man behind her growled.

Then the next second, there it was, the little Gray Wolf darting from behind the Benz. Bill hadn't stopped to refuel after all. There was still a chance, a slim one.

"No way for him to catch up now," scoffed Pete Eckles.

Meg ignored him. Taking a very deep breath, her hands clenched tight at her sides, she squeezed her eyes shut, imagined Bill flying over the other cars as she had pictured herself floating over Boulder Creek as a girl of twelve. Time stopped. Then suddenly, cheers erupted. Pandemonium broke out. Meg opened her eyes. And there was Bill in the Gray Wolf, all grin, surrounded by his fellow racers in their leather helmets. Corks exploded into the clear, blue sky. Mumm's extra dry spilled onto the sand.

Meg searched for some sign of Verna and Tess, then saw them, pushing through the crowd. She ran toward them, gave each a fierce hug.

"Wasn't Bill wonderful?" shouted a beaming Verna over the din.

Meg nodded, her entire face a smile. "I told you it would work."

Tess laughed. "You sure as hell did!"